BRAISE

ALSO BY DANIEL BOULUD

Cooking with Daniel Boulud

Daniel Boulud's Café Boulud Cookbook

Chef Daniel Boulud: Cooking in New York City

Daniel's Dish: Entertaining at Home with a Four-Star Chef

Letters to a Young Chef

ecco

An Imprint of HarperCollins*Publishers*

BRAISE

A JOURNEY THROUGH INTERNATIONAL CUISINE

DANIEL BOULUD
AND MELISSA CLARK

HarperCollins books may be purchased for educational, business, or sales promotional use. For information please write: Special Markets Department, HarperCollins Publishers, 10 East 53rd Street, New York, NY 10022.

A hardcover edition of this book was published in 2006 by Ecco, an imprint of HarperCollins Publishers.

FIRST ECCO PAPERBACK EDITION PUBLISHED 2013.

Designed by Marysarah Quinn

Photographs by Thomas Schauer

Library of Congress Cataloging-in-Publication Data has been applied for.

ISBN 978-0-06-223238-0

13 14 15 16 17 ❖/RRD 10 9 8 7 6 5 4 3 2 1

I'D LIKE TO DEDICATE THIS BOOK to all the chefs and cooks from around the globe who have worked in my kitchens over the years and have generously shared their recipes and their knowledge. You have all been a constant source of inspiration and contributed greatly to the flavor of this book.

And of course, as always, this book is for Alix and Micky.

ACKNOWLEDGMENTS

Just as it takes a strong brigade to run a restaurant, so, too, does it to produce a successful cookbook. With that said, I am incredibly thankful and grateful to the many people who contributed their time, energy, and culinary passion to bringing this project together.

Specifically, I would like to thank my talented and devoted chefs, Cyrille Alannic, Fabrizzio Salerni, Eric Bertoïa, Lior Lev Sercarz, and Mark Fiorentino, for the many (at times grueling!) hours they spent developing, preparing, baking, cooking, and testing each of the wonderful recipes that appear in this book. Each chef's expertise contributed not only to the flavor and diversity of each dish, but also in the visual presentation. In particular, I would like to thank Cyrille and Tiziana Agnello, our prop stylist, who each played a major role in styling each dish for our photography shoots.

I was also very lucky to have the photographer Thomas Schauer, who traveled all the way from Vienna to photograph this project. Thomas is an amazing artist whose innate skill and keen eye produced the vibrant and beautiful photography interspersed throughout the pages of this work.

On the editorial side, no one worked harder on this book than Katherine Yang, who coordinated the research, development, and testing of all the recipes—I will admit this was no easy task, especially given my hectic schedule and the constant demands of running several restaurants. Thank you, Katherine, for keeping me and the team on track.

Finally, a big thank you to Melissa Clark, my diligent co-author, who arrived at my doorstep on many an early morning, before the day unfolded, to help me put my thoughts and anecdotes onto paper.

And last but not least, thank you to the staff at Ecco: first and foremost, Dan Halpern, who believed in the idea of an international braising book, as well as Emily Takoudes.

CONTENTS

POULTRY AND RABBIT

FISH AND SEAFOOD 143

VEGETABLES AND BEANS 171

FRUIT AND OTHER DESSERTS 189

INTRODUCTION

GLOBAL BRAISING

Every chef has a dish so fundamental to his psyche that whenever he tastes, smells, or even just imagines its flavors, it immediately brings him back to where he had it first—usually, home.

For me, that dish is braised meat. The cut doesn't matter so much, or even the kind of meat (although at my family's home in Lyon it was most often chicken or beef). What is essential is the cooking method, which produces a dish with a caramelized, browned exterior giving way to tender, voluptuous chunks of meat that are so full of flavor they don't even need the velvety sauce surrounding them in the pot, though of course no one would dream of leaving it behind. Braised meat was what my grandmother and mother would make on a cold winter night to warm and satisfy the family. It was one of the first things I learned to make as an apprentice in France. There are few other dishes that stir my soul in the same way.

I'm certainly not alone. After traveling around the world, and sharing meals and thoughts with cooks of all cultures, I've come to realize that braising speaks to people almost everywhere. It's an age-old technique that appears all over the globe. There's almost no culinary tradition that doesn't have its own special repertoire of braised dishes.

So when I began thinking about writing a cookbook on braising, I didn't want to limit myself to the food of my own French and European background. I wanted to include influences, ingredients, and combinations reflecting a global perspective. And I realized that I had already begun the research in my kitchen at DANIEL. You see, we employ cooks of all nationalities, and when they first come to us, we always ask them to prepare for the staff a meal from their country—something they would make for their families at home. Often, the meal turns out to be a braised dish, starting from a cheap cut of meat (a practical constraint of a staff meal at a restaurant) that they turn into a wonderful dish! It's an authentic "slow food" experience, and I always learn something from it. All those lessons are apparent in this book.

For example, it was through such meals that I realized the French may not always be right about the presentation of green vegetables. The challenge for a French chef is to keep greens as bright-hued as possible during cooking. But after sampling an authentic Indian lamb curry made by an Indian cook, I realized that focusing on appearance may not always be best for the flavor of the greens. This lamb dish, made with spinach and mustard greens, was khaki-colored because of the addition of yogurt (the acid in yogurt browns the greens) and because the dish had been braised for a long time. But the flavor was phenomenally deep and rich. Similarly, I ate a North African appetizer of greens simmered with lemon that had taken on the color of green olives but had a magnificent flavor—fresh yet savory. I adapted both recipes for this book (see Cardamom-Spiced Coconut Lamb, page 86, and Spicy Merguez with Spinach and White Beans, page 92). And I decided that my goal in these pages would be to focus on taste instead of appearance, and on authenticity instead of adaptation.

This is not to say that every dish in this book, or even any dish, is strictly authentic. All of the recipes bear my mark in some way. Some of the dishes here are based quite closely on traditional braising recipes (such as the Brazilian national dish of black beans and meats called Feijoada, page 102), and some are a fusion of techniques and ingredients within a particular culture that are not indicative of any one dish (such as Asian Pork Belly with Ginger and Soy, page 48). But I'm sure you'll find all of them interesting and very likely delicious. I certainly do.

Braising is as close to alchemy as it is to cooking. It transforms inexpensive, tough cuts of meat, if not into gold, into succulent soft morsels. In fact, the cheaper, more sinewy, and more chewy the meat is to begin with, the more delectable its texture and the thicker the sauce after cooking. For this reason, braising is an extremely economical way to cook, especially if you are feeding a crowd. Unlike many other cooking techniques, braising tenderizes the connective tissue, dissolving the collagen into gelatin. Shot through with gelatin, the meat melts on your tongue. Thickened with gelatin, the sauce clings and shines. Braising is the only method that can accomplish this to such a supreme degree.

That's because in order to melt properly, the collagen needs just the right cooking environment: long, slow, moist heat. If the heat is high and dry, as in roasting and baking, the collagen evaporates before meeting the sauce. A roasted piece of meat may be extremely delicious, but it is delicious in a completely different way from braised meat.

Although braising is closely related to stewing, there are key differences. Both braises and stews are cooked in liquid at relatively low temperatures. But a braise calls for less liquid than stewing, and so it results in a more concentrated sauce. Then there is the size of the chunks of meat. Stews generally use smaller pieces of meat, whereas braises use large pieces, though there are exceptions to this rule, as to every rule.

Another key technique in braising that you don't always find in stewing is searing the meat (or vegetable, or fish) in fat before adding the liquid. This step builds the layers of taste in a dish, adding all the good, browned flavor of caramelization, which gives a little toastiness to the sauce. You cannot skip this step or skimp on it. Take your time to sear all sides of the meat well. They should be dark golden brown. Remember, the browner they are, without getting burned, the more flavor they will give the dish.

This step is the only time you will need to apply high heat during a braise. Otherwise, braises should be cooked gently, at relatively low temperatures. You will notice that I tend to braise between 275° and 325°F. That's warm enough to break down the collagen in meats and fish, but not hot enough to shrink or toughen the muscle fibers. You never want your braise to come above a very light simmer—in fact, just under a simmer is best. That's why I braise all my recipes in the oven. The heat is constant, without the variability of the stove top, so you won't have to worry about the liquid either getting too hot or cooling down. You can just leave your pot to cook and do something else.

That "something else" is probably one reason why braising is such a favored technique around the world. It doesn't matter that a recipe takes a long time in the oven if you are free to do other things meanwhile. I always joke that braising is a good technique for newlyweds. It gives them plenty of time to pursue other things while their dinner cooks. But it's great for anyone who is busy, and who isn't? If you are having a dinner party, braising allows you to make the rest of the meal while the entrée takes care of itself in the oven. Most braises are also excellent made a day or two ahead and then reheated. This gives the flavors a chance to come together. It also lets you easily take off any fat from the top of the sauce (see Some Tips for Braising, page xxi), since the fat will harden in the refrigerator. And most braises can also be frozen, so leftovers, if there are any, always have a place to go.

BRAISING EQUIPMENT

The most important piece of equipment that you will need for braising is a heavy braising pot with a cover. The pot should be deep enough to hold a large piece of meat or fish, but not so tall (like a stockpot) that the liquid doesn't evaporate properly. A Dutch oven is a good choice, as are any low-sided pots made for braising (called braisers).

If you have enough space and a large enough budget, you might even think about buying several braising pots. It's best if the ingredients fit as snugly as possible in the pot, leaving just enough room on all sides for the liquid. Ideally the pot should be about 1½ to 2 inches larger on all sides than the ingredients that you will be braising. This gives you enough room to brown the ingredients before adding the liquid. If your pot is bigger, it's OK. You might just have to adjust the thickness of the sauce at the end. Pots of different sizes will allow liquid to evaporate at different rates. For more about thickening or thinning a sauce, see Some Tips for Braising, page xxi. In the recipes we refer to the size of the pots as small, medium, and large. Roughly, small refers to a 3-quart pot, medium to a 5-quart pot, and large to a 6-quart or larger pot.

As for the material of the pot, enamel-coated cast iron is what I prefer to use at home. (At the restaurant we have special equipment for braising on a large scale.) Enamel-coated cast iron provides the most even heat. (You can use unlined cast iron as long as the ingredients you are cooking aren't particularly acidic. But any acid in the ingredients will react with the iron. Aluminum is also very reactive and should be avoided in such cases as well.)

Braising pots made of a copper core coated with stainless steel are good, too, provided they are very thick and heavy. The heavier the pot, the more evenly it will cook what's inside.

Although you can use ceramic, earthenware, and glass pots for braising in the oven, many are not flameproof, so you won't be able to use them on top of the stove for searing. If you want to use such a pot, make sure it can withstand direct heat before proceeding. You don't want to lose your sauce to a crack. Alternatively, you can sear your ingredients in a heavy skillet, deglaze the skillet with some of the liquid, and transfer everything to the pot of choice. I know that sometimes aesthetics plays a role in deciding what pot to use. An earthenware pot can make a nice presentation at the table.

Other than a pot, you won't need anything fancy for the recipes in this book, though you might consider investing in a good spice grinder or a mortar and pestle, or both. I think it's a good idea to have both; while their uses can overlap, they are also quite different. A mortar and pestle can handle both moist and dry ingredients, but a spice grinder can handle only dry ones. A spice grinder will give you a much finer powder than a mortar and pestle, which yields a coarser texture.

For quick, even slicing, a mandoline or a Japanese Benriner will come in handy, but you can always use a good sharp knife.

BRAISING INGREDIENTS

In Europe, we tend to braise in wine, beer, broth, or water. But when I was testing recipes for this book, I also included all kinds of condiments, including soy sauce, fish sauce, and chili sauce; citrus and other fruit juices; and coconut and other nut milks. I played with herbs and spices, mixing and combining them in ways that are traditional in their cultures, and also more experimental. You will notice that there are very few strictly traditional dishes here. Most are my own creations. But all the dishes spring from classic recipes that have been beloved in their cultures for decades or even centuries.

Since I availed myself of the contents of an international pantry, some of the ingredients can be hard to find. I've included tips, some history, and other information about unusual ingredients along with each recipe; a source list at the end of the book to help you obtain everything that won't be easily available at the super-market; and some ideas, as appropriate, for substitutions. These days, if it's out there, you can probably find it online.

Of course, when you buy produce, fish, and meats, always seek out the best quality you can get. I prefer something locally pro-duced to something that has to be shipped. If you can find some-thing in season, perhaps at a farmers' market, it will usually give you better flavor than something that had to travel thousands of miles to get to your supermarket. But there are exceptions here. The best indicator of quality, of course, is taste. If you can taste be-fore you buy, do so. Careful shopping will result in full-flavored in-gredients that will reward your braise in kind.

TECHNIQUE: SOME TIPS FOR BRAISING

MARINATING

To add flavor, marinate your meat before braising. Marinating breaks down the muscle fiber and allows the meat to absorb more of the savory braising liquid.

POTS

Use a high-quality heavy pot made of a material, such as cast iron or copper, that will conduct heat evenly.

SEARING

Before searing, dust moist, fatty cuts of meat (such as short ribs) with flour to create a crust that will seal in juices and flavor. With less succulent cuts (such as rabbit), pat the meat completely dry before browning to develop a deeper caramelization.

Sufficiently heating the oil before adding the meat ensures a good sear. To test the heat, touch a piece of meat lightly to the oil and listen for the telltale sizzle.

To make sure your dish achieves a rich color and flavor, don't overcrowd the pot. If not all the meat will fit into the pot, it's better to cook the pieces in batches and get a good sear.

CONSISTENCY OF THE SAUCE

Evaporation of the liquid in a braise will vary from oven to oven and pot to pot. If the sauce is too thin, ladle most of it into a small saucepan and simmer it on the stove top until it's reduced and thick. Then return it to the braising pot.

If the sauce is too thick, thin it with a little hot broth or wine, or whatever other liquid you used in cooking, then simmer it for 1 or 2 minutes to meld the flavors (or 5 or so minutes for wine, to evaporate the alcohol).

EXCESS FAT

If the dish seems too fatty or oily, the excess fat is easy to remove. The best way to do this is to refrigerate the cooled dish for several hours, or overnight. The fat will rise to the surface and harden there in a pale layer. Then just lift it off with a spoon.

Alternatively, simply let the braise cool for about 1 hour (this gives all the oils a chance to rise to the surface), then use a spoon to skim off the excess fat.

It's better not to trim all the fat from the meat before cooking. Fat adds a lot of flavor to the sauce, and you can always take the excess fat off later.

GARNISHING WITH FLAVOR

If the finished dish seems a little bland to your taste at serving time, mix together some good salt with a few pinches of the cooking spices you used in the braise (cumin, coriander, or what have you) and allow the individual diners to finish seasoning to their own liking.

A garnish of fresh herbs, citrus juices and grated citrus zest, mustard, horseradish, capers and chopped pickled vegetables, or vinegar will also perk up a flat-tasting braise. Do not be afraid to embellish.

SUBSTITUTION CHART FOR BRAISING

BEEF

BEEF SHOULDER: Any shoulder cut—blade pot roast, chuck eye pot roast, arm pot roast. Beef bottom round rump roast or beef top round roast such as brisket, boneless veal or pork shoulder cut, lamb shoulder.

BEEF SHORT RIBS: Chuck short ribs, baby back beef ribs, beef shanks, veal shanks, lamb shanks.

BEEF BRISKET: Rump roast, bottom round roast, any boneless beef shoulder cut, any boneless veal shoulder cut.

FLANK STEAK: Hanger steak, skirt steak.

GROUND BEEF: Ground lamb, ground pork.

BEEF SHANKS: Veal shanks, stew beef, short ribs.

OXTAIL: Beef shanks, beef short ribs, lamb shanks, veal shanks, lamb neck.

VEAL BREAST: Veal blade roast, bone-in pork belly.

VEAL SHOULDER: Any boneless cut from the shoulder, such as arm roast or blade roast. Veal rump roast, veal breast roast, rolled veal roast, beef shoulder, pork shoulder, lamb shoulder, pork loin roast.

PORK

PORK BUTT (SHOULDER): Pork center-cut loin roast, beef shoulder, veal shoulder, lamb shoulder, pork shanks, bone-in shoulder pieces.

PORK LOIN: Any boneless cut from the loin, such as top loin roast or blade roast. Boneless pork butt, pork shoulder roast.

BABY BACK PORK RIBS (FROM THE LOIN): Pork spareribs.

COUNTRY-STYLE RIBS (FROM THE LOIN): Pork spareribs, baby back pork ribs.

PORK BELLY: Veal breast.

PORK SPARERIBS (FROM THE BELLY): Baby back pork ribs, bone-in veal breast.

PORK SHANKS: Lamb shanks, bone-in pork shoulder, bone-in pork belly, veal shanks (osso buco).

LAMB

LAMB SHOULDER: Any boneless cut from the shoulder, such as eye roast or blade roast. Lamb leg, lamb shanks, lamb neck, veal shoulder, beef shoulder, bone-in cut from veal shoulder.

LAMB SHANK: Lamb neck, veal shanks, beef short ribs.

GROUND LAMB: Ground beef, ground pork.

VENISON SHOULDER (DEER, ELK, MOOSE, REINDEER): Beef shoulder (any cut), veal shoulder, lamb shoulder, pork shoulder, venison stew meat.

POULTRY

CHICKEN LEGS: Chicken breast, turkey legs.

WHOLE CHICKEN: Capon, Cornish hen, quail, duck, turkey, guinea hen.

CORNISH HEN: Capon, chicken, quail, pheasant, squab.

CAPON: Cornish hen, chicken.

PARTRIDGE: Pheasant, grouse, dove, quail, Cornish hen, squab.

TURKEY LEGS: Chicken legs, capon legs.

QUAIL: Partridge, squab, Cornish hen, grouse, chicken.

DUCK: Goose, chicken.

SQUAB: Quail, Cornish hen, grouse, partridge.

RABBIT: Chicken.

SEAFOOD

SMOKED SABLE: Smoked salmon, smoked cod, smoked sturgeon.

SKATE: Red snapper.

COD: Pollock, halibut, haddock, hake, ocean perch, tilapia, tilefish, sable (black cod).

GROUPER: Striped bass, mahi-mahi, black sea bass (flakier texture), red snapper (flakier texture).

RED SNAPPER: Striped bass, black bass, rockfish, grouper, halibut, catfish, tilapia, grouper.

STRIPED BASS: Blackfish, porgy, ocean perch, red snapper, rockfish, tilapia, grouper, sea bass, tilefish, halibut, salmon, blackfish.

TROUT: Shad, whitefish (flakier), sablefish (flakier), salmon, perch, butterfish, small sea bass, small striped bass, ocean perch.

MACKEREL: Shad, bluefish, herring, sea trout, small rockfish, porgy.

MONKFISH: Sea bass, cod, haddock, halibut, tilefish, mahi-mahi, blackfish, red snapper, lobster.

SCALLOPS: Cod cheeks, skate, monkfish.

SHRIMP: Crayfish, lobster, scallops, crab, prawns.

OCTOPUS: Squid, cuttlefish.

| BEEF CHEEK |

| TRIPE |

| TONGUE |

| PIG FEET |

| LAMB NECK |

| VEAL SWEETBREADS |

| OXTAIL |

MEAT

PALERON DE BOEUF AU VIN ROUGE

BRAISED BEEF SHOULDER WITH RED WINE AND BACON

| MAKES 6 TO 8 SERVINGS |

Paleron is a cut of beef from the shoulder, called chicken steak or flatiron steak here in the United States. It's a very beefy, hardy cut for braising, and it gives a nice rich broth for the sauce. In France, paleron de boeuf is a staple, the kind of dish someone's grandmother would make in the winter when she needed to warm up the family. If you are cooking for a crowd, double this recipe (you'll need a really big pot). There's no shame in leftovers, since it reheats so well. If you are short on time, you can skip the marinating.

4 pounds flatiron steak, or other cut of beef chuck

2 oranges

6 cups dry red wine

¼ cup cognac or brandy

¼ pound country bacon, cut into ½-inch-thick strips

2 garlic cloves, peeled and thinly sliced

Bouquet garni (4 sprigs fresh flat-leaf parsley, 1 sprig fresh thyme, 1 sprig fresh rosemary, and 1 bay leaf tied with kitchen string)

6 stalks celery, trimmed and cut on the bias into ½-inch-thick slices

4 large carrots, peeled, trimmed, and cut on the bias into ½-inch-thick slices

2 large onions, peeled and cut into ½-inch-thick slices or wedges

2 cups beef stock (page 209), low-sodium canned beef broth, or water

¼ cup vegetable oil

¼ cup (½ stick) unsalted butter

Coarse sea salt or kosher salt

1½ teaspoons crushed black pepper

2 tablespoons all-purpose flour

1. The day before you want to cook the beef, place it in a nonreactive bowl or Pyrex dish. Remove the zest of 1 orange using a vegetable peeler, including as little of the white pith as possible, and julienne. Juice both oranges and strain the juice. In a large bowl, combine the orange juice and zest, red wine, cognac, bacon, garlic, and bouquet garni. Pour the marinade over the beef, add the celery, carrots, and onions, cover, and marinate for at least 12 hours, or overnight, in the refrigerator.

2. Place a rack in the lower third of the oven and preheat the oven to 325°F.

3. Transfer the beef to a platter. Strain the marinade through a colander into a medium saucepan and reserve the vegetables and herbs. Pour the beef stock into the pan and bring to a boil. Lower the heat and keep at a slow, steady simmer.

4. Warm the vegetable oil and butter in a large cast-iron pot or Dutch oven over medium-high heat. Pat the beef dry and season all over with salt and the pepper. Dust the beef with the flour on all sides. When the oil is hot, add the beef to the pot and sear until golden brown on all sides, 12 to 15 minutes. Pour in the hot stock mixture and add the reserved vegetables and bouquet garni.

5. Cover the pot and transfer it to the oven. Braise, basting and turning the beef every 30 minutes, until the meat is fork-tender, 3 to 3½ hours. Discard the bouquet garni. If the sauce is too thin or is not flavored intensely enough, ladle most of it off into another pot and simmer it until it thickens and intensifies. Then add it back to the original pot and serve.

TENDER BEEF WITH HORSERADISH, PARSNIPS, AND CELERY ROOT

| MAKES 6 SERVINGS |

There's nothing that has quite the same extreme pungency as fresh horseradish. If you can't recall if you've ever eaten it, then you definitely have not. It's a forceful sensation you would remember, much more concentrated than the stuff in the jars. It's a classic accompaniment with braised fatty meat dishes, and for good reason. The sharpness is an excellent contrast to the richness of the meat.

You do need to take care when grating the horseradish, especially if your eyes are sensitive (though you will also feel it in your nose). If you use a food processor (and that's a good idea), whatever you do, don't lean over the machine when you take off the cover. Stand back!

---

1 (3-pound) beef bottom round

Coarse sea salt or kosher salt and freshly ground black pepper

1 tablespoon all-purpose flour

¼ cup extra-virgin olive oil

1 large onion, peeled and cut into large dice

20 juniper berries (see note)

¼ cup red wine vinegar

1 tablespoon tomato paste

¾ cup vodka

¾ cup dry red wine

2 medium parsnips, peeled, trimmed, and cut into large dice

1 large turnip, peeled, trimmed, and cut into large dice

¼ celery root, peeled, trimmed, and cut into large dice (about 1 cup)

3 bay leaves

2 tablespoons chopped fresh dill

5 ounces peeled, finely grated fresh horseradish (about ¾ cup; see note)

½ cup heavy cream

1. Center a rack in the oven and preheat the oven to 300°F.

2. Pat the beef dry and season with salt and pepper. Dust the beef with the flour. In a medium cast-iron pot or Dutch oven over high heat, warm the olive oil. Add the beef and sear until golden brown on all sides, 12 to 15 minutes. Transfer the beef to a plate.

3. Lower the heat to medium. Add the onion, juniper berries, and 1 teaspoon black pepper to the pot and cook, stirring, for 6 to 8 minutes, until the onions are translucent. Stir in the red wine vinegar and tomato paste and cook until almost all the liquid has evaporated. Pour in the vodka and red wine and bring to a boil. Add the parsnips, turnip, celery root, bay leaves, dill, ½ cup of the horseradish, and 2 cups water. Return the beef to the pot and bring to a simmer.

4. Cover the pot and transfer it to the oven to braise for 2½ hours, turning the meat two or three times.

5. Meanwhile, whip the heavy cream to medium peaks and stir in the remaining horseradish. Season to taste with salt and pepper. Serve the beef and vegetables with the horseradish whipped cream on the side.

JUNIPER BERRIES

These small purple fruits of a high-altitude evergreen tree have a clean, resinous taste and are used to flavor meats, pâtés, and marinades. They are also the flavoring behind gin. Juniper berries' refreshing taste makes them an excellent foil for fatty dishes and game meats like venison, and the berries play nicely against equally robust seasonings such as rosemary, garlic, and savory. In addition to gin, the berries are used in making various spirits and cordials, as well as a unique Finnish beer called *sahti*, in which juniper berries are used in place of (or in addition to) hops. Preferring colder climates, like those of North America, northern Europe, and the mountains of central Asia, juniper berries can take up to 3 years to reach full maturity, and they are always sold dried and whole. Juniper berries are available in supermarkets and specialty spice markets, or they can be purchased online (see Sources, page 210).

HORSERADISH

In the same family as cabbage and mustard, and a friend of both, the bitingly pungent horseradish root looks like a dirt-encrusted white carrot. It has to be peeled before cooking, and if it is tough, the root should be quartered lengthwise and the core cut away, jobs that will sting the eyes. The sharpness of raw horseradish, often mixed with vinegar or cream to be used as a relish, is lost when the root is cooked, as heat renders it a mild root vegetable with a pleasantly soft texture. Look for fresh horseradish in well-stocked produce aisles, particularly around the spring Jewish holiday of Passover, during which it is used to represent the bitterness of affliction.

BEEF SHOULDER
WITH JERUSALEM ARTICHOKES
AND CARROTS

| MAKES 6 TO 8 SERVINGS |

This is an easy, hearty recipe with Middle Eastern influence that you could make for your family on a Sunday night and then eat as leftovers during the week. Serve it with a little crisp salad of bitter greens, or maybe some sliced fresh fennel for crunch.

3 tablespoons extra-virgin olive oil

1 (3½-pound) beef shoulder; ask your butcher for the fattest part

Coarse sea salt or kosher salt and freshly ground black pepper

2 teaspoons paprika

2 teaspoons ground cumin

1 teaspoon ground ginger

½ teaspoon ground turmeric

½ teaspoon cayenne pepper

2 cups pearl onions, peeled (see note)

3 large carrots, peeled, trimmed, and roughly chopped

3 pounds Jerusalem artichokes, scrubbed (see note)

¼ cup chopped fresh cilantro

¼ cup diced preserved lemon (see note)

Freshly squeezed juice of 2 lemons

1. Center a rack in the oven and preheat the oven to 275°F.

2. Heat the olive oil in a medium cast-iron pot or Dutch oven over high heat. Season the beef with salt and pepper. Add the beef and sear until golden brown on all sides, about 15 minutes. Transfer the beef to a platter and reduce the heat to medium.

3. Add the paprika, cumin, ginger, turmeric, and cayenne to the pot and cook for 1 minute. Add the pearl onions, carrots, and Jerusalem artichokes, season with salt, and cook for 5 minutes more. Stir in 4 cups water and the cilantro, preserved lemon, and lemon juice. Return the beef to the pot and bring to a simmer.

4. Cover the pot and transfer it to the oven to braise for 2½ hours, turning the meat halfway through.

JERUSALEM ARTICHOKES

Also called sunchokes, Jerusalem artichokes are in fact tubers, not artichokes. Small and knobby, with a thin
brown skin that can be peeled or left
as is, Jerusalem artichokes are wonderfully versatile. Eaten raw, they are
similar in taste and texture to water
chestnuts; when roasted, boiled, or
sautéed they resemble a sweet, nutty
potato. Jerusalem artichokes are available in markets year-round but taste
best during their standard growing
season, which lasts from late fall
through early spring.

PRESERVED LEMON

A Moroccan standby, salt-preserved
lemons keep for at least 1 year. They
add a sweet lemony flavor to stews; or
they can be briefly boiled and then
used in dessert recipes. The pulp is
usually scraped away, while the rind
is chopped and used. You can make
your own preserved lemons, but you'll
need to do so 1 month before using
them; alternatively, you can find them
in Middle Eastern or gourmet food
stores or online (see Sources, page
210). To make your own, you'll need a
clean 1-quart jar. Cut 6 organic (un-
waxed) lemons into 6 wedges each,
leaving the wedges attached to one
another at the stem end. Pack each
lemon with 1 tablespoon kosher salt,
and place the lemons in the jar. Pour
any of the salt that has fallen onto
your work surface into the jar, then
top up with lemon juice (from about 8
more lemons). Cover and refrigerate
for 4 weeks, swirling and tipping the
jar once a week.

PEARL ONIONS

To peel pearl onions, bring a large pot
of water to a boil. Using a paring
knife, cut a small X in the root end of
each onion. Drop the onions into the
boiling water for 1 minute, then drain.
As soon as they are cool enough to
handle, slice off the root end with a
paring knife and slip off the papery
onion skin.

BEEF SHORT RIBS
WITH DAIKON RADISH AND SHIITAKE

| MAKES 4 TO 6 SERVINGS |

I grew up eating pot-au-feu (poached beef and vegetables) made with short ribs, so when I think of short ribs, I always imagine them poached, carved, and served off the bone in nice slices, maybe topped with a little broth and some coarse salt. But short ribs are also one of the most fantastic cuts for braising. They are meaty and full of gelatin and fat. When you have cooked them slowly, they will start to melt almost before you even get a bite into your mouth. Since you cook them on the bone, they have a lot of flavor, which the browning in a braise recipe will intensify, giving them a very earthy, caramelized, full taste. You can season braised short ribs any way you want, even strongly—as I do here, with a combination of dark soy sauce, ginger, star anise, and Szechuan pepper. They can take it!

When you are buying short ribs, tell the butcher you want them cut thick and lean (leanness is relative; even the leanest part of the short rib is pretty fatty). The pieces should be about 2 to 3 inches wide, weighing 1 pound each. Sometimes the butcher may precut the meat into smaller, thinner pieces. These will work too, but you might end up with more fat, which will dissolve into the sauce. Just skim it off with a spoon after cooking. If you have time, cook this the day before serving; let it cool, and refrigerate it overnight. That makes it very easy to take the fat off before you reheat the ribs.

---

3 tablespoons extra-virgin olive oil

3 pounds short ribs, trimmed of excess fat

Coarse sea salt or kosher salt and freshly ground black pepper

2 large red onions, peeled and cut into 1-inch cubes

1 (2-inch) piece fresh gingerroot, peeled and finely grated

½ pound shiitake mushrooms, cut into ½-inch-thick slices

2 star anise pods

1½ teaspoons ground Szechuan peppercorns (see note)

½ teaspoon ground cardamom

2 cups beef stock (page 209) or low-sodium canned beef broth

1. Center a rack in the oven and preheat the oven to 275°F.

2. In a medium cast-iron pot or Dutch oven over high heat, warm 2 tablespoons of the olive oil. Season the short ribs with salt and pepper and sear until golden brown on all sides, 15 to 20 minutes. Remove the short ribs and pour off all but 2 tablespoons of the fat from the pot.

3. Add the onions, gingerroot, and mushrooms and sauté, stirring, until the vegetables are softened, 5 to 6 minutes. Add the star anise, Szechuan pepper, and cardamom and cook, stirring, for 1 minute. Stir in the beef stock, bean paste, and soy sauce. Add the daikon radish and return the short ribs to the pot. Bring to a simmer.

4. Cover the pot and transfer it to the oven. Braise for 4 hours, or until the meat is very tender, checking the short ribs occasionally and spooning off any excess fat that rises to the surface. If the sauce is too thin or is not flavored intensely enough, ladle most of it off into another pot and simmer it until it thickens and intensifies. Then add it back to the first pot.

5. To serve: In a medium skillet over medium heat, warm the remaining 1 tablespoon olive oil. Add the scallions and garlic and cook until softened, 1 to 2 minutes. Sprinkle the scallion mixture and cilantro leaves over the short ribs and serve.

2 tablespoons fermented hot black bean paste (see note)

1 tablespoon dark soy sauce (see note)

2 pounds daikon radish, peeled, trimmed, and cut into 1/2-inch-thick slices

1 bunch scallions, trimmed and sliced

1 garlic clove, peeled and finely chopped

6 sprigs fresh cilantro, leaves only

Cucumber-Radish Rémoulade, for serving (see recipe below)

CUCUMBER-RADISH RÉMOULADE

| MAKES 4 TO 6 SERVINGS |

2 tablespoons mayonnaise

1 tablespoon Dijon mustard

2 teaspoons wasabi paste (see Sources, page 210)

Coarse sea salt or kosher salt and freshly ground black pepper

1 pound hothouse cucumbers, peeled, seeded, and cut into 1 1/2-by-1/4-inch sticks

1/2 pound red radishes, trimmed and cut into 1/8-inch-thick slices

3 tablespoons finely minced fresh chives

1. In a small mixing bowl, combine the mayonnaise, mustard, and wasabi paste. Season to taste with salt and pepper.
2. In a large mixing bowl, combine the cucumbers, radishes, and chives. Gently fold in the mayonnaise mixture and season with more salt and pepper. Serve immediately.

SZECHUAN PEPPERCORNS

Despite its name, the Szechuan peppercorn is not related to the black peppercorn but is in fact the dried seed of a plant related to the prickly ash tree. Used in Chinese cooking, most notably as one of the five spices in Chinese five-spice powder, the Szechuan peppercorn has a musky, piney aroma and a powerfully numbing heat. Szechuan peppercorns are often paired with fish, duck, or chicken, but they are also great in recipes that use dried fruit such as raisins or prunes. In 1968, the USDA began banning all imports of Szechuan peppercorns because the seeds were said to carry the citrus canker virus, harmful to citrus plants. Recently, however, the ban was lifted after producers began heat-treating their peppercorn crops to kill any traces of the virus. Szechuan peppercorns can now be purchased at specialty supermarkets or online (see Sources, page 210).

FERMENTED BLACK BEAN PASTE

Made from soybeans that have been salted or pickled (or both) and fermented, this pungent paste is prevalent in Asian (especially Chinese) cooking. The paste has a vast number of incarnations, including spicy varieties that have been enhanced with generous amounts of chopped dried chilies, and black bean garlic paste, loaded with chopped garlic. Black bean paste should not be confused with black bean sauce, which—although sometimes made with the paste—has a looser texture and a more complex flavor. Depending on the country of origin and the brand name, bean paste may be labeled under a variety of terms. Do not worry too much about finding exactly the right one, as any of them will work in most recipes. Black bean paste is available in jars or cans in many supermarkets and Asian markets or online (see Sources, page 210).

SOY SAUCE: LIGHT AND DARK

This carefully crafted staple—which has numerous varieties—is one of the few Asian condiments to enjoy nearly as much popularity in Western culture as in the East, where it's used in almost everything from stir-fries, sushi, soups, and stews to meat dishes. Originating in China approximately 3,000 years ago, soy sauce is believed to have slowly made its way to Japan and other Asian countries such as Vietnam and Thailand, where it acquired equal culinary significance. It is produced by crushing and then fermenting a mixture of steamed soybeans, roasted wheat, water, salt, and various bacteria and yeasts for a period as short as 6 months or, in the case of special aged soy sauces, as long as several years. Chinese soy sauce, made primarily with soybeans, tends to be darker in color and richer in flavor than its Japanese counterpart; Japanese soy sauce, containing larger amounts of wheat, has a sweeter, less earthy taste. (The exception is tamari, a variety of Japanese soy sauce, produced with very small amounts of wheat, which is sometimes said to be the "original" Japanese soy sauce because it more closely resembles Chinese soy sauce in flavor.)

Light and dark varieties of soy sauce also differ in taste and texture. Light soy sauce (sometimes called "thin" soy sauce), skimmed off the top of the soy sauce vat, is relatively salty and pale, and so it is suitable for vegetables, fish, and seafood. The darker kind, taken from the bottom of the batch, is fuller-bodied and has a rich molasses flavor more appropriate for heavier meat dishes. Light and dark soy sauce can be purchased at most supermarkets and Asian markets or online (see Sources, page 210). Tamari can be substituted for dark soy, and regular Japanese soy sauce (such as the ubiquitous Kikkoman) can be substituted for the light.

BEEF BRISKET WITH RED MISO AND WATERMELON RADISH

| MAKES 6 TO 8 SERVINGS |

Red miso has a unique character that enriches this braise, adding an earthy, funky, salty flavor to the meat. The recipe also calls for watermelon radishes, a red-fleshed, green-skinned variety that, when cut, resembles slices of watermelon. It's available seasonally at farmers' markets, or substitute black or daikon radish. If you've never had a radish any way but raw, the cooked radishes here are a nice surprise. They turn soft and really soak up the sauce. It's a terrific combination.

¼ cup extra-virgin olive oil

4 pounds beef brisket, trimmed of excess fat

1 large onion, peeled and chopped

2 tablespoons black sesame seeds (see note)

¼ cup red miso (see note)

¼ cup Chinese barbecue sauce (see note)

4 teaspoons red chili paste (see note)

6 garlic cloves, peeled and finely chopped

1 (4-inch) piece fresh gingerroot, peeled and finely grated

2 pounds watermelon radishes or black radishes, trimmed and halved, or daikon radish, peeled and cut into large chunks

1 bunch scallions, trimmed

1. Center a rack in the oven and preheat the oven to 275°F.

2. Heat the olive oil in a medium cast-iron pot or Dutch oven over high heat. Add the brisket and sear until golden brown on all sides, 10 to 15 minutes. Transfer the brisket to a platter.

3. Add the onion and sesame seeds to the pot and cook, stirring, for 5 minutes. Add the red miso, barbecue sauce, chili paste, garlic, and gingerroot and cook, stirring, for another 3 minutes. Stir in 1 cup water, return the brisket to the pot, and add the radishes.

4. Bring the liquid to a simmer, cover the pot, and transfer it to the oven. Braise for 3½ hours, turning the meat twice. Add the scallions and continue to braise until tender, about ½ hour more. If the sauce is too thin or is not flavored intensely enough, ladle most of it off into another pot and simmer it until it thickens and intensifies. Then return it to the first pot, and serve.

BLACK SESAME SEEDS

Black sesame seeds, as the name implies, have a darker color than their ivory-colored counterparts. In addition to the familiar nutty flavor of paler sesame seeds, black sesame seeds also taste slightly smoky. Sesame seeds can be purchased at specialty markets or online (see Sources, page 210).

MISO

A fermented paste made from soybeans and/or grains (rice, wheat, and barley), miso is a traditional Japanese food and comes in a wide variety of colors and flavors, although all miso is salted heavily during production. White miso, usually yellow in color, is made from rice and is fermented for less time than darker misos. As a result, it is milder, and well suited to light soups or sauces. The longer-aged red miso, usually made with barley, is much richer and more appropriate for heavier stews or meat dishes. Dark brown varieties are fermented the longest and have the deepest, most savory flavor. Look for unpasteurized miso, which will have a more interesting flavor and—like yogurt—offers the digestive benefits of active cultures. It is sold in refrigerated tubs in health food stores or Japanese markets, or it can be purchased online (see Sources, page 210).

CHINESE BARBECUE SAUCE

Often used in Chinese cooking for basting grilled meats and vegetables, Chinese barbecue sauce is a zesty mixture of hoisin sauce, soy sauce, black bean paste, and sugar. Its high sugar content means that it can burn; for this reason, it should be watched carefully during cooking, or used at low cooking temperatures. It can be purchased at Asian markets or online (see Sources, page 210).

RED CHILI PASTE

A simple mixture of crushed fresh hot chili peppers, garlic, and salt, red chili paste (or Thai chili paste) is frequently used as a condiment and an ingredient in Asian cooking. To make your own, remove the seeds (if you prefer to) from ½ pound of fresh red chili peppers. Heat a heavy pan over medium heat, and add the chilis, dry-roasting them until fragrant and lightly toasted, about 2 minutes. Finely chop the chilies and transfer them to a mortar and pestle. Add 1 teaspoon of salt and 1 finely chopped peeled garlic clove and grind until the mixture forms a soft paste. The chili paste can be stored in an airtight container in the refrigerator for up to 1 week. Red chili paste can also be purchased in Asian grocery stores or online (see Sources, page 210).

CORNED BEEF AND CABBAGE

| MAKES 6 TO 8 SERVINGS |

Corned beef is a cut of meat that has been cured lightly in salt. This is not a technique done in France, where the only meat we really cure before cooking is pork for bacon. But the salt cure gives the beef a nice firm, juicy texture and helps it keep its attractive pink color. The usual way to cook corned beef is to simmer it in plenty of water with some potatoes and cabbage. It's very homey and simple. In my version, I elevate the preparation by wrapping the meat in cabbage leaves before braising it slowly with an assortment of root vegetables. The meat ends up with a lot of flavor—and so do the vegetables. Then I serve it with a fresh horseradish cream, which lifts the dish in the same way that mustard lifts a corned beef sandwich. If you don't feel like making the horseradish cream, or if you can't find fresh horseradish, you could just serve this with a little mustard on the side, either mixed into sour cream or by itself.

---

1 savoy cabbage, outer leaves discarded, remaining leaves separated

3½ pounds corned beef, not too lean, not too fat (see note)

2 Yukon Gold potatoes, cut into large chunks

1 small rutabaga, peeled and cut into large chunks

1 medium carrot, peeled and cut into large chunks

1 medium turnip, peeled and cut into large chunks

1 small red onion, peeled and roughly chopped

1 small parsnip, peeled and cut into large chunks

2 bay leaves

3 sprigs fresh thyme

Spice sachet: 1 teaspoon black peppercorns, 1 teaspoon pink peppercorns (see note), and 10 whole allspice, tied in cheesecloth

3 cups beef stock (page 209), low-sodium canned beef broth, or water

½ cup sour cream

1. Center a rack in the oven and preheat the oven to 300°F.

2. Bring a large pot of water to a boil, and fill a large bowl halfway with ice cubes and cold water. Add the cabbage leaves to the boiling water and blanch just until the leaves are tender, 3 to 5 minutes. Using a strainer, transfer the cabbage leaves to the ice water bath and let cool completely. Drain the cabbage leaves and pat them dry with a paper towel.

3. Using half of the cabbage leaves, make a circle of overlapping leaves one-third larger in diameter than the corned beef. Put the corned beef in the center of the leaves and cover it with the remaining cabbage leaves. Wrap the cabbage leaves around the corned beef and tie securely with kitchen string.

4. Put the potatoes, rutabaga, carrot, turnip, onion, parsnip, bay leaves, and thyme on the bottom of a medium cast-iron pot or Dutch oven. Place the wrapped corned beef on top of the vegetables. (Alternatively, make a circle of overlapping leaves one-third larger in diameter than the corned beef on the bottom of the pot, put the corned beef in the center of the leaves, cover with the remaining cabbage leaves, and scatter the vegetables and herbs around.) Add the spice sachet and pour the stock into the pot.

5. Cover the pot and transfer it to the oven. Braise, basting the corned beef every 45 minutes, until the beef is very tender, about 3 hours. If the sauce is too thin or is not flavored intensely enough, ladle most of it off into another pot and simmer it until it thickens and intensifies. Then add it back to the first pot.

6. To serve: Mix together the sour cream, horseradish, mustard, and paprika. Remove the string from the corned beef and discard. Cut the corned beef into slices. Serve the beef and vegetables with the bread and the seasoned sour cream on the side.

IRISH SODA BREAD
| MAKES 6 TO 8 SERVINGS |

1 cup raisins

1/3 cup Irish whiskey (such as Jameson)

2 cups all-purpose flour

4 tablespoons unsalted butter or shortening, cut into small pieces

1 1/2 tablespoons sugar, plus additional for sprinkling

1 teaspoon baking soda

1/2 teaspoon fine sea salt

1/2 teaspoon freshly grated nutmeg

1/2 cup buttermilk, or as needed

1 egg

1. Bring the raisins and 2 cups water to a boil. Drain well. In a small bowl, combine the raisins and whiskey and let sit for at least 3 hours, or overnight.

2. Center a rack in the oven and preheat the oven to 350°F. Line a baking sheet with parchment paper.

3. In the bowl of a mixer fitted with the paddle attachment, combine the flour, butter, sugar, baking soda, salt, nutmeg, and rum-soaked raisins. Mix until the dough resembles coarse cornmeal.

4. On low speed, slowly pour in enough buttermilk so that the dough comes together. The mixture should be soft but should stay together.

5. Divide the dough in half and shape into two 5-inch balls. Transfer the balls to the prepared baking sheet. In a small bowl, whisk together the egg and 2 tablespoons water, and brush the tops of the balls with the egg wash. Using a serrated knife, cut an X in the top of each ball. Sprinkle each ball with sugar. Bake until golden brown, 35 to 40 minutes.

1 (2-inch) piece of fresh horseradish, peeled and grated (see note, page 5)

1 tablespoon Dijon mustard

1/2 teaspoon paprika

Irish Soda Bread, for serving (see recipe below)

CORNED BEEF

If you purchased your corned beef in the supermarket, it might be too salty. Taste a little. If it seems overwhelmingly saline, blanch it in boiling water for 2 minutes, then taste it again. If it's still too salty, repeat the blanching process using new cold water.

PINK PEPPERCORNS

Native to Brazil, pink (or red) peppercorns are the berries of an evergreen plant and are not related to black peppercorns. They are grown in the tropics but packaged in France (from which they are exported), and they can be found in gourmet food stores or online (see Sources, page 210). They have a pungent, piney, sweet flavor that could be described as somewhat peppery.

ROPA VIEJA

CUBAN-BRAISED FLANK STEAK WITH PEPPERS, TOMATOES, AND ONIONS

| MAKES 4 TO 6 SERVINGS |

This is a traditional Cuban recipe that calls for slowly braising flank steak until the meat practically falls apart—and looks to some people like worn-out old clothes that are coming apart and shredding at the ends. That's what the name means: old clothes. It sounds strange until you stop to think about it. But you won't have to think too much about the dish. Just eat it and enjoy! Fried Sweet Plantains are a nice accompaniment.

4 garlic cloves, peeled and chopped

2 jalapeño peppers, chopped

2 teaspoons dried oregano, preferably Cuban (see note)

1½ teaspoons coarse sea salt or kosher salt, plus additional

2½ to 3 pounds flank steak

1 to 2 tablespoons extra-virgin olive oil

1 tablespoon unsalted butter

2 medium Spanish onions, peeled, halved, and thinly sliced

2 large green bell peppers, peeled (peeling is optional), cored, seeded, and thinly sliced

1 red bell pepper, peeled (peeling is optional), cored, seeded, and thinly sliced

½ cup sherry

8 very ripe plum tomatoes, halved, cored, and seeded

2 bay leaves

Freshly ground black pepper

Lime wedges, for serving

Fried Sweet Plantains, for serving (optional; see recipe, opposite)

1. The day before you want to serve this dish, combine the garlic, jalapeños, oregano, and salt in a nonreactive container, such as a Pyrex bowl. Add the meat and rub the mixture all over it. Cover tightly with plastic wrap, and marinate overnight in the refrigerator.

2. Center a rack in the oven and preheat the oven to 275°F.

3. Heat 1 tablespoon of the oil and the butter in a medium cast-iron pot or Dutch oven over high heat. Scrape the rub off the flank steak, and reserve. Add the flank steak to the pot and sear both sides until golden brown, 5 to 7 minutes. Transfer the flank steak to a plate.

4. If there is not enough fat in the pot, add another 1 tablespoon olive oil. Add the onions and cook until light golden brown, 8 to 10 minutes. Add the bell peppers and cook for 5 minutes. Add the sherry and bring to a simmer, scraping up any browned bits on the bottom of the pot. Stir in the tomatoes, 1 cup water, and the reserved rub. Return the flank steak to the pot, nestle it in with the vegetables, and add the bay leaves and salt and pepper to taste. Bring to a simmer.

5. Cover the pot, transfer it to the oven, and braise until the meat is very tender, 3½ to 4 hours, turning the steak every hour or so. Serve slices of meat with the lime wedges and fried plantains, if desired.

FRIED SWEET PLANTAINS

| MAKES 6 SERVINGS |

¼ cup vegetable oil, plus additional

2 very ripe plantains (they should be nearly black all over), peeled and sliced ½ inch thick

Coarse sea salt or kosher salt

Heat half the oil in a large skillet. Add about half the plantains (as many as can fit in one layer) and fry until very dark golden brown on both sides, about 7 minutes. Drain on a plate lined with a paper towel. Season with salt. Repeat with the remaining plantains and oil, adding more oil if necessary. Serve with the Ropa Vieja.

CUBAN OREGANO

Originally from Africa, and also called Spanish thyme, this cousin of the more common oregano has purple stems and thick, slightly pointed leaves, sometimes with pale striped borders. It resembles oregano in flavor, though with a slight mintiness, and is a key ingredient in Cuban dishes such as black bean soup, as well as in some Asian cooking. It is available dried in some Latin stores, or try growing your own. It can do quite well as a houseplant (the botanical name is *Plectranthus amboinicus*).

CUBAN CREOLE STEW

BRAISED BEEF BRISKET WITH FRESH CHORIZO AND SQUASH

| MAKES 6 TO 8 SERVINGS |

This richly flavored one-pot meal incorporates the African, Spanish, and French influences that make up Creole cooking. Comprising tomatoes, lime juice, garlic, and cumin, the marinade for the brisket is very bright and savory, and it also tenderizes the meat. The plantains, squash, and sweet potatoes in the braise help thicken the sauce and lend sweetness, which I find works particularly well with the fresh chorizo. It's a fairly simple dish with a complex taste. Bear in mind that sweet potato doesn't freeze very well, so cook this dish for a crowd and finish it all up.

1 (3- to 4-pound) beef brisket

Coarse sea salt or kosher salt and freshly ground black pepper

10 plum tomatoes, halved

5 garlic cloves, peeled and chopped

2 bay leaves

Finely grated zest and freshly squeezed juice of 1 lime

1 teaspoon ground cumin

2 tablespoons extra-virgin olive oil

1 pound fresh chorizo, sliced (see note)

2 Spanish onions, peeled and chopped

3 green bell peppers, cored, seeded, and diced

1 (1-pound) calabaza squash, peeled, seeded, and cut into ½-inch dice

1 large (about ¾- to 1-pound) sweet potato or yam, peeled and cut into ½-inch dice

1 ripe plantain, peeled and cut into ½-inch dice

1. The day before you want to serve the dish, season the brisket with salt and pepper and place in a nonreactive container, such as a Pyrex bowl. In a blender, puree the tomatoes, garlic, bay leaves, lime zest and juice, and cumin. Pour this marinade over the brisket, cover tightly with plastic wrap, and refrigerate overnight.

2. Center a rack in the oven and preheat the oven to 275°F.

3. Scrape the marinade off the beef, reserving the marinade. In a medium cast-iron pot or Dutch oven over high heat, warm the olive oil. Add the beef and sear both sides until golden brown, 5 to 7 minutes. Transfer the beef to a platter. Add the sausage to the pot and brown for 1 minute. Add the onions, and cook until translucent, 5 to 7 minutes. Stir in the bell peppers and cook until softened, 4 to 5 minutes more.

4. Return the brisket to the pot. Add the reserved marinade, the squash, sweet potato, plantain, and 1 cup water. Bring to a simmer, cover, and transfer to the oven. Braise until the beef is fork-tender, about 4 hours. If the sauce is too thin or is not flavored intensely enough, ladle most of it off into another pot and simmer it until it thickens and intensifies. Then add it back to the first pot.

FRESH CHORIZO

A pork sausage that has different incarnations in Spain and Mexico, fresh chorizo in some form is available in most parts of America. Spanish chorizo is seasoned with garlic and smoked Spanish paprika (see page 163), which gives it a deep red color and a smoky taste, and then either soft-cured (at which point it is ready to use in cooking) or dry-cured (dry-curing renders it hard enough to simply slice and serve). Depending on the sweetness or spice of the paprika, the chorizo will vary in piquancy. Mexican chorizo, made with fresh pork, is moister and must be cooked before serving. It is added to everything from quesadillas to eggs. If fresh chorizo is unavailable, spicy Italian sausage, augmented if possible with a pinch of smoked Spanish paprika, is a passable substitute. Spanish fresh chorizo is available online (see Sources, page 210).

CARBONNADE À LA FLAMANDE

BEER-BRAISED BEEF SHOULDER WITH GINGERBREAD

| MAKES 8 TO 10 SERVINGS |

A classic carbonnade is made from slowly cooked beef and onions stewed in good Belgian beer. This version doesn't drift too far from that, though I do like to sweeten it a bit with some orange marmalade and crumbled gingerbread. Both melt into the sauce, so you don't exactly taste them, but they add a suave and spicy undercurrent that plays nicely against the bitterness of the beer. I also marinate the beef shoulder overnight in crème fraîche to tenderize it more.

5 pounds boneless beef shoulder, trimmed of all fat

Coarse sea salt or kosher salt and freshly ground black pepper

2 cups crème fraîche or sour cream

2 tablespoons extra-virgin olive oil

½ pound slab bacon, diced

3 medium onions, peeled, halved, and sliced

2 garlic cloves, peeled and thinly sliced

2 sprigs fresh thyme

2 bay leaves

¼ teaspoon crushed black pepper

4 (11.2-ounce) bottles Chimay beer or other Belgian-style beer

¼ cup Dijon mustard

2 tablespoons orange marmalade (optional)

1 cup gingerbread (Pain d'Épices, page 192) cut into ½-inch cubes or ¾ cup gingersnap crumbs

2 tablespoons red wine vinegar

2 tablespoons fresh flat-leaf parsley leaves

1. The day before you want to serve the dish, season the beef shoulder with salt and ground black pepper, and put the beef in a nonreactive container, such as Pyrex. Pour the 1 cup crème fraîche over it. Roll the beef shoulder to make sure it is completely covered with crème fraîche. Cover and refrigerate overnight.

2. The next day, center a rack in the oven and preheat the oven to 275°F.

3. In a large cast-iron pot or Dutch oven over high heat, warm the olive oil. Scrape the marinade off the beef shoulder, reserving it, and pat the beef dry. Add the beef shoulder to the pot and sear until dark golden brown on all sides, 20 to 25 minutes. Remove the beef from the pot and reserve.

4. Add the bacon to the pot and cook until it renders all of its fat, about 5 minutes. Add the onions and cook, stirring, until they turn a deep caramel color, about 20 minutes.

5. Add the garlic, thyme, bay leaves, crushed black pepper, and the reserved marinade. Add the beer and bring to a simmer, scraping up any browned bits that stick to the bottom of the pot. Whisk in 2 tablespoons of the Dijon mustard and the marmalade, if using. Return the beef to the pot, add 2 cups water and the gingerbread, and bring to a simmer.

6. Cover the pot and transfer it to the oven. Braise until the meat is tender, $2^{1}/_{2}$ to 3 hours, turning the meat once or twice. If the sauce is too thin or is not flavored intensely enough, ladle most of it off into another pot and simmer it until it thickens and intensifies. Then add it back to the first pot.

7. Meanwhile, just before serving, bring the red wine vinegar to a boil in a small saucepan, then reduce the heat to low and keep warm. In a small bowl, mix the remaining 1 cup crème fraîche with the remaining 2 tablespoons Dijon mustard. Drizzle the beef with the red wine vinegar and sprinkle with the parsley leaves. Serve the crème fraîche mixture on the side.

SMOKY BEEF CHILI

| MAKES 8 TO 10 SERVINGS |

What makes this chili the best of its kind is using my Homemade Chili Powder, ground from dried chilies. It gives this dish an enormous amount of flavor that builds from bite to bite. Make sure to have plenty of cold beer on hand, and serve corn tortillas and sliced cucumber and avocado alongside.

1. Center a rack in the oven and preheat the oven to 300°F.

2. Grate the zest of 1 of the limes, then juice both limes. In a large bowl, combine 3 cups water, the masa harina, and the lime zest and juice.

3. Heat the olive oil in a medium cast-iron pot over high heat. Add the beef cubes and ground beef and sear until golden brown on all sides, 10 to 12 minutes. Transfer the beef to a plate and wipe the inside of the pot clean with paper towels.

4. Lower the temperature to medium-high. Add the bacon to the pot and cook until it renders its fat, about 5 minutes. Add the onion, garlic, cumin, oregano, and salt and cook until the onions are softened, 10 to 12 minutes. Add the chili powder, stir to combine, and cook for 1 to 2 more minutes. Stir in the vinegar and Worcestershire sauce and bring to a simmer, scraping up any browned bits stuck to the bottom of the pot. Return the beef cubes and ground meat to the pot and add the tomatoes, bay leaf, and masa harina mixture. Bring to a simmer.

5. Cover the pot and transfer it to the oven to braise for 2 hours, stirring once or twice. Sprinkle with the cilantro leaves right before serving.

2 limes

2 tablespoons masa harina (see note)

2 tablespoons extra-virgin olive oil

4 pounds beef chuck roast: 2½ pounds cut into ½-inch cubes; 1½ pounds ground (ask your butcher to do this) or finely chopped

¼ pound slab bacon, cut into large chunks

1 large onion, peeled and cut into large cubes

4 garlic cloves, peeled and finely chopped

1 tablespoon ground cumin

1 tablespoon dried regular oregano or Mexican oregano (see note)

1 tablespoon coarse sea salt or kosher salt

¼ cup Homemade Chili Powder (see recipe, page 24), or more to taste

1 tablespoon red wine vinegar

1 tablespoon Worcestershire sauce

5 large tomatoes, roughly chopped

1 bay leaf

½ cup chopped fresh cilantro

HOMEMADE CHILI POWDER

| MAKES SCANT 1 CUP |

4 ancho chili peppers

4 pasilla chili peppers

4 guajillo chili peppers

2 chilies de árbol

2 pequín chili peppers

1 small habanero chili pepper

In a dry skillet over medium heat, toast the chili peppers (see notes) on all sides for 5 to 7 minutes, making sure that they are lightly toasted, but not burned. Transfer them to a plate to cool. Remove and discard the seeds from the peppers. Blend the peppers in a spice grinder.

MEXICAN OREGANO

Although similar in flavor, the spicier Mexican oregano is only loosely related to its ubiquitous Mediterranean cousin, Greek oregano. A relative of lemon verbena, Mexican oregano has a robust flavor that makes it an excellent partner for cilantro and cumin, and a natural choice for seasoning chili. Fresh Mexican oregano is often sold at farmers' markets—you can identify it by its grayish-green leaves and tiny white flowers. It is available both fresh and and dried in Latin American supermarkets or online (see Sources, page 210).

ANCHO CHILI PEPPERS

Blackish-purple in color, ancho chilies are the dried version of fully matured triangle-shaped poblano peppers. The most common variety of dried chili pepper in Mexico, ancho chilies are used extensively in Mexican cooking, their sweet, mild heat giving a kick to dishes such as chili con carne and enchiladas. When purchasing whole ancho chilies, you should avoid any that are brittle and lack luster; seek out peppers with a dark brownish-red sheen. Anchos are available whole and powdered at Latin American grocery stores or online.

PASILLA CHILI PEPPERS

Long, thin, glossy black dried pasilla peppers can be fairly hot, but once they have been toasted, the seeds and white veins can be removed, leaving them milder. Fried, crumbled pasilla is a traditional garnish for tortilla soup. Look for these peppers in Latin or other markets with a good selection of dried peppers, or order them online.

GUAJILLO CHILI PEPPERS

Dried guajillo chiles, which range in heat from moderate to very hot, have a long, thin shape and a thick, dark, leathery skin. They usually require longer soaking than other thinner-skinned chilies. This pepper is a favorite for flavoring Mexican salsas, soups, and stews (partly because it's rather inexpensive) and is most often used to make enchilada sauce. Guajillos are also sometimes used by North Africans to make harissa (see note, page 93). Dried guajillos are available whole or ground at Latin American markets or online.

CHILIES DE ÁRBOL

These long, thin red peppers, with a searing heat, are sold dried in many supermarkets, or you can buy them online.

PEQUÍN CHILI PEPPERS

Small, red, and exceedingly hot, pequín or bird's-eye peppers are any of several varieties of diminutive chilies, which in fact owe their seed dispersal to the hardy birds of Mexico that eat them. They are sold dried in Latin markets, or you can buy them online.

HABANERO CHILI PEPPERS

Small, squat peppers available fresh in colors ranging from light green to orange, red, and sometimes even dark purple, this thin, glossy-skinned chili is highly flavorful and very spicy. If it is unavailable, substitute the more easily found, equally hot Scotch bonnet pepper.

MASA HARINA

A Mexican flour made by drying and powdering hominy, corn kernels that have been boiled with lime. This pale white meal can be used for making tamales and tortillas. It is finer than cornmeal in texture and should have a sweet, cornlike fragrance. Be sure you have a fresh bag, as it can go rancid or become infested quite easily. It is widely available in grocery stores and Mexican markets, or you can order it online.

LAYERED BEEF AND ROOT VEGETABLES IN A SPICY COCONUT CURRY

| MAKES 6 SERVINGS |

This dish, featuring many Indian flavors, is a little unusual. Instead of calling for lamb as the base, I use beef, which is not so common in Indian cuisine. But I find it goes very well with the cardamom, cinnamon, and curry leaves that make up the aromatics in the pot. It's a fragrant dish, not spicy-hot, but very flavorful. Since you can make it in advance, it's perfect for when you are having a lot of friends coming over and you want to be able to spend time with them. Like many of the recipes in this book, it will braise while you socialize.

12 dried curry leaves (see note)

2 whole cloves

1 tablespoon peeled, grated fresh gingerroot

2 teaspoons ground cardamom

1 teaspoon ground cinnamon

1 teaspoon freshly ground black pepper, plus additional

½ teaspoon crushed red pepper flakes

2 pounds beef top butt or top sirloin, cut into ¼-inch-thick slices

½ cup plain whole-milk yogurt

2 teaspoons coarse sea salt or kosher salt, plus additional

¼ cup vegetable oil, plus additional if necessary

2 cups peeled, halved, and thinly sliced onions

2 garlic cloves, peeled and chopped

2 tablespoons white wine vinegar

2 cups carrot juice (see note)

½ pound turnips, peeled and sliced into ⅛-inch-thick rounds (see note)

½ pound celery root, peeled and sliced into ⅛-inch-thick rounds (see note)

1 pound Yukon Gold or Idaho potatoes, peeled and sliced into ⅛-inch-thick rounds (see note)

2 cups unsweetened coconut milk

1. The day before you want to serve this dish, use a mortar and pestle, spice grinder, or blender to grind the curry leaves and cloves. Transfer to a small bowl and mix in the gingerroot, cardamom, cinnamon, black pepper, and red pepper flakes.

2. Place the beef in a nonreactive bowl, such as Pyrex. Combine 3 tablespoons of the spice mix with the yogurt and salt. Toss the yogurt mixture with the beef. Cover the bowl tightly with plastic wrap and marinate in the refrigerator overnight. Refrigerate the remaining spice mix.

3. In a large nonstick skillet over high heat, warm 3 tablespoons of the vegetable oil. Remove the beef from the marinade and scrape off any marinade that clings to the meat (reserve the marinade). Sear the beef in batches, about 45 seconds on each side, adding additional oil if necessary. Transfer the beef to a bowl and set aside.

4. Reduce the heat to medium and heat the remaining 1 tablespoon vegetable oil. Add the onions and cook until translucent, about 5 minutes. Add the garlic and the remaining spice mix, and toss well. Pour in the vinegar, raise the heat to medium-high, and boil until the vinegar has mostly evaporated, about 2 minutes. Add the carrot juice, bring to a boil, and season to taste with salt and pepper.

5. Center a rack in the oven and preheat the oven to 300°F.

6. Arrange half of the beef on the bottom of a medium cast-iron pot or Dutch oven, then add a layer of turnips, a layer of celery root, and a layer of potatoes, seasoning each vegetable layer with salt and pepper. Repeat the layering once more, finishing with a layer of potatoes on top. Pour the carrot juice mixture and the coconut milk into the pot and cover with a piece of oiled parchment paper and the pot lid. Bring to a simmer.

7. Transfer the pot to the oven to braise for 2 hours. Uncover and braise until the meat is moist and stewlike, about 1 hour more. Sprinkle with cilantro leaves and grated coconut and serve.

Fresh cilantro leaves, for garnish

Grated fresh or desiccated coconut, for garnish

CURRY LEAVES
A small, glossy green leaf that resembles a bay leaf in both appearance and culinary usage, the curry leaf comes from citrus trees that grow in South Asia. Curry leaves add a savory flavor, for which bay leaves can be an adequate though approximate substitute. Curry leaves are sold fresh and dried in Indian food stores, or you can order them online (see Sources, page 210).

MANDOLINE
A French or Japanese mandoline is perfect for turning out paper-thin slices of vegetables. However, if you don't have either of these, a sharp knife works well too.

FRESH CARROT JUICE
If you have a juicer, this is your chance to put it to work. However, carrot juice is easily procured from a juice bar or can be purchased fresh, in bottles, from some natural food stores.

BRAISED GROUND BEEF WITH SPLIT PEAS, APRICOTS, AND APPLES

| MAKES 4 TO 6 SERVINGS |

Most people don't think of ground meat when they think of braising. But there are lot of classic braised dishes, like meatballs and even Bolognese sauce, that use it. You get much more flavor out of ground meat than a whole piece, and it stays moist and juicy in a sauce. This dish has a dense sweet-and-sour taste. The sweetness comes from the apples, apple juice, and apricots, while the apple cider vinegar keeps the sugar in check. You could serve this with something earthy on the side as a contrast, perhaps wild rice or kasha.

1 cup yellow split peas

2 pounds ground beef

Coarse sea salt or kosher salt and freshly ground black pepper

3 tablespoons extra-virgin olive oil

1 large onion, peeled and chopped

1 teaspoon Four-Spice Powder (see recipe, opposite)

1/4 teaspoon crushed red pepper flakes

2 Granny Smith apples, peeled, cored, and cut into 1/2-inch dice

1/2 cup dried apricots

1 teaspoon chopped fresh rosemary

1/2 cup apple cider vinegar

Freshly squeezed juice of 2 lemons

2 1/2 cups apple juice

Chopped fresh mint leaves, for serving

1. The day before you want to serve the dish, put the split peas in a bowl, cover with water by at least 2 inches, and refrigerate. The next day, drain before using.

2. Center a rack in the oven and preheat the oven to 300°F.

3. Season the ground beef with salt and pepper. Heat 1 tablespoon of the olive oil in a small cast-iron pot or Dutch oven over medium-high heat. Add the meat and cook until it loses its pink color, about 5 minutes. Transfer it to a bowl.

4. Lower the heat to medium and add the remaining 2 tablespoons olive oil to the pot. Add the onion, Four-Spice Powder, and red pepper flakes and cook for 4 to 5 minutes. Add the apples, apricots, split peas, rosemary, apple cider vinegar, and lemon juice and bring to a boil. Return the meat to the pan and add the apple juice and 1 cup water. Bring to a simmer.

5. Cover the pot, transfer it to the oven, and braise for 2 hours. Serve sprinkled with mint.

FOUR-SPICE POWDER

| MAKES ABOUT 2 TABLESPOONS |

Used by the French to season hearty, rustic food like charcu-terie, stews, and braised game, four-spice powder is tradition-ally a blend of cloves, pepper, nutmeg, and ginger. It is also used in the French-influenced cuisine of North Africa, where it fits in nicely with the tagines and stews of that region. This recipe makes only a small batch, but if you think you'll be using a lot of four-spice, you can double or triple it and store in an air-tight container in a cool, dry place for up to 6 months. Four-spice blends can also be purchased at specialty spice markets and on-line (see Sources, page 210).

2 teaspoons whole cloves

1 heaping tablespoon black peppercorns

2 teaspoons freshly grated nutmeg

1 teaspoon ground ginger

In a spice grinder or clean coffee grinder, finely grind the cloves and black pepper together. Transfer to a bowl and combine with the nutmeg and ginger.

BEEF SHANK WITH COCONUT AND AVOCADO

| MAKES 4 SERVINGS |

This is an unusual flavor combination for beef, but the creamy avocado matches wonderfully with the sweet coconut and raisins, all kept in check by the sherry vinegar and a squeeze of fresh lime at the end. It's unlikely that your guests will have had anything quite like it before, but they will probably ask you to make it for them again.

Since beef shank can be a little hard to deal with at home, you will need to ask your butcher for special help. Ask him to separate the meat from the shank and tie it together like a roast. Then he should cut the shank bone into four pieces. The meat gets cooked until it's very tender; then the bones are added to the pot at the end of cooking, so the marrow inside can soften. It's delicious to eat the marrow on the side with the shank meat, a real treat. If all this seems daunting, you can use a 4-pound piece of brisket instead. In that case, the cooking time might be less, so check the meat often with a fork to see when it's tender but not dry.

½ cup golden raisins

¾ cup sherry vinegar

1 tablespoon crushed red pepper flakes

1 teaspoon crushed black pepper

2 teaspoons cumin seeds, toasted (see note)

1 (6-pound) beef shank (see headnote for instructions)

Coarse sea salt or kosher salt

¼ cup extra-virgin olive oil

1 (14-ounce) piece of slab bacon: 12 ounces cut into 8 chunks; 2 ounces cut into ¼-inch-thick strips

3 medium carrots, peeled, trimmed, and cut into ½-inch pieces

1 large red onion, peeled, trimmed, and finely chopped

5 garlic cloves, peeled and thinly sliced

2 tablespoons tomato paste

¼ cup all-purpose flour

2 tablespoons grated peeled fresh gingerroot

1. Bring a small saucepan of water to a boil. Add the raisins, remove the saucepan from the heat, and let the raisins plump up in the hot water. Drain the raisins and combine them with the sherry vinegar. Let sit for 1 hour.

2. Meanwhile, combine the red pepper flakes, black pepper, and 1 teaspoon of the cumin seeds and rub the beef with this spice mixture and salt. Let sit at room temperature for at least 45 minutes. (You could also prepare this the day before and keep it in the refrigerator until needed.)

3. Center a rack in the oven and preheat the oven to 300°F.

4. Warm the olive oil in a large cast-iron pot or Dutch oven over medium-high heat. Add the beef and bacon chunks and sear the beef on all sides until golden brown, 12 to 15 minutes. Transfer the beef and bacon to a plate, leaving the fat in the pot.

5. Add the carrots, onion, and garlic to the pot and cook, stirring, until tender, about 10 minutes. Stir in the tomato paste and cook for 2 minutes. Stir in the flour and gingerroot and cook, stirring, for 2 minutes. Stir in the vinegar-and-raisin mixture and bring to a simmer, scraping up any brown bits sticking to the bottom of the pot. Add the beef stock, coconut milk, tomatoes, orange zest, and marjoram. Stir to combine; then return the beef and bacon to the pot and bring to a simmer.

6. Cover the pot and transfer it to the oven to braise until the meat is tender, about 4½ hours, turning the meat two or three times. If the sauce is too thin or is not flavored intensely enough, ladle most of it off into another pot and simmer it until it thickens and intensifies. Then add it back to the first pot. Add the reserved shank bones to the braise and let cook for 5 to 6 minutes, just until the marrow has softened and is warm.

7. Meanwhile, in a large skillet over medium-high heat, cook the remaining 2 ounces bacon until its fat is rendered. Add the coconut, avocados, peanuts, parsley, and remaining 1 teaspoon cumin seeds and toss until everything is warm, 2 to 3 minutes.

8. To serve: Remove the beef from the pot, untie, and cut into serving pieces. Transfer the beef to shallow bowls and add the broth, vegetables, and marrow bones. Sprinkle the avocado-peanut mixture around the beef and squeeze some orange and lime juice on top.

6 cups beef stock (page 209), low-sodium canned beef broth, or water

1 (13½-ounce) can unsweetened coconut milk

4 tomatoes, roughly chopped

Peeled zest of 3 oranges, ½ orange reserved for serving

2 sprigs fresh marjoram

1 cup unsweetened desiccated coconut

2 avocados, peeled, pitted, and cut into ½-inch chunks

1 cup unsalted roasted peanuts

6 sprigs fresh flat-leaf parsley, leaves only

1 lime, halved, for serving

TOASTING SPICES

To toast spices, place a small dry skillet over medium heat. Add the spices and cook, shaking the pan occasionally to prevent burning, until the spices are fragrant, 2 to 3 minutes. Immediately transfer the spices to a plate, to stop the cooking.

SPICY OXTAILS WITH PEARS AND SWEET POTATOES

| MAKES 4 TO 6 SERVINGS |

Everyone knows that the best meat is next to the bone, and with an oxtail, all the meat is next to the bone. There's not another part of the cow that concentrates as much flavor as the tail, and that is what makes oxtail so delicious. Sadly, I can't really serve oxtail on the bone at any of my restaurants. It's just too rustic. But it's a great, inexpensive cut to make at home for guests who don't mind using their hands. Don't try to eat oxtail with a fork and knife, or you will miss all the good bits stuck in between the vertebrae. Pick it up as you would a little roasted bird and chew all around. Of course the meat has to be cooked so it slips right off the bones, or it won't be tender enough. A long, slow braise, like this Asian-inspired one with sweet potatoes, pears, soy sauce, and ginger, is an ideal method.

1 tablespoon extra-virgin olive oil

4 pounds oxtails, cut into 1½- to 2-inch-thick slices, excess fat removed (see note, page 35)

Coarse sea salt or kosher salt and freshly ground black pepper

4 garlic cloves, peeled and finely chopped

1 (2-inch) piece fresh gingerroot, peeled and finely grated

1 tablespoon chili powder (purchased, or use the recipe on page 24)

2 Spanish onions, peeled and diced

½ cup dry vermouth

¼ cup light soy sauce (see note, page 11)

1 tablespoon hoisin sauce (see note)

1 teaspoon red chili paste

2 tablespoons packed light brown sugar

1 tablespoon toasted sesame seeds (see note)

2 pounds sweet potatoes or yams, peeled and cut into 1-inch cubes

4 Bosc pears, peeled, cored, and finely diced

2 bunches (about 12 large) scallions, trimmed and cut into thirds

1. Center a rack in the oven and preheat the oven to 275°F.

2. In a large cast-iron pot or Dutch oven over medium-high heat, warm the olive oil. Season the oxtails with salt and pepper and sear until golden brown on all sides, about 15 to 20 minutes. Transfer the oxtails to a plate and spoon off all but 1 tablespoon fat.

3. Decrease the heat to medium-low and add the garlic, gingerroot, and chili powder to the pot. Cook, stirring, for 3 minutes (be careful not to burn the chili powder). Add the onions and sauté until translucent, about 10 minutes.

4. Raise the heat to medium. Deglaze the pot by adding the vermouth and soy sauce and scraping up any browned bits clinging to the bottom of the pot. Stir in the hoisin sauce and red chili paste. Return the oxtails to the pot. Stir in 1 cup water, the sugar, and sesame seeds and bring to a simmer.

5. Cover the pot, transfer it to the oven, and braise for 3 hours, adding the sweet potatoes and pears after 1½ hours and the scallions after 2½ hours.

HOISIN SAUCE

This complex, salty Chinese condiment is a thin, sweetened, garlicky paste based on fermented soybeans. It is a dark, ruddy brown with a vinegar-bright flavor and is traditionally served with Peking duck, pancakes, and scallions. Bottles of hoisin are widely available in supermarkets and Asian food stores.

TOASTING SESAME SEEDS

To toast sesame seeds, place a small dry skillet over medium heat. Add the sesame seeds. Cook, shaking the pan occasionally to prevent burning, until the seeds are fragrant and golden, 4 to 5 minutes. Immediately remove the seeds from the skillet and transfer to a plate, to stop the cooking.

OXTAILS ASADO NEGRO
WITH PLANTAINS, PEPPERS, AND GARLIC

| MAKES 4 TO 6 SERVINGS |

Asado negro is normally a beef pot roast cooked with garlic and dark Mexican brown sugar, so it has a little sweetness to it. In this recipe I use oxtails because I love them, and just to do something a little different. It's a very casual, dense-tasting dish that you can serve with rice (see recipe, page 183) or tortillas.

4 pounds oxtails (see note)

Coarse sea salt or kosher salt and freshly ground black pepper

1 cup red wine

1 cup Madeira wine

½ cup grated Mexican sugar or packed dark brown sugar (see note)

¼ cup sherry vinegar

3 tablespoons Worcestershire sauce

2 sprigs fresh oregano, leaves only, chopped, or 1 tablespoon dried oregano

2 bay leaves

¼ cup extra-virgin olive oil

2 medium red onions, peeled and chopped

3 garlic cloves, peeled and chopped

1 green plantain, peeled and chopped

1 red bell pepper, cored, seeded, and chopped

1 yellow bell pepper, cored, seeded, and chopped

1 green bell pepper, cored, seeded, and chopped

2 cups beef stock (page 209) or low-sodium canned beef broth

1. The day before you want to make the dish, season the oxtails with salt and pepper and arrange them in a single layer in a nonreactive bowl or Pyrex dish. Combine the red wine, Madeira, sugar, sherry vinegar, Worcestershire sauce, oregano, and bay leaves and mix until the sugar has dissolved. Pour this marinade over the oxtails, cover tightly with plastic wrap, and refrigerate overnight.

2. Center a rack in the oven and preheat the oven to 275°F.

3. Remove the oxtails from the marinade, scrape off any oregano that is still clinging to them, and reserve the marinade. In a large cast-iron pot or Dutch oven over medium-high heat, warm 2 tablespoons of the olive oil. Add the onions, garlic, plantain, and bell peppers, season with salt and pepper, and sauté until the onions are translucent, 5 to 8 minutes. Transfer the vegetables to a plate.

4. Add the remaining 2 tablespoons olive oil to the pot and increase the heat to high. Add the oxtails and sear on all sides until deeply browned, 15 to 20 minutes. Add the reserved marinade and the beef stock and season to taste with salt and pepper. Bring the mixture to a simmer and cook gently until the liquid has reduced by half, about 6 minutes.

5. Return the vegetables to the pot, taste, and adjust the seasoning if necessary. Cover the pot and transfer it to the oven. Braise, turning the oxtails two or three times, until they are very tender, about 2 hours. If the sauce is too thin or is not flavored intensely enough, ladle most of it off into another pot and simmer it until it thickens and intensifies. Then add it back to the first pot and serve.

OXTAIL

Oxtail is one of the less meaty parts of a cow, but it is supremely delicious nonetheless. It contains a lot of gelatin and marrow, thanks to the high proportion of bones and tendons, and when it is braised, these make the meat meltingly soft and flavorful. You can buy skinned, segmented oxtail in most butcher shops and stores that sell meat to a Latin or Asian clientele.

MEXICAN SUGAR

Piloncillo in Spanish, Mexican sugar is an unrefined brown sugar that is pressed into conical cakes and has hardened by the time it reaches your home. It is typically grated but can also be melted or pulverized before use. Look for Mexican sugar in Latin markets or order it online (see Sources, page 210).

VEAL BREAST BRAISED WITH CINNAMON AND GREEN OLIVES

| MAKES 6 SERVINGS |

In this fragrant braise, typical Spanish ingredients—serrano ham, olives, cinnamon, and sherry—combine to make a lovely, elegant sauce for a tender veal breast. Most people think of tapioca as a thickener for pies, but it also works very well in sauces. The translucent little pearls practically disappear as they simmer, and they give the sauce a particularly satiny, tongue-coating texture.

3 tablespoons extra-virgin olive oil

1 (3½-pound) bone-in veal breast

Coarse sea salt and kosher salt and freshly ground black pepper

2 small red onions, peeled and sliced

½ teaspoon crushed black pepper

6 garlic cloves, peeled and chopped

½ cup dry sherry

4 plum tomatoes, blanched and peeled, if desired, and chopped (see note)

½ cup Spanish green olives, pitted and halved

4 (3-inch) cinnamon sticks

½ pound serrano ham, thinly sliced and cut into 2-inch pieces (see note)

¼ cup quick-cooking tapioca

1. Center a rack in the oven and preheat the oven to 275°F.

2. Heat the olive oil in a medium cast-iron pot or Dutch oven over high heat. Season the veal with salt and pepper. Add the veal and sear on all sides until golden brown, about 20 minutes. Remove the veal and lower the heat to medium.

3. Add the onions and crushed black pepper to the pot and cook for 4 minutes. Add the garlic and cook for 3 minutes more. Deglaze the pot by adding the sherry, bringing it to a simmer, and stirring up all the browned bits stuck to the bottom of the pot. Add the tomatoes, olives, and cinnamon sticks and cook for 2 to 3 minutes. Add 2 cups water, the ham, and tapioca and return the veal to the pot. Bring to a simmer.

4. Cover the pot, transfer it to the oven, and braise until the meat is tender, about 3 hours. If the sauce is too thin or is not flavored intensely enough, ladle most of it off into another pot and simmer it until it thickens and intensifies. Then add it back to the pot with the veal.

5. Remove the meat from the bone in chunks and place it in warm bowls. Top with the vegetables and sauce and serve.

PEELING TOMATOES

Bring a pot of water to a boil. Cut a small X in the base of each tomato, add the tomatoes to the boiling water, and blanch for 5 to 10 seconds. Drain the tomatoes and hold them under cold water to cool. Using a small knife, core and peel the tomatoes. Cut each tomato in half crosswise and remove the seeds.

SERRANO HAM

Produced in the mountainous regions of southwestern Spain, dry-cured serrano ham expresses a more assertive, complex taste than its Italian counterpart, prosciutto. Salted and then hung to age for at least 1 year, serrano ham is easily recognizable by the dark green, almost black mold that partially coats its exterior. This should not be a deterrent, however, as the mold both protects the meat and enhances its flavor. In Spain, serrano ham is cut into ragged 2-inch shavings and served by itself as a tapas item or in sandwiches and salads. It should be stored in a cool, dry place and is best served at room temperature. It is available at specialty markets or online (see Sources, page 210). If serrano ham is not available, prosciutto is a good substitute.

VEAL SHOULDER
FORESTIÈRE AU RIESLING

VEAL SHOULDER WITH WILD MUSHROOMS AND RIESLING

| MAKES 6 SERVINGS |

Veal and mushrooms are a wonderful combination because veal can absorb a lot of flavor from other ingredients, and mushrooms have an intense earthiness that works extremely well with this delicate meat. You can use whatever mushrooms are available. A combination is nice if you can get only farm-raised "exotic" mushrooms like shiitake, oyster, and cremini, plus some white buttons. But if you are lucky enough to find fresh morels or chanterelles, use them alone and open a bottle of wine you've been saving for a special occasion. This dish really deserves it.

---

1 (4-pound) boneless veal shoulder roast, trimmed of all fat

6 garlic cloves, peeled and quartered

Coarse sea salt or kosher salt

2 tablespoons finely chopped fresh savory or marjoram (see note)

1½ teaspoons cracked green peppercorns

3 tablespoons vegetable oil

2 tablespoons unsalted butter

1 cup shallots, peeled and cut into ¼-inch-thick slices

1 leek, trimmed and washed (see headnote, page 179), white part sliced ¼ inch thick, greens reserved

2 pounds turnips, peeled and cut into ¼-inch-thick slices

½ pound oyster mushrooms, trimmed and split

½ pound white button mushrooms, trimmed

¼ pound lobster (see note), shiitake, or cremini mushrooms, trimmed and cut into ¼-inch-thick slices

Freshly ground black pepper

1¼ cups white wine, preferably a dry Riesling or sauvignon blanc

1. Center a rack in the oven and preheat the oven to 325°F.

2. Make 1-inch-deep incisions all over the veal with a very sharp pointed knife. Force the garlic quarters into the incisions and rub the roast well with salt, 1 tablespoon of the savory (or marjoram), and the cracked green peppercorns.

3. Heat the vegetable oil in a medium cast-iron pot or Dutch oven over high heat. Add the veal and sear until golden brown on all sides, 10 to 15 minutes.

4. Add the butter, shallots, and sliced leek to the pot and cook, stirring, for 5 minutes. Add the turnips and cook until light golden brown, about 10 minutes. Add the mushrooms and cook, stirring, until they begin to release their liquid, about 10 minutes. Add salt and pepper to taste. Deglaze the pot by pouring in the white wine, bringing it to a simmer, and scraping up any browned bits stuck to the bottom of the pot. Add the bouquet garni and transfer the pot to the oven.

5. Braise, uncovered, for 45 minutes, basting and turning the roast several times.

6. Add 1 cup of the cream to the pot, cover, and continue to braise until the veal is tender, about 1 hour, basting and turning the veal every 20 minutes. Remove the pot from the oven and let the meat rest for 20 minutes. Transfer the veal to a large serving platter and keep warm.

7. Place the pot with the liquid over medium-high heat and let the sauce reduce until thickened somewhat, 5 to 10 minutes. Meanwhile, in a small bowl, whisk together the remaining 1/4 cup cream with the egg yolks. Remove the pot from the heat and stir in the cream–egg yolk mixture. Pour the sauce and vegetables around the veal. Garnish with the parsley leaves and the remaining table-spoon of savory and serve.

Bouquet garni (2 sprigs fresh flat-leaf parsley, 1 sprig fresh rosemary, 1 sprig fresh thyme, and 1 bay leaf wrapped in a leek green and tied)

1 1/4 cups heavy cream

3 large egg yolks

1/2 cup fresh flat-leaf parsley leaves, for garnish

LOBSTER MUSHROOMS

With a flaming orange color suggestive of a cooked lobster's shell, the lobster mushroom is not a true mushroom. A parasitic mold that uses other mushrooms as its host (adding good flavor in the process), it has a firm, meaty texture and a delicate taste that makes it a nice match for meat, seafood, or vegetables. The lobster mushroom grows wild in the coastal forests of the northeastern and northwestern United States and may occasionally (although not usually) choose a toxic mushroom as its host. For this reason, it is important to purchase your mushrooms from a reputable purveyor. When buying lobster mushrooms, avoid mushrooms that are soggy or covered with white mold, and wipe the mushrooms with a damp paper towel before cooking, discarding the stems. If you cannot find lobster mushrooms, you can use any firm mushroom, such as portobello, cremini, or hen-of-the woods (also called maitake), as a substitute. Lobster mushrooms are available at specialty markets from midsummer to late fall.

SAVORY

A relative of mint, with slightly peppery, thin, dark green leaves, summer savory is an herb that can be used fresh or cooked and is cultivated throughout Europe and North America, though for some reason it is hard to find in food markets. You can buy savory fresh at farmers' markets in the summer, or find plants at a nursery and grow your own. Fresh marjoram or thyme, or a combination, is a suitable, if distant, substitute. Dried savory is sold in some spice markets and has a mustier, stronger, but acceptable flavor.

VEAL SHOULDER GOULASH

| MAKES 4 TO 6 SERVINGS |

Goulash is part of the French repertoire de cuisine, so I learned how to make it when I was a fifteen-year-old apprentice. But until recently, I hadn't made it many times since I was a teenager. Then I sampled a version that was slightly different from the classic. The paprika-flavored sauce was thickened with vegetables and simmered until it became almost like a savory jam or compote clinging to the meat. It was just wonderful, and it reminded me how good this dish can be. My current version is just as rich and hearty, but with a little more of a sauce, which is perfect to mix with a bit of sour cream at the end.

1 (2½-pound) boneless veal shoulder

Coarse sea salt or kosher salt

2 tablespoons unsalted butter

½ teaspoon freshly ground black pepper

5 ounces slab bacon, roughly chopped

¼ cup paprika

1 onion, peeled and chopped

4 garlic cloves, peeled and chopped

1 teaspoon caraway seeds

1 teaspoon dried marjoram

5 plum tomatoes, chopped

1 green bell pepper, cored, seeded, and roughly chopped

1 red bell pepper, cored, seeded, and roughly chopped

1 yellow bell pepper, cored, seeded, and roughly chopped

1 pound Yukon Gold potatoes (about 2), roughly chopped

2 bay leaves

2 sprigs fresh thyme

Sour cream, for serving

1. Center a rack in the oven and preheat the oven to 300°F.

2. Season the veal with salt. In a small cast-iron pot or Dutch oven over high heat, melt the butter. When the butter begins to foam, stir in the black pepper. Add the veal shoulder and sear on all sides. After about 7 minutes, sprinkle the bacon around the veal shoulder. Continue cooking until the veal is golden brown, about 15 minutes total cooking time. Transfer the veal shoulder to a platter.

3. Lower the heat to medium-high. Add the paprika, onion, garlic, caraway seeds, and marjoram and cook, stirring, until the onion is translucent, 6 to 7 minutes. Add the tomatoes and bell peppers and cook, stirring, for 4 minutes. Pour in 2 cups water and stir to incorporate the brown bits from the bottom of the pot. Add the potatoes, bay leaves, and thyme and stir to combine. Return the veal to the pot and bring to a simmer. Cover the pot and transfer it to the oven.

4. Braise until the veal is tender, about 2½ hours. Serve with the sour cream on the side.

DB'S VEAL MATAMBRE

STUFFED VEAL WITH QUAIL EGGS AND SPINACH

| MAKES 6 SERVINGS |

In Argentina, matambre is made from a butterflied piece of flank steak wrapped around a stuffing of spinach, carrots, and hard-cooked hen's eggs. In my version, I make miniature, individual-sized matambres out of pounded veal and quail eggs. It's a fun presentation to serve at an elegant meal.

When buying quail eggs, I always get a few extra just in case any of their delicate shells break on the way home from the market. It's also insurance against any "floaters." (Remember that if they float, they are not fresh, so discard them!)

1. Bring a small pot of water to a boil. Put the quail eggs into a fine-mesh strainer and gently lower the strainer into the water. Boil the quail eggs for 3 minutes (discard any that float to the surface). Cool the eggs under cold running water, and shell.

2. Put 1 of the veal tenderloins, the heavy cream, vinegar, hen's egg, garlic, parsley, oregano, red pepper flakes, cumin, and salt and pepper to taste in the bowl of a food processor and mix just until combined. It is important not to blend the meat too fine, or the stuffing will not be tender. Transfer the mixture to a bowl, cover it tightly with plastic wrap, and refrigerate until needed.

3. Cut the remaining tenderloin on the bias into six ½-inch-thick slices. Lay a large piece of plastic wrap on a flat surface. Put 1 slice of the veal tenderloin in the center of the plastic wrap and cover it with a second large piece of plastic wrap. Gently flatten the veal with a meat pounder or mallet into a disk about 7 inches in diameter, making it as round and thin as possible. Repeat with the remaining 5 veal slices.

4. Divide the veal stuffing into 6 equal portions. Put a veal disk on a flat work surface and season both sides with salt and pepper. Put a portion of the veal stuffing in the center. Using the back of a spoon, spread the stuffing over the meat, leaving a 2-inch border all around. Evenly

8 quail eggs (see note)

2 (1-pound) veal tenderloins or veal breasts

¼ cup heavy cream

3 tablespoons red wine vinegar

1 large hen's egg

3 garlic cloves, peeled

2 tablespoons fresh flat-leaf parsley leaves

1 tablespoon dried oregano

½ teaspoon crushed red pepper flakes

1 teaspoon ground cumin

Coarse sea salt or kosher salt and freshly ground black pepper

3 red bell peppers, cored and seeded: 1 cut into ¼-inch dice; 2 julienned

1 small carrot, peeled and cut into ¼-inch dice

2 stalks celery, cut into ¼-inch dice

¼ cup extra-virgin olive oil

½ cup beef stock (page 209) or low-sodium canned beef broth

½ pound spinach leaves, trimmed

Sweet Potato Salad, for serving (see recipe, page 42)

sprinkle one-sixth of the diced red bell pepper, carrot, and celery over the stuffing. Put 1 quail egg in the center. Fold some of the stuffing and vegetables over the quail egg and then wrap the entire tenderloin around the quail egg, shaping it into a round ball with the ends securely tucked in. Tie with kitchen string. Repeat with the remaining veal slices, stuffing, vegetables, and quail eggs.

5. Center a rack in the oven and preheat the oven to 275°F.

6. In a small cast-iron pot or Dutch oven over medium-high heat, warm the olive oil. Add the veal and sear on all sides until golden brown, 10 to 12 minutes. Transfer the veal to a platter.

7. Add the julienned red bell peppers to the pot and cook, stirring, until soft, about 10 minutes. Return the veal to the pot, add the beef stock, and bring to a simmer.

8. Cover the pot and transfer it to the oven. Braise for 1 hour 45 minutes. Uncover the pot, add the spinach, and continue to braise until the spinach is wilted, 10 to 15 minutes more. If the sauce is too thin or is not flavored intensely enough, ladle most of it off into another pot and simmer it until it thickens and intensifies. Then add it back to the first pot.

9. Serve immediately, with the Sweet Potato Salad, if desired.

SWEET POTATO SALAD

| MAKES 6 SERVINGS |

1 large sweet potato, peeled and thinly sliced

2 tablespoons celery leaves, taken from the heart of the celery

2 tablespoons fresh flat-leaf parsley leaves

1 tablespoon extra-virgin olive oil

Coarse sea salt or kosher salt and freshly ground black pepper

Bring a small pot of water to a boil. Add the sweet potato slices and blanch for 30 seconds to 1 minute. Drain. Toss the sweet potatoes with the celery leaves, parsley leaves, and olive oil. Season to taste with salt and pepper.

PORK BUTT WITH HAZELNUTS, GOLDEN RAISINS, AND JERUSALEM ARTICHOKES

| MAKES 8 TO 10 SERVINGS |

Cut from the leg, pork butt has a lot of flavor but not a lot of fat. That makes it ideal for braising, since the liquid (in this case chicken stock) keeps the meat moist during cooking. The texture of the braised pork butt reminds me of roast fresh ham, which is also cut from the leg. The butt is a delicious, lean chunk of meat that can take either a lot of seasoning or just a little. Here, I keep it pretty simple. After braising it with Jerusalem artichokes and raisins, I cover the meat with a crust of hazelnuts and bread crumbs that gets browned and crunchy when run under the broiler just before the butt is served with its savory sauce. It doesn't really need an accompaniment, but a little crisp salad wouldn't be out of place.

1. In a medium pot, bring 4 cups water to a boil. Add the raisins, reduce the heat, and simmer for 5 minutes. Drain. Transfer the raisins to a small bowl and cover with the cognac. Cover the bowl tightly with plastic wrap and let sit at room temperature for 1 hour, or refrigerate overnight, or for up to 5 days.

2. Mix together the hazelnuts, bread crumbs, 3 tablespoons of the butter, chopped thyme, and lemon zest, and salt and pepper to taste. Divide the mixture in half and roll each half out between two pieces of parchment paper or plastic wrap into a 1/4-inch-thick rectangle. Refrigerate until firm, about 2 hours, or up to 3 days.

3. Put a rack in the lower third of the oven and preheat the oven to 325°F.

4. Drain the raisins and reserve the cognac. If there is any excess fat on the pork butt, trim it off and discard. Cut the pork butt in half and season with salt and pepper. In a medium cast-iron pot or Dutch oven over medium-high heat, warm 2 tablespoons of the olive oil and 2 tablespoons of the butter. Add the pork, garlic, shallots, and 2 of the sprigs of thyme and sear the pork until golden brown on all sides, about 10 minutes.

1 cup golden raisins

1/2 cup cognac or brandy

1/4 cup toasted, peeled, and crushed hazelnuts (see note)

1/4 cup fresh bread crumbs (see note)

7 tablespoons unsalted butter, softened

4 teaspoons chopped fresh thyme leaves, plus 4 whole sprigs of thyme

1/2 teaspoon finely grated lemon zest

Coarse sea salt or kosher salt and freshly ground black pepper

1 (5-pound) boneless pork butt

1/4 cup extra-virgin olive oil or vegetable oil

1 head garlic, split in half crosswise

4 shallots, peeled and quartered

1 cup dry white wine

3 cups chicken stock (page 208) or low-sodium canned chicken broth

2 pounds Jerusalem artichokes, peeled (see note, page 7)

1 pound cipollini onions, peeled

5. Deglaze the pot by adding the reserved cognac and scraping up any browned bits clinging to the bottom of the pot. Bring the cognac to a boil, and let reduce until almost all the liquid in the pot has evaporated. Add the white wine and chicken stock and return to a boil. Transfer the pork to a plate. Strain the contents of the pot through a colander set over a bowl, reserving the liquid and discarding the garlic, shallots, and thyme.

6. Put the pot back on the stove over medium-high heat and melt the remaining 2 tablespoons butter with the remaining 2 tablespoons olive oil. Add the Jerusalem artichokes and onions and cook, stirring, until light golden brown, about 10 minutes. Add the pork back to the pot along with the reserved liquid and remaining 2 sprigs of thyme and bring to a simmer. Add the raisins, cover, and transfer the pot to the oven.

7. Braise for 2 hours, or until the meat is tender. (At this point, the pork can be cooled and refrigerated overnight, if you wish. This cooling will allow any fat in the braising liquid to come to the top for easy removal. The pork can then be reheated in a 325°F oven for about 30 minutes.)

8. Preheat the broiler. Remove the hazelnut crust from the refrigerator. Transfer the pork to a baking sheet and top each pork half with a piece of crust. Broil until the crust is golden brown, about 3 minutes. If the sauce is too thin or is not flavored intensely enough, ladle most of it off into another pot and simmer it until it thickens and intensifies. Then add it back to the original pot. Slice the pork, serving equal pieces of the crust. Spoon the braising liquid over the pork and serve.

MILK-BRAISED PORK LOIN
WITH HAZELNUTS AND PEPPER

| MAKES 6 SERVINGS |

This rustic, homey dish from Italy tastes much better than it looks. In the oven, the milk caramelizes and reduces into curds, which add wonderful flavor to the pork but aren't very pretty when you pull the pork out of the oven. Serve it to good friends who will appreciate substance over beauty.

1. Center a rack in the oven and preheat the oven to 300°F.

2. Season the pork with salt and pepper. In a medium cast-iron pot or Dutch oven over high heat, melt the butter. Add the pork and sear until golden brown on all sides, about 12 minutes. Transfer the pork to a platter.

3. Lower the temperature to medium-high. Add the carrots, celery, and onion to the pot and cook, stirring, until the onion is translucent, about 12 minutes. Add the remaining ingredients, return the pork to the pot, and bring to a simmer.

4. Cover the pot and transfer it to the oven. Braise until tender, about 2 hours 15 minutes for the pork loin or 1 hour 15 minutes to 1½ hours for the pork tenderloins.

5. Transfer the pork to a platter. Remove and discard the bay leaves. If you'd like a more attractive sauce, use a hand blender or a standing blender or food processor to puree the remaining liquid and vegetables until smooth, and season to taste with salt and pepper. Cut the pork into slices, pour the sauce over the meat, and serve.

1 (3-pound) pork loin or 2 (1½-pound) pork tenderloins

Coarse sea salt or kosher salt and freshly ground black pepper

3 tablespoons unsalted butter

6 carrots, peeled, trimmed, and roughly chopped

6 stalks celery, trimmed and roughly chopped

1 large onion, peeled and roughly chopped

2½ cups whole milk

½ cup hazelnuts, toasted (see note, opposite)

1 teaspoon crushed black pepper

2 bay leaves

½ teaspoon pink peppercorns (see note, page 15)

3 sprigs fresh savory (see note, page 39)

TEXAS-STYLE BARBECUED
BABY BACK RIBS

| MAKES 6 SERVINGS |

I love barbecue. Everyone has a favorite recipe for barbecue. You will discover that each person is fiercely loyal to their region's specialty. My preference is Texas-style barbecue, where the ribs are rubbed with a spice blend composed mostly of black pepper and then mopped with a sauce. My rub has black pepper, but I also add other spices and herbs to the mix to give it more flavor, such as the smoked paprika and espresso (in the sauce), which give the ribs their smoky taste. Any leftover spice rub can be stored and kept in an airtight container for up to 3 months.

If you have time, make the Jalepeño Cheddar Corn Bread recipe that follows. My bread baker, Mark Fiorentino, has been making corn bread for us to eat for many years. It's the best corn bread I have ever eaten. It's moist, not dry like most corn breads. And don't be afraid of the jalapeños. They add a nice spiciness without being too hot—although of course you can use less or leave them out all together if you prefer.

FOR THE RIBS:

2 racks (4 pounds) baby back ribs, cut into 2-rib pieces

1 onion, peeled and halved

1 leek, white part only, washed (see headnote, page 179)

1 stalk celery

1 carrot

3 juniper berries (see note, page 5)

2 bay leaves

1 tablespoon coarse sea salt or kosher salt

1 teaspoon freshly ground black pepper

FOR THE RUB:

3 tablespoons smoked Spanish paprika (see note, page 163)

1 tablespoon cumin seeds

2 tablespoons regular oregano or dried Mexican oregano (see note, page 25)

1 tablespoon black peppercorns

1. Place the ribs in a large pot with the onion, leek, celery, carrot, juniper berries, bay leaves, salt, and black pepper and pour in enough water to cover. Bring the water to a boil, lower to a simmer, and cook for 30 minutes. Using tongs, transfer the ribs to a plate and pat dry.

2. Strain the liquid in the pot through a fine-mesh sieve. Return the strained liquid to the pot, bring it to a boil, and cook, skimming the fat from the surface occasionally, until the liquid has reduced to 2½ cups. Remove from the heat.

3. To make the rub, grind all the rub ingredients together in a spice grinder. Rub 2 tablespoons of the mixture over the ribs.

4. To make the sauce, combine all the sauce ingredients with the reduced poaching liquid.

5. Center a rack in the oven and preheat the oven to 300°F.

6. In a large cast-iron pot or Dutch oven over high heat, heat the oil. Add the ribs to the pot and sear until caramelized on all sides, 5 to 10 minutes, making sure that the ribs do not burn. Add the sauce and bring to a simmer. Cover the pot, transfer it to the oven, and braise until the ribs are meltingly tender, about 1 hour 45 minutes. If the sauce is too thin or is not flavored intensely enough, ladle most of it off into another pot and simmer it until it thickens and intensifies. Then return it to the pot with the ribs. Serve with the corn bread.

JALAPEÑO CHEDDAR CORN BREAD

| MAKES 8 TO 10 SERVINGS |

2 cups all-purpose flour

3/4 cup coarse cornmeal

2 teaspoons baking powder

1 teaspoon coarse sea salt or kosher salt

9 tablespoons unsalted butter, at room temperature

3/4 cup sugar

4 eggs, at room temperature

1/2 cup crème fraîche or sour cream

1/3 cup whole milk

1 (8-ounce) can corn, drained

1/2 cup grated cheddar cheese

1/3 cup pickled jalapeño peppers, chopped

1. Center a rack in the oven and preheat the oven to 350°F. Grease a 9-by-13-inch baking pan.

2. In a large bowl, whisk together the flour, cornmeal, baking powder, and salt. In the bowl of an electric mixer fitted with the paddle attachment, beat the butter and sugar until smooth. Beat in the eggs one at a time. Add half the dry ingredients and beat to combine. Beat in the crème fraîche and milk, and then the remaining dry ingredients. Use a rubber spatula to fold in the corn, cheddar cheese, and jalapeños.

3. Pour the batter into the prepared pan. Bake until a knife inserted into the center of the bread comes out clean, about 40 minutes.

2 tablespoons packed dark brown sugar

2 tablespoons chili powder, mild or hot, to taste

2 teaspoons garlic powder

2 teaspoons onion powder

2 teaspoons dry mustard

Finely grated zest of 1 lemon

FOR THE SAUCE:

1 large onion, peeled and diced

4 garlic cloves, peeled and minced

1 jalapeño pepper, finely chopped

1/3 cup chili sauce, mild or hot, to taste

3/4 cup Worcestershire sauce

1/2 cup molasses

1/4 cup cider vinegar

1 tablespoon finely grated peeled fresh gingerroot

1 teaspoon coarse sea salt or kosher salt

3/4 cup espresso or strong coffee

1 tablespoon vegetable or extra-virgin olive oil, for searing the ribs

Jalapeño Cheddar Corn Bread, for serving (see recipe, left)

ASIAN PORK BELLY
WITH GINGER AND SOY

| MAKES 6 TO 8 SERVINGS |

In the United States, some people can be hesitant about pork belly. They think that they might not like it, or maybe that you mean the inside of the belly, the tripe. But when you tell them it's pretty much the same cut as bacon, they come around. Almost everyone here likes bacon.

Still, there are several differences between pork belly and bacon. One is the cut. Bacon is cut from the thinner side of the pig's belly, down toward the leg. The meaty, thicker part near the breast is what I use for this recipe and for Oaxacan Pork Belly with Pineapple and Plantains (page 51). The thinner section of the belly has more narrow stripes of fat and meat, with the emphasis on the meat—just like what you see in a slice of bacon. Here, both the meat and the fat are about 1 inch thick, and the ratio of meat to fat is, ideally, fifty-fifty. Don't be put off by all that fat. The fat is extremely tasty, the best part of the dish, and it breaks my heart to see people leaving fat on their plates. When gently braised at a low temperature, the fat in the pork belly reaches a melt-in-the-mouth state of being that doesn't exist with any other kind of meat. It's like softened butter. There's more gelatin in the breast half of the pork belly, and this dissolves in the braise too, giving the sauce body and a glossy appearance that you can't get with other thickeners. There's also more cartilage, which helps keep the meat moist.

Another difference between pork belly and bacon is that bacon is cured in salt and then usually smoked. The pork belly you need for braising is fresh and uncured (unsalted). This is really important, since you can buy salted, cured pork belly. But don't. This recipe is intended for the fresh meat, which you will probably have to order specially from your butcher.

When this dish comes out of the oven, the meat looks like shining, polished mahogany and has a heady, pungent fragrance. It's great to eat hot, but you can also eat it cold the next day. That may sound strange, but it's delicious. During my entire youth, until I left home, every day we had saucisson and pork belly on the table, which we ate with a little mustard. We would cure our own fresh belly with salt, poach it slowly, cool it, and serve it cold. My grandmother, who lived to be eighty-seven, ate pork belly every morning for breakfast. And, like most Frenchwomen, she was never fat.

If you have time to make it, this dish goes well with Homemade Pickled Ginger (see recipe on page 50).

1. The day before you want to serve this dish, use a sharp knife to score the top of the pork belly in a 1-inch-wide diamond pattern. Transfer the pork belly to a nonreactive container, such as a Pyrex bowl. In another bowl, combine the beef stock, vinegar, soy sauce, gingerroot, scallions, brown sugar, salt, hoisin, and star anise. Pour this marinade over the pork belly, cover, and refrigerate overnight.

2. Center a rack in the oven and preheat the oven to 275°F.

3. In a medium cast-iron pot or Dutch oven over medium-high heat, warm the oil. Scrape the marinade from the pork belly, reserving the marinade. Add the pork belly to the pot and sear until golden brown on all sides, 5 to 20 minutes.

4. Turn the pork fat side up in the pot and add the spring onions and carrots. Pour the reserved marinade on top. Bring to a simmer, cover, and braise in the oven for 4 to 5 hours, until the belly is very soft and tender. If the sauce is too thin or is not flavored intensely enough, ladle most of it off into another pot and simmer it until it thickens and intensifies.

5. To serve, transfer the pork to a platter and strain the cooking liquid, discarding the solids. Skim the fat from the liquid (or use a gravy separator). Sprinkle the chives and cilantro over the meat and serve with some of the cooking liquid and Homemade Pickled Ginger.

1 (3½- to 4-pound) fresh, uncured pork belly (see headnote)

2 cups beef stock (page 209) or low-sodium canned beef broth

½ cup rice wine vinegar (see note)

¼ cup dark soy sauce (see note, page 11)

¼ cup peeled, finely grated fresh gingerroot

1 bunch scallions, trimmed and sliced

3 tablespoons packed dark brown sugar

Coarse sea salt or kosher salt

1½ teaspoons hoisin sauce (see note, page 33)

1 star anise pod

1 tablespoon extra-virgin olive oil

8 spring onions, trimmed

4 large carrots, peeled and cut into ¾-inch-thick slices

1 small bunch fresh chives, finely chopped

1 small bunch fresh cilantro, leaves only

Homemade Pickled Ginger (see recipe, next page)

RICE WINE VINEGAR

Also called rice vinegar, this mild, clear vinegar has a sweet, slightly grainy or nutty flavor at its best. A staple in Japanese and Chinese kitchens, it can be found wherever Asian sauces are sold. White wine vinegar diluted with water (about ¾ vinegar to ¼ water) can be substituted in a pinch. Be sure to use unseasoned rice wine vinegar—*not* the seasoned kind, which contains sugar and salt and is used for making sushi rice.

HOMEMADE PICKLED GINGER

3/4 pound fresh gingerroot, peeled and thinly sliced

1/2 cup sugar

3 tablespoons kosher salt

1/2 cup red wine vinegar

1/2 cup white wine vinegar

4 red or black plums, quartered and pitted

In a medium bowl, pour boiling water over the gingerroot to cover. Let stand for 30 minutes, then drain. In a medium saucepan, bring 1/2 cup water and the remaining ingredients to a boil; pour the mixture over the gingerroot, and let cool. Refrigerate for 24 hours before using. The pickled ginger will keep, tightly covered in the refrigerator, for up to 2 weeks.

OAXACAN PORK BELLY
WITH PINEAPPLE AND PLANTAINS

| MAKES 6 TO 8 SERVINGS |

In this recipe for sweet-and-sour pork belly, the chilies and apple cider vinegar cut the richness of the fat belly, while the plantains add starch and the pineapples and Granny Smith apples give a little sweetness. It's a memorable combination of flavors and textures. Serve it with warm tortillas.

1. The day before you want to serve this dish, remove the stems (if any) from the guajillo and ancho chilies. For each chili, make a slit down one side and remove the seeds and veins. Spread out and flatten the chilies out as much as possible. Cover with boiling water and let soak until fleshy and soft, about 15 minutes. Drain well. Transfer the chilies to a blender, add 1 cup water, the cider vinegar, chopped tomatoes, chopped pineapple, oregano, bay leaves, avocado leaves, and canela, and blend until smooth. Strain the marinade through a fine-mesh strainer.

2. Using a sharp knife, score the top of the pork belly in a 1-inch-wide diamond pattern. Season the pork belly with the salt. Transfer it to a large cast-iron pot or Dutch oven. Arrange the plantains, onions, apples, the tomato wedges, and the pineapple chunks around the pork and pour in the marinade. Cover tightly and refrigerate overnight.

3. Center a rack in the oven and preheat the oven to 300°F.

4. Scrape as much of the marinade off the pork belly as possible onto the fruit and vegetables. Cover the pot with its lid and transfer it to the oven. Braise for 2 hours, basting every 30 minutes, making sure to use only the liquid to baste the pork belly. (If the vegetables are not kept submerged, they will burn.) Uncover the pot and braise until the pork is fork-tender, about 3 hours more, basting the pork belly every hour.

10 guajillo chilies (see note, page 25)

6 ancho chilies (see note, page 25)

½ cup apple cider vinegar

8 large tomatoes: 4 roughly chopped; 4 cut into 8 wedges each

1 ripe pineapple, peeled and cored: ½ roughly chopped; ½ cut into 1-inch chunks

2 teaspoons dried Mexican oregano (see note, page 25) or regular oregano

3 bay leaves

2 dried avocado leaves (see note)

1 (1-inch) piece canela or cinnamon stick (see note)

1 (6-pound) piece bone-in fresh pork belly (see headnote, page 48)

2 tablespoons coarse sea salt or kosher salt

3 ripe plantains, peeled and cut into 1-inch-thick slices

2 large white onions, peeled and cut into 1-inch cubes

2 Granny Smith apples, peeled, cored, and cut into 8 wedges each

AVOCADO LEAVES

The deep green, anise-scented leaves of the avocado tree are a primary ingredient in Mexican cooking and are used both fresh and dried. Used fresh, they serve as wrappers for tamales, barbecued meats, and fish dishes. Dried, they are crumbled and added to soups, stews, and beans. In the United States, they are usually found dried at Latin American markets, or they can be purchased—fresh and dried—online (see Sources, page 210).

CANELA

Also called Mexican or Ceylon cinnamon—*canela* means cinnamon in Spanish—this thin, delicate bark is prized for its floral, complex taste, considered far superior to that of its frequent substitute, cassia. Cassia, the coarse bark of the laurel tree, is, like cinnamon, sold in tightly curled quills, and is often used interchangeably with cinnamon. It is even sold as cinnamon in the United States. However, cassia is darker in color than the pale brown Mexican cinnamon, and because of its higher volatile oil content, it is more assertive in flavor. Canela, originally from Ceylon (present-day Sri Lanka), is used in Asian, African, Indian, and Latin American cooking. Its fragility makes it quite perishable, and it should ideally be freshly ground (in a spice grinder or clean coffee grinder) as needed to add flavor to soups, stews, moles, and pastries. It can be purchased at specialty supermarkets or online (see Sources, page 210). Regular "cinnamon" (cassia) can be used as a substitute if you can't get Mexican cinnamon.

SPICY PORK CHOPS WITH BLACK BEAN SAUCE

| MAKES 4 SERVINGS |

Fermented black beans are intensely sour, salty, and funky, and they can overpower a dish if used with an open hand. But if used with parsimony, they add wonderful depth and tang—as they do in this dish. Combined with lemongrass, tamarind, and fish sauce, these are pork chops as you've probably never had them before—but will crave again and again. Poaching the chops before braising helps to keep them moist and tender.

1. At least a day before cooking, combine the chops, onion, carrot, celery, bay leaf, salt, and 1 quart water in a large pot and bring to a boil. Lower the heat and simmer for 20 minutes, skimming the foam as needed. Transfer the chops to a platter and let cool.

2. Strain the poaching liquid through a fine-mesh sieve into a large saucepan, discarding the vegetables. Bring the liquid to a boil and reduce it to 2 cups. Cover and refrigerate until ready to use.

3. In a small, preferably light-colored, saucepan (such as a lined copper pot or an enameled cast-iron one), dissolve the sugar in 1 tablespoon water. Cook the sugar water over medium-high heat until it becomes a dark caramel, about 7 minutes. Remove from the heat, stand back, and immediately add ¼ cup water (the caramel will bubble like mad). Stir to combine, and then let cool.

4. Arrange the pork chops in a nonreactive bowl, such as Pyrex. In a medium bowl, mix together the cooled caramel, soy sauce, fish sauce, tamarind paste, plum sauce, black vinegar, bean paste, lemongrass, ginger, cilantro, garlic, and black pepper. Pour this marinade over the pork chops. Cover tightly with plastic wrap and refrigerate overnight.

5. Center a rack in the oven and preheat the oven to 300°F.

4 pork chops (about 2 pounds)

1 onion, peeled and quartered

1 carrot, peeled and cut into chunks

1 stalk celery, cut into chunks

1 bay leaf

1½ teaspoons coarse sea salt or kosher salt

2 tablespoons sugar

3 tablespoons soy sauce (see note, page 11)

1 tablespoon Thai or Vietnamese fish sauce (see note)

1 tablespoon tamarind paste (see note)

1 tablespoon plum sauce (see note)

1 tablespoon black vinegar (see note)

2 teaspoons fermented black bean paste (see note, page 10)

2 teaspoons minced lemongrass (see note)

1 teaspoon ground ginger

5 sprigs fresh cilantro, chopped

2 garlic cloves, peeled and finely chopped

¼ teaspoon crushed black pepper

6. Transfer the pork chops, marinade, and the 2 cups of poaching liquid to a medium cast-iron pot or Dutch oven and bring to a simmer. Cover, transfer to the oven, and braise, basting the pork chops every 20 minutes, until the meat is fork-tender, 45 minutes to 1 hour. If the sauce is too thin or is not flavored intensely enough, ladle most of it off into another pot and simmer it until it thickens and intensifies. Then add it back to the pot with the pork chops.

CHICKEN BASQUAISE
WITH ARTICHOKES (PAGE 114)

MONKFISH WITH SAVOY CABBAGE AND JUNIPER BERRIES (PAGE 160)

SHRIMP WITH ZUCCHINI, ONIONS,
COCONUT, AND TAMARIND
(PAGE 166)

PESCADO VERACRUZANA (PAGE 152)

OCTOPUS WITH GINGER, GARLIC, AND SOY SAUCE   (PAGE 168)

DUCK WITH GREEN PICHOLINE OLIVES (PAGE 138)

SEA SCALLOPS WITH SALSIFY,
SHIITAKE MUSHROOMS,
AND WHITE MISO
(PAGE 164)

SMOKED SABLE CHOWDER (PAGE 144)

SKATE CIOPPINO
(PAGE 146)

MACKEREL WITH
HERB CURRY (PAGE 158)

THAI OR VIETNAMESE FISH SAUCE

An essential ingredient in Southeast Asian cooking, Thai or Vietnamese fish sauce (*nuoc mam* in Vietnamese and *nam pla* in Thai) is prepared from fermented anchovies and other tiny fish and has a strong, salty flavor and pungent aroma that can intimidate those unaccustomed to cooking with it. Combined with other Asian ingredients, however, fish sauce lends a subtle, complex flavor that enriches many soups, noodles, and sauces. You can use Thai and Vietnamese brands interchangeably. Fish sauce can be found in Asian markets or purchased online (see Sources, page 210).

TAMARIND AND TAMARIND CONCENTRATE

Tamarind, an evergreen tree native to Africa, is now grown in most of the world's tropics. The sticky brown pulp of its long seedpods is used predominantly in Latin American, Indian, and Southeast Asian cooking, to which its tangy, slightly fruity taste contributes a bright acidity similar to lemon juice. The pods are often sold whole, or sometimes the pulp and seeds are removed from the pod and formed into a brick (called tamarind paste). To use either the pods or the paste, you need to mix the pulp and seeds with warm water and strain the resulting paste. Or look for jars of tamarind concentrate—a more intense, seed-less, and convenient product. You'll find tamarind products in Asian, Indian, and South American groceries, or you can buy them online (see Sources, page 210).

PLUM SAUCE

A Chinese sauce of plums, vinegar, and sugar, usually seasoned with some ginger and chili, this sweet and tangy condiment is served as a dipping sauce in Cantonese restaurants and is also used in Chinese cooking as a partner for goose and duck. It is widely available in grocery stores and Asian markets. Two reliable brands are Lee Kum Kee and Koon Chun.

BLACK VINEGAR

A thick, dark, slightly salty Chinese vinegar made from a mixture of fermented grains, black vinegar becomes smoky-sweet when aged. It adds depth to hearty sauces and glazes. Balsamic vinegar is a good, if more expensive, substitute, though it lacks the slight funk and saline taste of the black vinegar. If you have a choice, look for the high-quality Chinkiang vinegar. Black vinegar is sold in Asian markets, or you can order it online (see Sources, page 210).

LEMONGRASS

Extensively cultivated in the tropics and subtropics, this perennial blade-like grass is most commonly used in Thailand, Vietnam, and Laos. Its long, thin stalks release a lemony flavor when chopped, and they are often added to curries, soups, confections, and teas. Lemongrass also serves as an excellent seasoning for poultry and seafood. It is very fibrous in texture, so the tough outer leaves and woody stalk must be trimmed before use (both can be saved and added to Asian-inspired stocks or teas). It can be purchased dried or powdered, but lemongrass is most flavorful when fresh. In addition to its culinary uses, lemongrass oil is also often extracted for aromatherapy and medicinal purposes. It has variously been used to treat flatulence, muscle aches, and stress, and it is familiar to many people because of its effectiveness as an insect repellent (also known as citronella). Fresh lemongrass stalks can be purchased in Asian markets or online (see Sources, page 210).

MEXICAN BABY BACK RIBS WITH JALAPEÑOS AND EPAZOTE

| MAKES 4 TO 6 SERVINGS |

There are certain flavors I remember from my trips to Mexico that have stayed with me over the years. Epazote is one of them. It's a soft green herb with a musky, oregano-like, minty flavor that's also very earthy. Even with all the other ingredients in this rich, complex recipe for baby back ribs—the herbs and chilies, citrus, and spices—the epazote still comes through. It's available in specialty markets, but if you can't find it, you can use cilantro instead. Your finished braise may not taste exactly the same as mine, but the tender, falling-off-the-bone ribs will be delicious no matter what.

2 racks (about 4 pounds) baby back ribs, each rack cut into 4 sections

3 cups freshly squeezed orange juice

2 yellow onions, peeled and quartered

1 head garlic: cloves separated, peeled, and crushed

2 jalapeño peppers, seeded, if desired, and chopped

Freshly squeezed juice of 2 limes, plus juice of ½ lime

2 tablespoons white wine vinegar

2 tablespoons annatto seeds (see note)

1 tablespoon coarse sea salt or kosher salt

1 tablespoon dried Mexican oregano (see note, page 25) or regular oregano

1 tablespoon coriander seeds

1 tablespoon pink peppercorns (see note, page 15)

4 whole allspice

3 whole cloves

1 (1-inch) piece canela or cinnamon stick (see note, page 52)

2 tablespoons extra-virgin olive oil, plus additional for serving

1 small bunch fresh epazote or cilantro, leaves only (see note)

Freshly ground black pepper

1. The day before you want to cook the ribs, place them in a nonreactive bowl or Pyrex dish. In a medium bowl, combine the orange juice, onions, garlic, jalapeños, juice of 2 of the limes, and the vinegar. Pour this marinade over the pork ribs, cover tightly with plastic wrap, and refrigerate overnight.

2. Center a rack in the oven and preheat the oven to 275°F.

3. In a spice grinder, finely grind the annatto seeds, salt, oregano, coriander seeds, pink peppercorns, allspice, cloves, and canela.

4. Remove the pork ribs from the marinade, scraping off as much of the marinade as possible and reserving the marinade. Season the pork ribs with the ground spices. Heat the olive oil in a medium cast-iron pot or Dutch oven over medium-high heat. Add the pork ribs, in batches if necessary, and sear on all sides until golden brown, 10 to 12 minutes. Adjust the heat as needed to make sure that the spices do not burn.

5. Pour the reserved marinade into the pot with the ribs and bring to a simmer. Cover and braise in the oven, basting the pork ribs every 30 minutes, until tender, 2½ to 3 hours. If the sauce is too thin or is not flavored intensely enough, ladle most of it off into another pot and simmer it until it thickens and intensifies. Then add it back to the braising pot.

6. Meanwhile, in a small bowl, combine the epazote, the remaining lime juice, a drizzling of olive oil, and salt and pepper to taste. Sprinkle over the pork ribs before serving.

ANNATTO SEED

Also referred to as achiote seed, the rust-colored seeds of the achiote tree are a familiar seasoning in Latin American, Asian, and Caribbean cooking. Earthy and slightly bitter in flavor, annatto seed is often used more for color than for flavor—when soaked in hot water or sautéed in oil, achiote releases its bright reddish-orange hue, coloring soups, stews, seafood, and meats. In the United States, annatto seed is used as a coloring agent for cheese and butter. Whole or ground annatto seed can be purchased at Mexican grocery stores or online (see Sources, page 210).

EPAZOTE

A mildly licorice-scented wild herb reminiscent of tarragon or anise, epazote is common in Latin American cooking and is identifiable by its strong, resinous flavor and flat, serrated leaves. Although native to Mexico, epazote is also used in parts of South America and the Caribbean. It is most often used as a seasoning for soups, beans, and quesadillas. Epazote is also referred to as Mexican tea and wormseed, and it is often touted for its medicinal use as a remedy for gas caused by consuming beans. Latin Americans almost always cook with fresh epazote. If you can't find it fresh, however, it can be purchased dried at specialty stores or online (see Sources, page 210).

BEER-BRAISED PORK SHANK WITH CUMIN AND CHAYOTE

| MAKES 6 TO 8 SERVINGS |

Pork shank is a rustic cut of meat that does well if you match it with earthy ingredients. Here, I braise it South American–style with dark beer, cumin and other spices, vegetables such as chayote and carrots, and some citrus juice and zest. The result is a homey stew that's very warming in the winter but will also be good in the summer if you serve it with more cold dark beer.

1 (8- to 10-pound) pork shank, tied (ask your butcher to do this for you)

Finely grated zest and freshly squeezed juice of 2 oranges

Finely grated zest and freshly squeezed juice of 2 lemons

Finely grated zest and freshly squeezed juice of 2 limes

3 tablespoons coarse sea salt or kosher salt

1½ tablespoons paprika

1 tablespoon ground cumin

1 tablespoon packed dark brown sugar

½ teaspoon cayenne pepper

¼ cup extra-virgin olive oil

6 cups dark beer (such as Negra Modelo)

1 cup quinoa, rinsed under cold water (see note)

3 large carrots, peeled and roughly chopped

1 large Spanish onion, peeled and roughly chopped

1 chayote, peeled and roughly chopped (see note)

1 small head garlic: cloves separated, peeled, and finely chopped

15 sprigs fresh flat-leaf parsley, chopped

2 jalapeño peppers, seeded, if desired, and chopped

2 bay leaves

1. The day before you want to serve the dish, use a small paring knife to pierce the pork shank all over. In a large bowl, combine all the citrus zest and juice, the salt, paprika, cumin, brown sugar, and cayenne. Rub this citrus-spice mixture all over the pork shank, cover tightly with plastic wrap, and refrigerate overnight.

2. The next day, center a rack in the oven and preheat the oven to 300°F.

3. In a large cast-iron pot or Dutch oven over high heat, warm the olive oil. Add the pork shank and sear until golden brown on all sides, 15 to 20 minutes. Transfer the pork to a plate. Remove all but 2 tablespoons of fat from the pot. Add the beer, quinoa, carrots, onion, chayote, garlic, parsley, jalapeños, and bay leaves and bring to a simmer.

4. Return the pork to the pot. Cover and braise in the oven until cooked through but moist, 3 to 3½ hours. If the sauce is too thin or not flavored intensely enough, ladle most of it off into another pot and simmer it until it thickens and intensifies. Then add it back to the braising pot.

5. Carve the meat off the shank and serve with some of the sauce.

QUINOA

An ancient grain cultivated in the South American Andes for over 5,000 years, quinoa has a nutty, delicate flavor that is enhanced by gentle toasting before cooking. Similar in appearance to millet, quinoa is generally ivory-colored, but brown, orange, and yellow varieties are also grown. Commercially sold quinoa is prewashed to remove the grain's bitter coating (called saponin), a natural defense against birds and insects; however, a thorough rinse at home, in cold water, is still a good idea. A relative of spinach, quinoa has a high concentration of essential amino acids, making it a great source of calcium and protein. Steamed, quinoa inflates to a light, fluffy texture. It is an excellent addition to soups, stews, salads, and baked goods, and it can be ground into a substitute for wheat flour. It is available at specialty markets, at health food stores, or online (see Sources, page 210).

CHAYOTE

Also called vegetable pear, this round green gourd, native to Central America, has an inward-turning seam along one side. You'll find chayote in Mexican soups, stews, and fritters; stuffed; and even sweetened and used in desserts. It has white, crisp flesh and a tough pale green skin. The single almond-like seed is a delicacy; when cooked it softens like a lima bean, but with a gentle, nutty flavor. Look for chayote in Latin or Asian markets.

HAM HOCKS
IN JAMAICAN JERK SAUCE

| MAKES 4 TO 6 SERVINGS |

At DANIEL, even though we're open, it's a little bit more relaxed on the weekend after-noons among the back-of-the-house staff than it usually is during the week. Sometimes a small group will get together and have someone make a run down to a great Jamaican take-out restaurant on Fourteenth Street. Spicy, delicious, and full of great flavor, Jamaican Jerk Chicken is everyone's favorite.

A true jerk sauce from Jamaica is very complex, and there's nothing else quite like it. It has both warm and hot spiciness—warmth from the cinnamon, allspice, nutmeg, and clove, and heat from the chilies. You could also rub this sauce onto chicken and either grill it or broil it. It will be very tasty. But the ham hocks, with all the collagen from the meat, make the sauce particularly dense. Make sure to buy fresh, uncured ham hocks.

You'll love this served over red beans and rice (see page 182).

---

5 pounds fresh ham hocks (4 to 6 hocks), trimmed of excess fat (ask your butcher to do this for you)

1/3 cup light soy sauce (see note, page 11)

1/2 cup dark rum

6 tablespoons sherry vinegar

1/4 cup Worcestershire sauce

6 garlic cloves, peeled

4 ají amarillo chili peppers, 1 to 2 Scotch bonnet peppers, or 3 tablespoons ají amarillo paste, to taste (see note)

1 (2-inch) piece fresh gingerroot, peeled and finely grated

1 1/2 teaspoons coarse sea salt or kosher salt, plus additional

2 teaspoons ground allspice, preferably Jamaican

1 1/2 teaspoons freshly grated nutmeg

1 1/2 teaspoons ground cinnamon or canela (see note, page 52)

1 whole clove

2 tablespoons vegetable or extra-virgin olive oil

1. The day before you want to serve the dish, bring a large pot of pot of water to a boil, add the ham hocks, and boil for 10 minutes. Drain the ham hocks and transfer them to a nonreactive container, such as a Pyrex bowl. In a blender or food processor, combine the soy sauce, rum, sherry vinegar, Worcestershire sauce, garlic, chili peppers or paste, gingerroot, salt, allspice, nutmeg, cinnamon, and clove and blend until smooth. Pour this marinade over the ham hocks, cover, and refrigerate overnight.

2. Center a rack in the oven and preheat the oven to 275°F.

3. In a large cast-iron pot or Dutch oven over medium-high heat, warm the oil. Add the onions and a pinch of salt and cook, stirring, until the onions are translucent, 12 to 15 minutes (adjust the heat to keep the onions from taking on any color). Pour in the white wine and add the carrots, celery, and thyme. Bring the liquid to a boil, stir-ring to scrape up any cooked-on bits from the bottom of the pot, and boil for 5 minutes.

4. Add the ham hocks and marinade to the vegetables and pour in 1 cup water (or enough to cover the vegetables and hocks by two-thirds). Bring the liquid to a boil and cook for 2 to 3 minutes, skimming off any foam or solids that rise to the surface.

5. Cover the pot, place it in the oven, and braise until the ham hocks are tender, about 3 hours, turning once.

6. Transfer the hocks and vegetables to a plate and let them cool slightly, then pick off the meat from the hocks. Strain the sauce and defat it, using a gravy separator. (Alternatively, skim the fat from the strained sauce with a spoon—or chill the strained sauce in the refrigerator until the fat has solidified and can be discarded, then reheat the sauce before serving.) Taste the sauce, and season with salt if needed. Serve the meat and vegetables over rice (see recipe, page 183), drizzled with a little of the sauce.

3 large onions, peeled and roughly chopped

1 cup dry white wine

4 medium carrots, peeled and cut into ½-inch dice

4 stalks celery, trimmed and cut into ½-inch dice

4 sprigs fresh thyme, leaves only

AJÍ AMARILLO, AJÍ MIRASOL

Ají is the Peruvians' word for chili pepper, and Peru offers some distinctly flavorful varieties. Ají amarillo is a hot, sharp-flavored, yellow-orange pepper (red when dried), also grown in Mexico. Ají mirasol (used dried) is mild, sweet, and dark red, with a slight apricot-like flavor. Both are available in some Latin stores and are sometimes sold as paste. They can also be bought online (see Sources, page 210).

HAM HOCKS WITH LYCHEES
AND BOK CHOY

| MAKES 4 SERVINGS |

In the United States, ham hocks are normally smoked, along with the rest of the ham, and are used to flavor a big pot of greens or soup, especially in the South. But I also like to cook with fresh, uncured hocks, because they have a lot of flavor and are inexpensive. They're also unusual, since you don't see them on their own very often. As much as I love them, you do need to seek out nice, thick, relatively meaty ones. Hocks that are just skin and bones are no fun to eat. But with good ham hocks, this intensely flavored, pan-Asian-inspired recipe won't disappoint anyone. Serve it with regular (see recipe, page 183) or sticky rice.

4 pounds fresh ham hocks, trimmed of excess fat (ask your butcher to do this for you)

2 tablespoons vegetable or extra-virgin olive oil

1 large onion, peeled and chopped

5 garlic cloves, peeled and chopped

1 (2-inch) piece fresh gingerroot, peeled and smashed

1 (20-ounce) can lychees in syrup

3 tablespoons light soy sauce (see note, page 11)

2 tablespoons packed dark brown sugar

2 tablespoons chopped fresh cilantro

1 tablespoon crushed red pepper flakes

1 tablespoon Thai or Vietnamese fish sauce (see note, page 55)

1 teaspoon red chili paste (see note, page 13)

4 baby bok choy (about 1 pound), tough stem ends trimmed

1 pound bitter melons (about 2 to 3 melons), quartered lengthwise, seeded, and cut into 1-inch cubes (see note)

2 bunches scallions, trimmed and cut into 2-inch lengths

1. Bring a large pot of water to a boil. Add the ham hocks and cook for 10 minutes. Drain.

2. Center a rack in the oven and preheat the oven to 275°F.

3. In a large cast-iron pot or Dutch oven over medium-high heat, warm the oil. Add the onion, garlic, and gingerroot and cook, stirring, until the onion is translucent, 5 to 7 minutes. Add the ham hocks, lychees and syrup, soy sauce, brown sugar, cilantro, red pepper flakes, fish sauce, and chili paste. Bring to a simmer.

4. Cover the pot, transfer it to the oven, and braise for 3 hours, turning the hocks two or three times during cooking.

5. Add the bok choy and bitter melon, and continue to braise, covered, for 1 hour 15 minutes. Add the scallions, cover, and braise for an additional 15 minutes. Serve over rice.

BITTER MELON

Also called bitter gourd or bitter cucumber, this bumpy, cucumber-shaped vegetable lives up to its name. Very bitter in flavor, bitter melon has a light or dark green skin (depending on the variety) and a white, spongy interior. Prized in Indian and Asian cooking, bitter melon can be cooked in every conceivable manner—fried, stuffed, sautéed, braised, stir-fried, and baked. It is also great at balancing intense flavors and cutting sweetness and fat, pairing well with a wide array of vegetables, fish, and meat. Bitter melon should be refrigerated and used quickly, as it will spoil after several days. It is available at many Asian markets.

PORK AND SWISS CHARD CAILLETTES WITH TOMATO SAUCE

| MAKES 6 TO 8 SERVINGS |

A *caillette* is a little meatball or sausage that's wrapped in something to help it keep its shape. Here I secure a lightly spiced mix of pork loin, liver, fatback, chestnuts, and greens with a casing of bacon and caul fat. The bacon adds a smoky flavor, and the caul fat helps keep the meatballs moist and juicy (and together in one piece) while they cook in a pot with tomatoes and wine. Traditionally in France you can eat a caillette either hot or cold. I prefer it hot—that's when it's at its most tender. But try it both ways and decide for yourself.

1 pound pork loin, ground and well chilled

1 pound pork liver, ground and well chilled

½ pound pork fatback, ground and well chilled (see note)

7 ounces slab bacon: 4 ounces finely chopped; 3 ounces thinly sliced

½ pound peeled fresh chestnuts or dry-packed bottled, vacuum-sealed, or frozen peeled chestnuts, finely chopped

2 teaspoons finely chopped fresh thyme

1 tablepoon finely chopped fresh sage

1 tablespoon coarse sea salt or kosher salt

1 teaspoon crushed black pepper

3 tablespoons extra-virgin olive oil

1 red onion, peeled and chopped

8 garlic cloves, peeled and minced

½ pound Swiss chard, stemmed and roughly chopped

½ pound spinach, stemmed

½ pound caul fat (see note)

4 stalks celery, roughly chopped

2 carrots, peeled and roughly chopped

1 large onion, peeled and roughly chopped

1. Center a rack in the oven and preheat the oven to 300°F.

2. In a large bowl, toss together the pork loin, pork liver, fatback, and chopped bacon. Add the chestnuts, thyme, sage, salt, and black pepper to the meat and mix well. Refrigerate until needed.

3. Heat 1 tablespoon of the olive oil in a large skillet over medium heat. Add the red onion and garlic and cook until translucent, 5 to 6 minutes. Add the Swiss chard and continue to cook until the chard is tender, about 10 minutes. Add the spinach and cook until wilted, about 3 minutes. Remove from the heat and let the greens cool.

4. When the greens have completely cooled, add them to the bowl of ground meat and stir to combine. Using your hands, roll the mixture into 2- to 3-inch meatballs. You should have 12 to 15 meatballs. Wrap each meatball in a layer of caul fat.

5. Heat the remaining 2 tablespoons olive oil in a medium cast-iron pot or Dutch oven over medium-high heat. Add the celery, carrots, and onion and cook until the onion is translucent, about 10 minutes. Stir in the tomato sauce, then pour in the white wine, bring to a boil, and boil for 1 minute. Add the chopped tomatoes and stir to combine. Place the meatballs in the pot and place a piece of the sliced bacon on top of each meatball. Bring to a simmer.

6. Cover the pot, transfer it to the oven, and braise until the meat is cooked through, about 1 hour. (Do not overcook; if you do, the liver in the meatballs will become dry and tough.) Spoon the tomato sauce over the tops of the meatballs and serve.

2 tablespoons tomato sauce

2 cups dry white wine

1 pound ripe tomatoes, halved, seeded, and finely chopped

FATBACK

Frequently used to flavor such Southern favorites as collard greens and black-eyed peas, fatback is the layer of fat that runs along the pudgy back of a pig. Although fatback is often rendered into lard for frying, slivers can also be wrapped around roasted meats, terrines, and pâtés, lending wonderful flavor and moisture. Usually purchased fresh (unsmoked and unsalted), fatback is sometimes available cured. Stored in the refrigerator, fresh fatback will keep for about a week; salt-cured will keep for up to 1 month. For these recipes, you will need the fresh kind. Ask your local butcher to order fatback for you, or purchase it online (see Sources, page 210).

CAUL FAT

This fragile, lacy membrane surrounding the stomach and organs of animals (usually pork) is often used as a covering for pâtés, terrines, and sausages, and lends moisture and flavor to a dish as it cooks. Caul fat usually dissolves completely during slow cooking. It is highly perishable and should be purchased in small amounts and used immediately or frozen for future use. Although you may have to ask for it, many butchers do sell caul fat, or it can be purchased online (see Sources, page 210).

STUFFED CABBAGE WITH PORK AND CHESTNUTS

| MAKES 8 SERVINGS |

This dish takes a little time to put together but makes an extremely elegant presentation. A whole cabbage is disassembled, blanched, and then put back together with a very savory forcemeat stuffing between the leaves. After braising, the stuffed cabbage is sliced into wedges, which look beautiful with their layers of green leaves and golden brown meat filling. Of course, it's a lot more complicated than the stuffed cabbages my grandmother would make. She'd just tuck ground leftover meat between the leaves of a loose cabbage, or roll up the leaves with the filling inside. This version is much more impressive, though you can try the simplified variation (see note on page 69) if you'd prefer.

FOR THE CABBAGE:
2 large heads savoy cabbage

FOR THE STUFFING:
4 slices white bread, crusts removed, sliced ½ inch thick and quartered

¾ cup heavy cream

2 tablespoons unsalted butter

4 medium carrots, peeled and cut into ⅛-inch dice

1 medium celery root, peeled and cut into ⅛-inch dice

1 cup finely chopped dry-packed bottled or vacuum-sealed peeled chestnuts

2 garlic cloves, peeled and finely chopped

2 sprigs fresh thyme, leaves only, finely chopped

Coarse sea salt or kosher salt and freshly ground pepper

5 ounces slab bacon, diced

2 chicken livers, cleaned and halved

1 large onion, peeled and cut into ¼-inch-thick slices

5 large white mushrooms, trimmed and cut into ¼-inch-thick slices

1½ pounds boneless pork shoulder, cut lengthwise into 5 strips

1. For the cabbage: Fill a 4- to 5-quart Dutch oven with salted water and bring to a boil. Pull off the leaves from each cabbage, trying to keep each leaf whole, and plunge them into the salted water to blanch for 5 to 6 minutes, or until they are tender enough to bend easily. (The larger, dark green outer leaves may take 1 or 2 minutes longer to cook until pliable.) Transfer the leaves to a colander and run them under very cold water to cool them and set their color. When the leaves are cool, cut away the tough ribs—it's best to cut them out in a V pattern—and then dry the leaves between layers of paper towels.

2. To make the stuffing: Soak the bread in the heavy cream in a large bowl.

3. Melt the butter in a small sauté pan over medium heat. When it is hot, add the carrots, celery root, chestnuts, garlic, and thyme. Season with salt and pepper and cook, stirring, until the vegetables just soften but don't color, 5 to 8 minutes. Transfer the vegetables to a plate to cool.

4. Warm a large skillet over medium heat and when it is hot, add the bacon. Cook, stirring, until the bacon renders its fat and starts to brown. Add the chicken livers and onion and cook for about 10 minutes. Add the mushrooms, season with salt and pepper, and continue to cook and stir until the liver and vegetables are browned and cooked through, about 10 minutes more.

5. Using a slotted spoon, transfer the ingredients to a bowl and set the bowl over ice, or put it in the refrigerator. Leave whatever cooking fats are in the skillet and return the pan to medium-high heat. Toss in the cut-up pork shoulder, season with salt and pepper, and cook, stirring, until the meat is well browned, about 15 minutes. Add the pork to the ingredients over ice and cool. In order to grind the stuffing, everything has to be really cold. (You can make the stuffing up to this point a day ahead and keep the ingredients well covered in the refrigerator.)

6. Pass the chilled meat mixture, the fatback, and the soaked bread (reserve any cream) through the medium blade of a meat grinder. Alternatively, use a food processor and gently pulse the meat until it reaches small dice (don't overprocess to a paste). Transfer the ground stuffing to a large bowl and, mixing with a wooden spoon, add the carrot and celery root mixture, along with whatever cream (if any) remains from soaking the bread, the egg, 1½ teaspoons salt, ¼ teaspoon freshly ground pepper, the Four-Spice Powder, and chopped parsley. Because the meat in the stuffing is not fully cooked, the best way to check on the seasoning is to make a small patty, cook it well in a pan, and then taste it. Add more salt and pepper to the stuffing as needed.

7. Center a rack in the oven and preheat the oven to 300° F.

1½ ounces pork fatback, cut into chunks

1 large egg, lightly beaten

¼ teaspoon Four-Spice Powder (see recipe, page 29)

1 small bunch fresh flat-leaf parsley, leaves only, finely chopped

TO ASSEMBLE:
Kitchen twine

4 slices bacon

¾ cup veal demi-glace, homemade or store-bought (see note)

¾ cup chicken stock (page 208) or low-sodium canned chicken broth

1 tablespoon extra-virgin olive oil

1 tablespoon unsalted butter

Coarse sea salt or kosher salt and freshly ground pepper

8. To assemble the cabbage (see photographs): Place 4 pieces of kitchen twine a little longer than the bacon in a crisscross pattern on a flat work surface. Place bacon strip on top of each piece of twine.

9. Using the largest, darkest, sturdiest, best-looking cabbage leaves, make a circle of 5 leaves (or more, depending on the size of the leaves) slightly overlapping over the bacon. The best way to do this is to arrange the leaves so that they make a circle about 20 inches in diameter with the V cut out of each leaf toward the center of the circle. Place a small leaf in the center of the circle. Repeat, making a second layer of cabbage over the first. Spoon about one-third of the stuffing into the center of the circle and then, with the back of the spoon, press the stuffing into a patty that's about 8 inches in diameter. Cover this first layer of filling with another double circle of cabbage leaves, but this time make the circle about 10 inches in diameter. Spoon about one-third of the remaining filling over the leaves and top with another layer of leaves. Repeat until you have three layers of filling separated by cabbage leaves. The cabbage layers will get smaller as you go, and so the last layer of stuffing will be less a layer than a ball. Pull up the edges of the cabbage, then the bacon strips, and then the kitchen twine. Twist and squeeze to shape the stuffed cabbage into a ball. Tie the cabbage securely with the kitchen twine.

10. Wrap the cabbage in a layer of cheesecloth or in a kitchen towel, twisting and squeezing the cabbage ball to tighten it further. Remove the cheesecloth or kitchen towel. Once tied, the cabbage has the shape of a round pumpkin or a muskmelon.

11. Add the demi-glace and chicken stock to an oven-proof skillet, roasting pan, or cast-iron pot just large enough to hold the cabbage. Carefully transfer the stuffed cabbage to the pan and brush the outside of it with the olive oil. Finally, crown the cabbage with the butter. Put the pan over medium heat and bring the demi-glace and stock to a boil, basting the cabbage a few times.

12. Cover the pan, slide it into the oven, and braise, basting frequently, until an instant-read thermometer inserted into the center of the cabbage reaches 150°F, about 1½ hours.

13. Carefully transfer the cabbage to a warm serving platter and remove the string. Skim the fat from the sauce, add ⅓ cup water, and bring to a boil, stirring to scrape up any browned bits on the bottom of the pan. Season to taste with salt and pepper and strain the sauce through a fine-mesh sieve over the cabbage. Let the cabbage rest for about 5 minutes before carving and serving.

CABBAGE ROLLS

To make individual cabbage rolls, lay out 1 large, sturdy cabbage leaf on a clean work surface. Place 2 heaping teaspoons of the stuffing in the middle of the bottom of the cabbage leaf. Fold the right and left sides of the cabbage leaf over the filling toward the center. Fold the bottom edge up toward the center, away from you, and roll until the cabbage leaf is completely wrapped. Wrap each roll in a slice of bacon. Sear, and then braise for about 45 minutes, until an instant-read thermometer inserted into the center reads 150°F.

PORK SHOULDER WITH GUINNESS, DRIED CHERRIES, AND SWEET POTATOES

| MAKES 6 TO 8 SERVINGS |

Pork shoulder is a classic for braising—the meat turns nearly spoonable but still slices nicely, and leftovers are great for sandwiches. In this recipe I've combined the pork with dried cherries and sweet potatoes, balancing their sweetness with the slightly bitter taste of Guinness stout and molasses.

5 cups Guinness stout

1 cup dried cherries

⅓ cup balsamic vinegar

2 tablespoons vegetable or extra-virgin olive oil

1 (5½-pound) pork shoulder roast

Coarse sea salt or kosher salt and freshly ground black pepper

3 large red onions, peeled and sliced

½ teaspoon crushed black pepper

4 garlic cloves, peeled and finely minced

1 tablespoon tomato paste

5 whole allspice, crushed

2 bay leaves

¼ cup molasses

3 tablespoons packed dark brown sugar

2 pounds sweet potatoes or yams, peeled and roughly chopped

1. Bring the stout, cherries, and vinegar to a simmer in a saucepan. Transfer to a bowl, cover tightly with plastic wrap, and let sit for at least 1 hour, or refrigerate overnight.

2. Center a rack in the oven and preheat the oven to 300°F.

3. Warm the oil in a large cast-iron pot or Dutch oven over high heat. Season the pork shoulder with salt and ground black pepper and sear on all sides until golden brown, 12 to 15 minutes. Transfer the pork shoulder to a platter. Remove all but 2 tablespoons of the fat in the pot.

4. Add the onion and the crushed black pepper to the pot and sauté for 7 minutes. Add the garlic and continue cooking until the onions are translucent, about 3 minutes. Stir in the tomato paste and cook for 2 to 3 minutes longer. Add the pork shoulder, the marinated cherries and liquid, allspice, bay leaves, molasses, brown sugar, 1 teaspoon salt, and 2 cups water. Bring the mixture to a simmer.

5. Cover the pot, transfer it to the oven, and braise for 1 hour, turning the pork once during cooking. Add the sweet potatoes and continue to braise for 2 more hours, turning two more times. If the sauce is too thin or is not flavored intensely enough, ladle most of it off into another pot and simmer it until it thickens and intensifies. Then add it back to the first pot.

6. Slice the pork and serve with the sauce on top.

LAMB SHOULDER À LA GARDIANE

BRAISED LAMB SHOULDER WITH POTATO AND FENNEL

| MAKES 6 SERVINGS |

This dish—lamb braised with fennel, tomatoes, lemon, and potatoes—is typical of Provence. I use Meyer lemons (see note) because I like their milder, more floral taste, but regular lemons will work well, too, and they are definitely what we would use in France. Even though the recipe already has potatoes, you can still serve it with a little bread to absorb the aromatic juices, and perhaps a peppery green salad on the side. Bring the lamb to the table on a platter, and carve it in front of your guests for a very impressive presentation.

½ cup fresh bread crumbs (see note, page 44)

10 garlic cloves, peeled: 2 cloves chopped; 8 cloves sliced

2 sprigs fresh rosemary: 1, leaves chopped; 1 left whole

2 sprigs fresh sage: 1, leaves chopped; 1 left whole

5 tablespoons extra-virgin olive oil

1 (4½-pound) bone-in center-cut lamb shoulder roast, trimmed

Coarse sea salt or kosher salt and freshly ground black pepper

1 pound fingerling potatoes, scrubbed

2 Meyer lemons or 1 regular lemon, scrubbed and thinly sliced

3 fennel bulbs, trimmed and halved

1 stalk celery, diced

1 tablespoon coriander seeds, crushed

4 tomatoes, peeled (if desired—see note, page 37), halved, and cored

2 cups chicken stock (page 209) or low-sodium canned chicken broth

2 tablespoons tomato paste

1. Place a rack in the lower third of the oven and preheat the oven to 300°F.

2. Combine the bread crumbs with the chopped garlic, chopped rosemary, and chopped sage; drizzle with 2 tablespoons olive oil; and season with salt and pepper. Toss to combine. Set aside. Using kitchen twine, tie together the remaining sprigs of rosemary and sage to make an herb bouquet; set aside.

3. Season the lamb with salt and pepper. In a large cast-iron pot or Dutch oven over medium-high heat, warm the remaining 3 tablespoons olive oil. Add the lamb and sear on all sides until golden brown, 7 to 10 minutes. Transfer the lamb to a platter and keep warm.

4. Add the potatoes, lemons, fennel, celery, sliced garlic, coriander seeds, and reserved herb bouquet to the pot. Sauté, stirring, for 5 to 6 minutes. Stir in the tomatoes, chicken stock, and tomato paste. Return the lamb to the pot, sprinkle the bread crumbs evenly over the top, and bring to a simmer.

5. Cover the pot, transfer it to the oven, and braise for 1 hour. Using a pastry brush, baste the lamb, being careful not to disturb the crumb crust. Uncover and bake for an additional 30 minutes, until the top is crusty and golden. Transfer the lamb and vegetables to a large, warm serving platter and serve immediately.

MEYER LEMONS

Brought to the United States from China during the early twentieth century, Meyer lemons have a thin, edible skin and a sweeter, more delicate flavor than the hardy lemon found in supermarkets. Believed to be a cross between a lemon and a mandarin orange, Meyer lemons are typically in season from December through April. Although Meyer lemons are mostly used as an ornamental plant in Asia, American chefs prize them for the complex taste they lend to both sweet and savory dishes. Meyer lemons can also be preserved in salt. Look for lemons with a rich orange-yellow color, which indicates that the fruit has been allowed to ripen fully on the tree.

ROYAL SHOULDER OF LAMB WITH SAFFRON, RAISINS, AND PISTACHIOS

| MAKES 6 SERVINGS |

With plenty of saffron and crème fraîche, this luxurious dish earns its traditional, princely title, derived from Moghul cuisine. Although it's made with hot chilies and ample spices, the flavor is more heady and aromatic than fiery. Serve it for a special occasion with the Lemon-Coriander Basmati Pilaf (see recipe, opposite).

1 teaspoon saffron threads (see note)

½ teaspoon cornstarch

1 cup plain whole-milk yogurt

1 cup crème fraîche

½ cup almond flour or finely ground blanched almonds

½ cup seedless green grapes

1 (2-inch) piece fresh gingerroot, peeled and grated

1 tablespoon sugar

2 teaspoons coarse sea salt or kosher salt

2 teaspoons black cumin seeds (see note)

8 black cardamom pods, or substitute regular cardamom pods (see note)

6 garlic cloves, peeled

Finely grated zest and freshly squeezed juice of 2 lemons

2 small dried hot red chili peppers

2 whole cloves

1 (4½-pound) bone-in lamb shoulder (ask your butcher for a cut from the front of the shoulder), trimmed

2 tablespoons vegetable oil

1 small onion, peeled and minced

1 cup celery hearts cut on the bias into 1-inch pieces, leaves reserved for garnish

½ cup pistachios, toasted (see note, page 44)

1. The day before you want to serve this dish, bring ½ cup water and the saffron to a boil in a small saucepan. Whisk in the cornstarch. Let the mixture infuse for 10 minutes.

2. Combine the saffron mixture with the yogurt, crème fraîche, almond flour, grapes, gingerroot, sugar, salt, cumin seeds, cardamom pods, garlic, lemon zest and juice, chilies, and cloves in a blender and mix until smooth. Put the lamb in a nonreactive bowl or Pyrex dish. Pour this marinade on top, cover tightly with plastic wrap, and marinate in the refrigerator overnight.

3. Place a rack in the lower third of the oven and preheat the oven to 300°F.

4. Remove the lamb from the marinade, scraping off and reserving the marinade. In a medium cast-iron pot or Dutch oven over medium-high heat, warm the vegetable oil. Add the lamb to the pot and sear on all sides until golden brown, 7 to 10 minutes. Add the onion and celery, turn the lamb over, lower the heat to medium, and continue to cook for 5 minutes. Add the pistachios, raisins, cinnamon stick, ½ cup water, and the reserved marinade, stir to combine, and bring to a simmer.

5. Cover the pot, transfer it to the oven, and braise for 1½ hours, turning the meat once halfway through. Remove the lid and continue to braise for 1 hour more.

6. Sprinkle the celery heart leaves over the lamb and serve, accompanied by the Lemon-Coriander Basmati Pilaf, if desired.

LEMON-CORIANDER BASMATI PILAF

| MAKES 6 SERVINGS |

1 lemon

2 tablespoons unsalted butter

1 small onion, peeled and finely chopped

2 cups basmati rice, rinsed

½ teaspoon crushed coriander seeds

1 cup milk

2 teaspoons coarse sea salt or kosher salt

½ cup raisins, soaked in hot water for 20 minutes, drained

1 (3-inch) cinnamon stick

Lemon-Coriander Basmati Pilaf (optional; see recipe, left)

Finely grate the zest of one half of the lemon and juice the entire lemon. In a medium saucepan over medium heat, melt the butter. Add the onion and cook, stirring occasionally, until tender, 3 to 5 minutes. Add the rice and sauté for 3 minutes. Stir in the lemon zest and juice and the coriander seeds. Add 3 cups water and bring to a boil. Add the milk and salt and return to a boil. Reduce the heat to low, cover, and simmer for 15 minutes. Remove from the heat and let sit, covered, for 5 minutes before serving.

SAFFRON THREADS

Saffron is the most expensive spice available, and generally considered worth the cost because of its fine flavor and color and because a little goes a long way. It consists of the fiery-looking stigmas of crocus flowers, hand-harvested and dried. These flowers are cultivated for their precious orange strands in many countries, and some of the most highly regarded saffron comes from Kashmir. A few threads reconstituted in warm water, then added to a dish along with their brightly dyed soaking water, will infuse the ingredients with a warm, floral, slightly sweet flavor. Often a part of rice dishes, as well as a key ingredient in French bouillabaisse, saffron is best used with restraint—aside from being very expensive, it can become soapy-tasting when overused. Look for dried but not crumbled strands of a bright hue in gourmet markets.

BLACK CUMIN SEEDS

True black cumin, a spice with a sweet cumin flavor that is used in Indian and Arabic cooking, is rare and looks similar to typical cumin seeds in shape. It can be found in Indian and Middle Eastern stores, or online (see Sources, page 210).

BLACK CARDAMOM PODS

Also known as brown cardamom, this spice is traditionally used to flavor meat stews, vegetables, and pilafs in the Middle East, Asia, and Africa. It is a relative of green cardamom, although black cardamon has a somewhat more pungent taste whereas the green variety is rather sweet. It also has a more camphorous aroma and a larger, dark brown, three-sided seed coating that contains its black seeds. Its flavor is best released through long, slow cooking. Look for this spice in Asian, Indian, and Middle Eastern markets, or order it online (see Sources, page 210).

LAMB SHANKS WITH WALNUTS AND POMEGRANATE

| MAKES 6 SERVINGS |

Lamb shanks are a classic meat for braising, and there's a good reason why. Browned and then cooked slowly in a little liquid, they soften and soak up the essence of whatever you cook them with, so they are always flavorful and tender.

Before you go to the butcher, it's good to know that there are front shanks and back shanks, and the shanks from the back legs are normally better, with a bit more muscle on the bone and less fat. You may want to call ahead and order the back shank. But if there is only front shank to be had, don't walk away empty-handed. Just take care that the pieces you choose are not too bony.

I like lamb shanks braised, but not swimming in sauce. So in this recipe, I finish the braise uncovered. That method gives the sauce—in this case made with pomegranate juice—a chance to really thicken, and the meat caramelizes a little on the outside, so that it takes on a slightly roasted flavor. If there is still too much sauce but the meat is already tender, you can just keep cooking until the sauce reduces enough. That's one thing about lamb shank meat—even when it is falling off the bones, you can let it go on cooking and it won't dry out.

4 lamb shanks, (about ¾ to 1 pound each), shank bone trimmed

Coarse sea salt or kosher salt and freshly ground black pepper

3 tablespoons extra-virgin olive oil

4 garlic cloves, peeled and chopped

1 sprig fresh sage

1 teaspoon ground sumac (see note)

½ teaspoon crushed red pepper flakes

½ teaspoon fennel seeds

2 medium red onions, peeled and sliced

1 medium fennel bulb, trimmed, halved lengthwise, and sliced crosswise

1 tablespoon tomato paste

2 cups pomegranate juice (see note)

1 (15-ounce) can chickpeas, rinsed and drained

½ cup golden raisins

1. Center a rack in the oven and preheat the oven to 275°F.

2. Season the lamb shanks with salt and pepper. Heat the olive oil in a large cast-iron pot or Dutch oven over high heat. Add the lamb shanks and sear on all sides until well browned, 12 to 15 minutes. Transfer them to a plate and reduce the heat to medium.

3. Add the garlic, sage, sumac, red pepper flakes, and fennel seeds to the pot and cook, stirring, for 1 minute. Add the red onions and sliced fennel bulb and cook until softened, 10 to 12 minutes. Stir in the tomato paste and cook for 3 minutes. Add the pomegranate juice, chickpeas, raisins, walnuts, and pomegranate molasses, return the lamb shanks to the pot, and bring to a simmer.

4. Cover the pot, transfer it to the oven, and braise until the lamb is nearly tender, about 1½ hours, turning the shanks twice while cooking. Remove the lid, turn the shanks again, and continue to cook uncovered until the lamb is caramelized on top and the sauce is thick. Serve with the pomegranate seeds sprinkled on top.

½ cup chopped toasted walnuts (see note, page 44)

1 tablespoon pomegranate molasses (see note)

Seeds of 1 pomegranate (to remove the seeds, quarter the pomegranate)

SUMAC

Widely used for cooking in the Middle East and the Mediterranean, sumac is the dried and ground berries of a wild bush that grows in both of these regions. Sumac is typically purchased as a coarse reddish-purple powder, and it has a sour, astringent taste that can substitute for lemon, tamarind, or vinegar. It frequently seasons stews, casseroles, and meat dishes. Sumac berries are also sometimes crushed and soaked in hot water to make a juice used for salad dressings, sauces, and chicken or fish kebabs. Dried, powdered sumac can be purchased at specialty spice markets or online (see Sources, page 210).

POMEGRANATE JUICE

The large, round, red pomegranate has been an integral part of Middle Eastern and Mediterranean cooking for thousands of years, making appearances in Greek mythology, Homer's *Odyssey,* and the Bible. It is still growing wild in its native Iran. The ruby-red seeds of this sweet, tangy fruit can be consumed out of hand, or the fruit can be juiced and (if desired) reduced to a syrup for use in soups, tagines, and desserts. In India, pomegranates are sold dried whole and powdered and are used as a souring agent for vegetable and lentil

dishes. Despite their popularity abroad, pomegranates have historically been little more than a novelty food in North American culture, perhaps because it takes a long time to separate the small, juice-filled arils (or seeds) from their honeycombed membrane. In recent years, however, the pomegranate has seen a tremendous increase in popularity in the United States, in great part owing to recent studies citing its powerful antioxidant properties. Bottled pomegranate juice and frozen concentrated juice are now widely available in supermarkets; you can also purchase whole pomegranates (in markets from October through December) and make your own juice at home.

To juice a pomegranate, roll the unpeeled fruit on a work surface to soften the seeds and release some of the juice. Carefully cut the pomegranate in half (you may want to wear an apron and gloves, as the vibrantly colored juice does stain) and, using your hands or a citrus reamer, carefully squeeze the juice into a deep bowl. Strain the juice before using. One pomegranate yields approximately ½ cup of juice.

POMEGRANATE MOLASSES

Called *robb-e-anar* in its homeland, Iran, this thick, purple-red syrup is simply the concentrated juice of the pomegranate. To add a sweet, sharp depth of flavor to food, Middle Eastern and Mediterranean recipes often pair pomegranate molasses with game or walnuts, or both. Don't confuse pomegranate molasses with grenadine, a sugary pomegranate-flavored syrup that is used in cocktails and is rarely made from real pomegranates. To make your own pomegranate molasses, simmer 2 cups pure pomegranate juice in a nonreactive saucepan over medium heat, uncovered, until it has reduced to about ¼ cup and is thick enough to coat the back of a spoon, 20 to 25 minutes. The molasses can be stored in an airtight container in the refrigerator for up to 3 months. Pomegranate molasses can also be purchased at Middle Eastern markets or online (see Sources, page 210).

LAMB SHANKS WITH MINT, PRUNES, AND BOURBON

| MAKES 4 SERVINGS |

Here's another preparation for lamb shanks—this one gets its sweet taste from the prunes and bourbon. It's the kind of recipe you might want to double, since you can serve it to a crowd and be sure that everyone will love it. And you probably already have most of the ingredients at home.

1½ cups pitted prunes

1¼ cups bourbon

½ cup apple cider vinegar

5 sprigs fresh mint, plus additional mint leaves for garnish

2 bay leaves

2 (2-inch) strips fresh lemon zest

1 sprig fresh thyme

¼ cup extra-virgin olive oil

4 lamb shanks (about ¾ to 1 pound each), fat trimmed and shank trimmed close to the bone (have your butcher do this for you)

Coarse sea salt or kosher salt

2 teaspoons crushed black pepper

2 small red onions, peeled and sliced

4 stalks celery, cut into 2-inch-long pieces

2 green bell peppers, cored, seeded, and thinly sliced

3 carrots, peeled, trimmed, and roughly chopped

3 garlic cloves, peeled and finely chopped

Freshly squeezed juice of 1 lemon

1. In a large pot, bring the prunes, bourbon, and vinegar to a simmer. Remove from the heat and let sit at room temperature for at least 1 hour, or cover and refrigerate overnight.

2. Center a rack in the oven and preheat the oven to 300°F.

3. Wrap and tie the mint sprigs, bay leaves, lemon zest, and thyme in cheesecloth or stuff them into a large tea ball.

4. Heat the olive oil in a large cast-iron pot or Dutch oven over high heat. Season the lamb shanks with salt and 1 teaspoon of the crushed black pepper. Add the lamb shanks to the pot and sear until golden brown on all sides, about 12 to 15 minutes. Transfer the lamb shanks to a plate and lower the heat to medium-high.

5. Add the onions to the pot and cook until translucent, about 8 minutes. Add the celery, bell peppers, carrots, and garlic and cook, stirring, for 5 minutes. Return the lamb shanks to the pot and add the prune marinating liquid (save the prunes for later), the lemon juice, 1 cup water, the herb sachet, the remaining 1 teaspoon black pepper, and salt to taste. Bring to a simmer.

6. Cover the pot, transfer it to the oven, and braise for 2 hours, turning the shanks at least twice. Add the prunes and continue to braise until the lamb is very tender, about 30 minutes more. Serve garnished with the mint leaves.

LAMB SHANKS ROGAN JOSH

INDIAN-SPICED LAMB SHANKS IN YOGURT SAUCE

| MAKES 6 SERVINGS |

For this dish, I took inspiration from a traditional Indian curry made with cubes of lamb. The shank meat really takes in the flavor of the spices, and the marrow in the bone adds richness to the sauce, which is already creamy with yogurt. It's quite a festive, luxurious dish, especially if you serve it with the Mint and Ajwain Pancakes (see recipe, page 83), which were inspired by Chinese scallion pancakes, although they are less greasy. Or, a simple rice pilaf is also nice here—and easier.

1. The day before you want to serve the dish, use a spice grinder to finely grind the cardamom, black and white peppercorns, allspice, cloves, paprika, salt, cumin, coriander, cinnamon, cayenne, and bay leaf. Place the shanks in a nonreactive container such as a Pyrex bowl and rub with 2 tablespoons of the oil and then with the spice mixture. Cover the shanks tightly with plastic wrap and let marinate in the refrigerator overnight.

2. Using a food processor or blender, blend ⅓ cup water with the diced red bell pepper, garlic, yogurt, and gingerroot until smooth.

3. Position a rack in the lower third of the oven and preheat the oven to 300°F.

4. In a medium saucepan, bring 3 cups water to a boil and keep at a slow, steady simmer.

5. Warm the remaining 3 tablespoons oil in a large cast-iron pot or Dutch oven over medium-high heat. Add the shanks to the pot and sear, adjusting the heat and turning the meat so that the spices do not burn, until golden brown on all sides, 12 to 15 minutes. Transfer the lamb to a plate.

6. Add the sliced red bell peppers and onions to the pot and cook, stirring, until the vegetables begin to soften but do not brown, about 5 minutes. Return the browned

12 green cardamom pods

10 black peppercorns

10 white peppercorns

3 whole allspice

2 whole cloves

2 tablespoons Indian paprika or sweet paprika (see note)

1 tablespoon coarse sea salt or kosher salt

1½ teaspoons cumin seeds

1 teaspoon coriander seeds

2 (3-inch) cinnamon sticks or 1 teaspoon ground cinnamon

½ teaspoon cayenne pepper

1 bay leaf

6 lamb shanks (about ¾ to 1 pound each), bone trimmed (ask your butcher to do this)

5 tablespoons vegetable or extra-virgin olive oil

3 red bell peppers, cored and seeded: 1 diced; 2 sliced into ¼-inch-thick strips

6 garlic cloves, peeled

½ cup plain whole-milk yogurt

2 tablespoons grated peeled fresh gingerroot

2 medium onions, peeled, halved lengthwise, and cut into ¼-inch-thick slices

½ teaspoon garam masala (see note and recipe below)

Mint and Ajwain Pancakes, for serving (see recipe, opposite)

GARAM MASALA

Garam masala is an Indian spice mixture, typically made of cardamom pods, cinnamon sticks, cloves, black peppercorns, cumin seeds, and coriander seeds (but can include other spices as well) that have been toasted and then ground together. It can be purchased at any store with a good selection of spices or online (see Sources, page 210). As with all ground spices, garam masala should be used fresh, so buy small quantities and replace it often, or make your own.

lamb to the pot, stir in the bell pepper–yogurt mixture, and sprinkle the garam masala on top. Pour in the hot water and bring to a simmer.

7. Cover the pot, transfer it to the oven, and braise for 2½ hours, turning the shanks twice while cooking.

GARAM MASALA

| MAKES ½ CUP |

¼ cup cumin seeds

¼ cup coriander seeds

2 tablespoons black peppercorns

2 (2-inch) cinnamon sticks, broken up

1 tablespoon green cardamom pods, crushed with the side of a knife

1 teaspoon whole cloves

3 cloves mace

1 tablespoon ground nutmeg

Heat a large heavy wok or skillet over medium heat for 2 minutes, then add the spices. Toast, stirring constantly, until fragrant and brown but not burned, 7 to 9 minutes. Transfer to a bowl to cool, then grind in a clean electric coffee grinder or spice grinder. Store airtight in a cool, dry place for up to 6 months.

MINT AND AJWAIN PANCAKES

| MAKES 8 PANCAKES |

2 cups all-purpose flour, plus additional for kneading

2 teaspoons ajwain seeds (see note), toasted, or dried thyme

2 teaspoons garam masala (see note and recipe, opposite)

1 teaspoon coarse sea salt or kosher salt

2 tablespoons unsalted butter, melted

¼ cup chopped fresh mint leaves

1. In the bowl of an electric mixer fitted with the dough hook, combine the flour and 1 cup water and knead on medium-low speed for 5 minutes, sprinkling in a little more flour if necessary to yield a smooth, soft dough. Alternatively, stir together with a rubber spatula, then knead by hand on a floured board for 5 to 10 minutes (our baker's suggestion: put on a CD and knead to two songs). Use your hands to form the dough into a ball. Place the ball in a lightly greased bowl. Cover the dough with lightly greased plastic wrap and let it rest for at least 30 minutes, but no more than 90 minutes.

2. Turn the dough out onto a lightly floured work surface and divide it into 8 equal pieces. Roll each piece of dough into a ball with the floured palm of your cupped hand, using slight pressure. Roll the ball quickly in a circular motion until it is smooth, adding as little extra flour as possible. As you work, cover the finished balls of dough with a damp kitchen towel or lightly greased plastic wrap.

3. In a small bowl, combine the ajwain, garam masala, and salt. Use a floured rolling pin to roll a ball of the dough into a 6-inch disk. Brush the disk with some of the melted butter, then sprinkle the dough with a scant ¾ teaspoon of the spice mixture and 1½ teaspoons of the mint. Starting from one end of the disk, roll the dough up like a jelly roll; then twist it into a spiral, like a snail shell. Flatten the snail a little with the palm of your hand, then roll it into 6-inch disk. Repeat with the remaining dough to make 8 pancakes, keeping them covered with a damp towel or plastic wrap as you work.

4. Heat your heaviest skillet over medium-high heat for 2 minutes. Cook the pancakes one at a time, turning once, until golden brown, about 2½ minutes on the first side and about 2 minutes on the second side. Transfer the pancakes to a napkin-lined basket and cover to keep soft and warm. Or reheat in a moderate oven as needed.

INDIAN PAPRIKA

Indian paprika is very similar to Hungarian sweet paprika, which is a more readily available substitute. Each is a sweet, slightly earthy red powder made of dried mild red peppers. The brilliant vermilion hue of paprika is what gives rogan josh its distinctive redness. Look for paprika at stores that stock a good selection of spices and have a high turnover, to ensure that the spice is fresh and sweet rather than dusty-smelling and faded-looking. As with all ground spices, store paprika in a cool, dry place and use it within 6 months to 1 year.

AJWAIN SEEDS

Used in Indian cooking to season breads, ajwain seeds (also known as carom) look similar to caraway seeds, to which they are related. Their herbaceous flavor is reminiscent of oregano or thyme. The small gray-brown seeds are sold in Indian food stores and in the herb and spice section of well-stocked markets, or they can be ordered online (see Sources, page 210).

CARDAMOM-SPICED COCONUT LAMB

| MAKES 6 SERVINGS |

Lamb shoulder, cut into cubes, makes a good stew-like braise. Here, Indian spices give it a lot of character that sets it apart from the usual lamb stew. If you have time to make the Mustard Greens and Spinach Purée (see recipe, opposite), that is a perfect accompaniment, since it's a little bit milder than the stew and helps soften the chilies. But rice (see recipe, page 183) and a nice little salad would work well, too.

8 black cardamom pods (see note, page 77)

3 whole cloves

2 teaspoons cumin seeds

1½ teaspoons coriander seeds

1½ teaspoons ground turmeric

¼ cup vegetable oil

2½ pounds lean lamb shoulder, cut into 1-inch cubes and patted dry

Coarse sea salt or kosher salt and freshly ground black pepper

2 medium onions, peeled and finely chopped

½ teaspoon sugar

3 garlic cloves, peeled and finely chopped

1 (1-inch) piece fresh gingerroot, peeled and finely grated

6 fresh or dried curry leaves (see note, page 27)

3 small green chili peppers (such as jalapeños), seeded and chopped

4 plum tomatoes, cut into ¼-inch dice

1 tablespoon all-purpose flour

1 cup red lentils

¼ cup unsweetened desiccated coconut, toasted (see note)

Finely grated zest and freshly squeezed juice of 1 lime

1. Position a rack in the lower third of the oven and preheat the oven to 325°F.

2. Bring 5 cups water to a boil and keep at a slow, steady simmer.

3. In a spice grinder, finely grind the cardamom pods, cloves, cumin seeds, coriander seeds, and turmeric.

4. In a medium cast-iron pot or Dutch oven over medium-high heat, warm 3 tablespoons of the vegetable oil. Season the lamb with salt and pepper and sear the lamb, in batches, on all sides until golden brown, 7 to 10 minutes. Transfer the meat and any accumulated juices to a bowl.

5. Warm the remaining 1 tablespoon oil in the pot over medium-high heat. Add the onions and sugar and cook, reducing the heat to medium-low and stirring, until the onions are light golden brown, 10 to 12 minutes. Add the ground spices, garlic, ginger, curry leaves, and chilies and cook, stirring, 2 to 3 minutes more. Return the heat to medium-high, add the tomatoes, flour, simmering water, and lamb and juices, and bring to a simmer.

6. Cover the pot, transfer it to the oven, and braise for 30 minutes. Add the lentils, stir to combine, and braise for another 45 minutes. Taste and adjust the seasoning if necessary. To serve, sprinkle the lamb with the coconut and lime zest and juice.

STUFFED CABBAGE WITH PORK
AND CHESTNUTS (PAGE 66)

LAYERED BEEF AND ROOT VEGETABLES
IN A SPICY COCONUT CURRY (PAGE 26)

PORK BUTT WITH HAZELNUTS, GOLDEN RAISINS,
AND JERUSALEM ARTICHOKES (PAGE 43)

MEXICAN BABY BACK
PORK RIBS WITH
JALAPEÑOS AND EPAZOTE
(PAGE 56)

SMOKY BEEF CHILI
(PAGE 23)

SPICY MERGUEZ WITH SPINACH
AND WHITE BEANS
(PAGE 92)

HAM HOCKS WITH LYCHEES AND BOK CHOY (PAGE 62)

VEAL SHOULDER
FORESTIÈRE AU RIESLING (PAGE 38)

MUSTARD GREENS AND SPINACH PURÉE

| MAKES 6 SERVINGS |

1 tablespoon vegetable or extra-virgin olive oil

3 garlic cloves, peeled and chopped

1 pound spinach, stemmed and tough center ribs removed

1/2 pound mustard greens, trimmed

Coarse sea salt or kosher salt and freshly ground black pepper

2 teaspoons garam masala (see note and recipe, page 82)

1/4 cup plain whole-milk yogurt

In a large skillet over medium-high heat, warm the oil. Add the garlic, spinach, and mustard greens and cook, stirring, until the greens are wilted, 6 to 7 minutes. Season with salt, pepper, and the garam masala. Transfer the greens to a blender, add the yogurt, and blend until smooth.

TOASTING COCONUT

Grated fresh or dried (desiccated) coconut will toast nicely in a dry pan. To toast the coconut, put it in a heavy pan over medium heat and cook, tossing constantly, until it has begun to color slightly and the edges are browned, 1 to 2 minutes. Transfer immediately to a plate to stop the cooking; coconut burns quickly. The toasted coconut sold in bags in the supermarket has been sweetened. Avoid it.

INDIAN-STYLE RATATOUILLE
WITH SPICY GROUND LAMB

| MAKES 6 TO 8 SERVINGS |

Ratatouille was one of my comfort foods during my childhood in France, and my mother would make it all the time. It was one of the things she loved to cook in the late summer, in huge pots, maybe 25 pounds at a time. Then she would freeze small containers, and we'd eat it all year long. The thing about ratatouille is this: the bigger the batch, the better the stew, since the flavors can come together more slowly when you are cooking in volume. For me, the perfect ratatouille is one where the vegetables each keep their own distinct shape and flavor, never cooking down into mush. But, at the same time, they should be meltingly soft and tender, not crisp. Sometimes at the restaurant we do a "ratatouille *minute*," a quicker version using diced vegetables. The cubes always hold their shape and it presents nicely, but it never really captures what a good ratatouille is all about—the flavor.

This dish, inspired by the cuisines of India, has some of the elements of a good Provençale ratatouille—the zucchini, eggplant, tomatoes, and bell peppers—but differs in profound ways. First of all, there's the ground lamb, which flavors the vegetables and gives them another, more complex dimension. In France, ratatouille is normally vegetarian, and its richness comes from olive oil, not meat. Then there is the spicing. My mother used just a lot of garlic and a little basil. Here, I use jalapeño peppers, garam masala, turmeric, grated gingerroot, saffron, and cilantro. So really, it tastes nothing like my mother's dish, but it is, of course, nearly as good as hers in its own way.

---

2 pounds ground lamb

1 large egg

½ cup fresh bread crumbs (see note, page 44)

6 garlic cloves, peeled and finely chopped

2 teaspoons garam masala (see note and recipe, page 82)

¼ cup vegetable oil

2 medium eggplants (about 2 pounds), trimmed and cut into 2-inch cubes

3 medium zucchini, trimmed and cut into 1-inch cubes

3 green bell peppers, cored, seeded, and finely chopped

1 bunch scallions (about 8), trimmed and thinly sliced

1. Center a rack in the oven and preheat the oven to 300°F.

2. Mix the ground lamb with the egg, bread crumbs, about 1 garlic clove, and 1 teaspoon of the garam masala. Form into meatballs the size of golf balls.

3. Warm 2 tablespoons of the vegetable oil in a large skillet over medium heat. Add the meatballs to the pan and cook until golden brown on all sides, 7 to 8 minutes. Using a slotted spoon, transfer the meatballs to a paper towel–lined plate.

4. Warm the remaining 2 tablespoons vegetable oil in a medium cast-iron pot or Dutch oven over medium heat. Add the eggplant and cook for 5 minutes. Add the zucchini and cook for 5 more minutes. Add the remaining garlic, the bell peppers, scallions, jalapeños, gingerroot, turmeric, saffron, cayenne, and salt and pepper to taste and cook, stirring, until the vegetables soften, 4 to 5 minutes. Add the coconut milk and ½ cup water and bring to a simmer.

5. Add the meatballs, cover, and transfer to the oven to braise for 30 minutes.

6. Before serving, sprinkle the cilantro, lemon zest, lemon juice, and the remaining 1 teaspoon garam masala over the dish.

2 jalapeño peppers, seeded and minced

1 (2-inch) piece fresh gingerroot, peeled and finely grated

½ teaspoon ground turmeric

½ teaspoon saffron threads (see note, page 77)

2 pinches of cayenne pepper

Coarse sea salt or kosher salt and freshly ground black pepper

½ cup unsweetened coconut milk

3 tablespoons coarsely chopped fresh cilantro

Finely grated zest and freshly squeezed juice and of 1 lemon

CALABASH STUFFED WITH SPICY GROUND LAMB

| MAKES 6 SERVINGS |

With its rounds of green squash stuffed with fragrant lamb, this wonderfully tasty dish makes a very nice presentation at the table. Serve it with white rice or couscous.

1 (2-pound) calabash or winter melon, trimmed (see note)

1 large slice white bread (½ inch thick), torn into small pieces

¼ cup whole milk

1½ pounds ground lamb

1 large egg, lightly beaten

Coarse sea salt or kosher salt and freshly ground black pepper

2 tablespoons light soy sauce (see note, page 11)

1 teaspoon Thai or Vietnamese fish sauce (see note, page 55)

1 teaspoon ground turmeric

2 tablespoons extra-virgin olive oil

1 onion, peeled and diced

4 garlic cloves, peeled and thinly sliced

1 (2-inch) piece fresh gingerroot, peeled and finely grated

2 teaspoons annatto seed (see note, page 57)

1 whole clove

½ star anise pod

1 apple (your choice), peeled, cored, and diced

1 medium carrot, peeled, trimmed, and diced

1 bunch scallions, trimmed, thick scallions halved lengthwise

1 stalk lemongrass, trimmed and finely minced (see note, page 55)

3 sprigs fresh Thai basil (see note)

3 sprigs fresh cilantro

1. Center a rack in the oven and preheat the oven to 275°F.

2. Cut the calabash crosswise into ½- to ¾-inch-thick disks. Lay the calabash disks flat and use a round cookie cutter a little smaller than the diameter of the disks to cut the melon slices into equal-sized skinless rounds. Alternatively, use a knife to do this. Use a melon baller or small spoon to scoop out most of the seeds from the center of each melon slice, but leave a thin wall at the bottom of each slice to form a shallow cup.

3. Place the bread in a bowl, cover it with the milk, and let soak until the bread is completely soft, about 5 minutes.

4. Place the ground meat in a large bowl and stir in the egg, soaked bread, and milk. Season with 1 tablespoon salt and a few grinds of pepper. Mix gently until just combined.

5. Stuff the melon cups with the ground lamb filling, forming a small mound on top—do not compact the filling too much.

6. In a small bowl, stir together the soy sauce, fish sauce, and turmeric.

7. Heat the olive oil over medium heat in a very wide cast-iron pot or ovenproof skillet with a cover. (Alternatively, you can use two pots that will fit side by side in the oven, dividing the ingredients equally between them; the melon slices will need to fit into one layer.) Add the onion and garlic and cook, stirring, about 5 minutes, adjusting the heat if necessary to keep the vegetables from browning. Add the gingerroot, annatto seed, clove, and star anise and cook, stirring, until fragrant, 3 to 4 minutes more. Add the stuffed melon cups to the pot and scatter the apple, carrot, scallions, lemongrass, Thai basil, cilantro, green chili, and soy sauce mixture over the top. Bring the liquid to a simmer.

8. Cover the pot and transfer it to the oven. Braise until the melon and lamb filling are tender, about 1½ hours.

1 green chili pepper (such as jalapeño or serrano), minced, or ¼ teaspoon red chili paste (see note, page 13)

CALABASH, OR WINTER MELON

Large, with dark green, white-mottled skin, calabash—also called winter melon, because it ripens in the fall—has very white flesh with a mild flavor and nice crunch. It is used in Chinese stir-fries and soups, and it has a flavor similar to summer squash. It is usually sold sliced (whole melons can be as large as 30 pounds) in Asian markets.

THAI BASIL

Common in Southeast Asian cooking, Thai basil (also sometimes referred to as sweet basil) is a licorice-flavored herb frequently used to sweeten curries, stir-fries, and salads. Though its leaves are similar in color and shape to the deep green Italian basil sold in American supermarkets, Thai basil has distinguishing purple flower buds and stems. (The buds are also edible.) Thai basil should not be confused with holy basil, which is also Thai in origin but has a minty, peppery flavor quite different from that of Thai basil. Thai basil can be purchased in Asian markets or online (see Sources, page 210).

SPICY MERGUEZ WITH SPINACH AND WHITE BEANS

| MAKES 4 TO 6 SERVINGS |

Merguez is a very spicy North African sausage usually made from lamb or a combination of lamb and beef. People in France, especially Paris, love these sausages and eat them grilled and stuffed into a baguette, with pommes frites and maybe some harissa (hot sauce) spooned on top. This combination is called merguez frites, and we French eat it on the streets the way Americans eat hot dogs. Delicious!

You can buy merguez at butcher shops and large supermarkets, in links or rolled into a coil. The coil makes a very nice presentation. Just secure it with toothpicks before searing and braising, then remember to take them out before serving.

1/4 cup plus 1 tablespoon extra-virgin olive oil

4 pounds spinach, stems removed, washed and dried

2 medium onions, peeled and cut into small cubes

6 garlic cloves, peeled and finely chopped

2 tablespoons chopped fresh mint leaves

2 tablespoons chopped fresh cilantro leaves

1 tablespoon harissa (see note) or 1/4 teaspoon cayenne pepper

1 teaspoon freshly ground black pepper

1/2 teaspoon Four-Spice Powder (see recipe, page 29)

1/2 pound dried cannellini beans or black-eyed peas, soaked overnight in cold water and drained

2 pounds merguez sausage: 1 long link or individual links

1/4 cup freshly squeezed lemon juice (about 2 lemons)

Coarse sea salt or kosher salt

1. Center a rack in the oven and preheat the oven to 300°F.

2. Heat 1/4 cup of the olive oil in a wide cast-iron pot or Dutch oven over high heat. Add the spinach, little by little, and cook, stirring continuously, until all the spinach has wilted and browned slightly and all the liquid has evaporated, 20 to 30 minutes.

3. Add the onions, garlic, mint, cilantro, harissa (or cayenne), black pepper, and Four-Spice Powder and cook, stirring, for 5 minutes.

4. Pour in 4 cups water and add the cannellini beans (or black-eyed peas). Stir, bring to a simmer, and cover. Braise in the oven for 2 hours, or until the beans are nearly tender.

5. Meanwhile, heat the remaining 1 tablespoon olive oil in a medium skillet over medium heat. Sear the merguez on all sides, about 10 minutes. Transfer to a plate lined with a paper towel to drain.

6. Stir the lemon juice into the beans and place the seared merguez on top. Cover and continue to braise until the beans are tender and the sausage is cooked through, about 30 minutes more. Season with salt to taste.

HARISSA

Both a condiment and a seasoning for soups and tangines, harissa is an essential ingredient in North African cooking, particularly in Tunisia, Algeria, and Morocco. It gets its hot, smoky essence from a mix of dried chili peppers, cumin, coriander, garlic, caraway, olive oil, and occasionally tomatoes. The sauce is such an important part of Tunisian cooking that connoisseurs claim to be able to distinguish between the flavor of chilies that have been dried in the sun, the shade, or an oven. It can be purchased at specialty supermarkets or online (see Sources, page 210).

LAMB NECK WITH COMICE PEARS AND WHEAT BERRIES

| MAKES 4 TO 6 SERVINGS |

Lamb neck isn't the kind of ingredient you can easily find in your local supermarket. Even many butchers will have to order it specially. But it's a nice cut for braising because of all the connective tissue in the spine, which gives a lot of gelatin to thicken the sauce. It's a very traditional cut in the Middle East, and this recipe reflects that. The braise has a fragrant, fruity taste from the Comice pears (or apples) and all the spices—such as cardamom, mace, allspice, and saffron. They really melt into the meat and the sauce and add wonderful flavor.

If you can't find lamb neck, you can substitute lamb shanks. And if you have time to soak the wheat berries in cold water in the refrigerator overnight, you can skip the blanching.

¾ cup wheat berries (see note)

2½ teaspoons cumin seeds

1 teaspoon black peppercorns

1 teaspoon saffron threads (see note, page 77)

¼ teaspoon cayenne pepper

¼ teaspoon ground mace

6 cardamom pods

4 whole allspice

2 whole cloves

4 pounds lamb neck, trimmed and cut into 2-inch pieces (as for osso buco; ask your butcher to do this); or substitute 2-inch pieces of lamb shank

Coarse sea salt or kosher salt and freshly ground black pepper

3 tablespoons extra-virgin olive oil

2 large red onions, peeled and cut into 1-inch cubes

1 to 2 jalapeño peppers, to taste, seeded and chopped

1 tablespoon grated peeled fresh gingerroot

1. Center a rack in the oven and preheat the oven to 300°F.

2. Bring a small pot of water to a boil. Add the wheat berries, immediately turn off the heat, and let the wheat berries sit, uncovered, for 10 minutes. Drain them in a colander and rinse under cold running water to stop the cooking.

3. In a spice grinder or with a mortar and pestle, finely grind the cumin seeds, black peppercorns, saffron, cayenne, mace, cardamom, allspice, and cloves.

4. Season the lamb neck with salt and pepper. Heat 1½ tablespoons of the olive oil in a medium cast-iron pot or Dutch oven over high heat. Add the lamb and sear until golden brown on all sides. Transfer the lamb to a plate. Spoon off all of the fat in the pot. Heat the remaining 1½ tablespoons olive oil over medium heat. Add the ground spices, red onions, jalapeños, gingerroot, and orange zest, season with salt, and cook, stirring, for 8 minutes. Add the garlic and cook for 2 more minutes. Add the turnips and pears and cook for 3 to 4 minutes.

Transfer the pears to a plate. Return the lamb neck to the pot, add the orange juice and 5 cups water, and bring to the simmer.

5. Cover the pot, transfer it to the oven, and braise for 1 hour, basting the lamb neck once. Return the pears to the pot, add the wheat berries, and braise for 1 more hour, basting once. Garnish with the cilantro and serve.

Finely grated zest of 1 orange

1 tablespoon chopped peeled garlic

4 medium turnips, peeled and halved

4 ripe Comice or Anjou pears or apples, peeled, quartered, cored, and cut into large cubes

Freshly squeezed juice of 2 oranges

1 tablespoon chopped fresh cilantro leaves

WHEAT BERRIES

Whole wheat berries are shaped somewhat like small coffee beans, with an indentation along one side. The berry (technically the grain) consists of the starchy endosperm; the small, nutrient-rich germ at one end; and the bran, the brown outer covering—so the wheat berry is a whole grain of high nutritional value. Wheat berries are used whole in many cuisines and can be found in natural food stores or in Indian and Middle Eastern markets. Roasted green (immature) wheat berries, called *freekah*, are an Arabic delicacy. Green spelt (a wheat variety), called *Grünkern*, is used in German cooking. Farro is an Italian product made by slightly polishing the bran of the wheat berry, making it less fibrous and somewhat faster cooking.

VENISON SHOULDER
WITH SAUCE GRAND VENEUR

BRAISED VENISON IN A PEPPERY RED CURRANT SAUCE

| MAKES 4 TO 6 SERVINGS |

Venison shoulder is beefy, gamy, and shot through with gelatin, which nourishes the meat inside while it braises, keeping it moist. As with most game meats, the robustness of venison calls for marinating overnight, which I do with red wine that I've reduced first so it's strong and a little dense. Then I cook the venison slowly and for a long time so that the result is tender, juicy, and not at all tough. It's a wonderful piece of meat, something for a special occasion on a cold winter night, maybe during the holiday season. A nice accompaniment to this dish could be the Red Cabbage with Apples and Honey (page 174) or the Spiced Sweet Potatoes with Almonds (page 178).

2 bottles (750 ml each) full-bodied red wine

3 pounds venison shoulder or stew meat, cut into cubes

Coarse sea salt or kosher salt and freshly ground black pepper

½ cup ruby port wine (see note)

¼ cup red wine vinegar

6 ounces slab bacon, cut into 6 pieces

3 stalks celery, cut into 1-inch pieces

2 large carrots, peeled, trimmed, and cut into 1-inch pieces

8 shallots, peeled, trimmed, and halved

1 large onion, peeled and quartered

1 head garlic, halved crosswise

1 orange, quartered

3 sprigs fresh basil

2 sprigs fresh thyme

2 bay leaves

2 teaspoons crushed black pepper

10 juniper berries, crushed (see note, page 5)

2 whole cloves

1 (3-inch) cinnamon stick

1. The day before you want to serve this dish, bring the red wine to a simmer in a medium saucepan over medium-high heat and let it reduce by half. Remove from the heat.

2. Season the venison with salt and pepper and put it into a nonreactive bowl such as a Pyrex dish. Combine the reduced wine, the port, vinegar, bacon, celery, carrots, shallots, onion, garlic, orange, basil, thyme, bay leaves, crushed black pepper, juniper berries, cloves, and cinnamon. Pour the mixture over the venison, cover tightly with plastic wrap, and refrigerate overnight, turning the meat over a few times.

3. Remove the venison from the marinade. Strain the marinade through a colander, reserving the liquid and reserving the bacon, vegetables, herbs, and spices separately.

4. Put a rack in the lower third of the oven and preheat the oven to 275°F.

5. In a medium cast-iron pot or Dutch oven over medium-high heat, warm the oil and butter. Add the venison to the pot and sear on all sides until golden brown, about 20 minutes. Transfer to a plate. Add the reserved bacon, vegetables, herbs, and spices to the pot and cook, stirring, for 15 minutes. Sprinkle the flour over the vegetables and cook for 2 to 3 minutes more. Pour the reserved marinade and the stock into the pot, add the venison back to the pot, stir to combine, and bring to a simmer.

6. Cover the venison with a round of buttered parchment paper 1 inch less in diameter than the pot and with a 2-inch hole in the center, and transfer the pot to the oven. Braise until tender, 1½ to 2 hours. If the sauce is too thin or is not flavored intensely enough, ladle most of it off into another pot and simmer it until it thickens and intensifies. Then add it back to the original pot. Stir in the crème fraîche and red currant jelly and serve.

2 tablespoons extra-virgin olive oil

2 tablespoons unsalted butter

2 tablespoons all-purpose flour

1½ cups chicken stock (page 208), low-sodium canned chicken broth, or water

2 tablespoons crème fraîche

1½ tablespoons red currant jelly (or substitute lingonberry, black currant, or raspberry jam)

RUBY PORT WINE

This young, fruity port wine is a good choice for cooking, since it's less aged, and therefore less expensive, than its vintage and tawny counterparts. Be absolutely sure to avoid "cooking port." It's an inferior product that contains salt and becomes biting when cooked down.

BRAISED VEAL SWEETBREADS
WITH FENNEL AND TOMATO

| MAKES 4 TO 6 SERVINGS |

I think braising is the best way to cook sweetbreads. It's certainly the lightest way, compared with, say, panfrying them and serving them with a creamy sauce, which is how they often are prepared in restaurants. Here, I coat the sweetbreads (which, for the record, are the thymus gland of a calf) with cornmeal before searing them. This helps keep them crisp even when they are braising. You'll notice that the braising temperature, at 350°F, is slightly higher than usual for this book. This also promotes a crisp crust, and the dense flesh of the sweetbreads can take the higher heat. Since sweetbreads are mild and delicate on their own, you can cook them with almost anything and they will absorb the flavors. This recipe, seasoned with saffron and anise (and, optionally, fennel pollen) and spiked with pastis, was inspired by Provence.

3 pounds sweetbreads, about 4 (8- to 10-ounce) pieces or 8 (4- to 6-ounce) pieces

4 fennel sticks (see note) or 4 licorice sticks (see note, page 199)

2 teaspoons coarse sea salt or kosher salt

2 teaspoons fennel seeds

1 teaspoon white peppercorns

1 teaspoon fennel pollen, optional (see note)

½ teaspoon saffron threads (see note, page 77)

½ teaspoon cayenne pepper

1 star anise pod

½ cup polenta or cornmeal

2 tablespoons extra-virgin olive oil

2 tablespoons unsalted butter

12 garlic cloves, peeled

4 small fennel bulbs, trimmed and quartered

1 cup dry white wine

2 tablespoons Pernod or pastis

1. The day before you want to serve this dish, trim the sweetbreads of any fat and veins (or ask your butcher to do this for you). Put the sweetbreads into a large bowl of ice water and refrigerate them for 24 hours, changing the water twice during this period. Drain and rinse the sweetbreads well.

2. Put a rack in the lower third of the oven and preheat the oven to 350°F.

3. Using a small paring knife, make a small hole in each sweetbread and push a fennel stick into it. (Use half a fennel stick if necessary.)

4. In a spice grinder, finely grind together the salt, fennel seeds, white peppercorns, fennel pollen (if you are using it), saffron, cayenne pepper, and star anise. Season the sweetbreads with this spice mixture and roll each one in the polenta, coating all sides and shaking off any excess.

5. Warm the olive oil and butter in a medium cast-iron pot or Dutch oven over medium-high heat. Add the sweetbreads, garlic, and fennel and sear until the sweetbreads and fennel are light golden brown on all sides, 10

to 15 minutes. Deglaze by adding the white wine and pernod, bringing to a boil, and scraping up any browned bits stuck to the bottom of the pot. Let simmer until the liquid is reduced by half, about 5 minutes.

6. Add the chicken stock and tomatoes, bring to a simmer, transfer the pot to the oven, and braise, uncovered, turning the sweetbreads once, until tender, 30 to 40 minutes.

1 cup chicken stock (page 208), low-sodium canned broth, or water

4 plum tomatoes, peeled if desired, halved, and seeded (see note, page 37)

FENNEL STICKS

Also called fennel branches, fennel sticks are the dried twigs of the mild, anise-flavored fennel plant, long prized in European and Asian cuisine for its versatility. The fennel plant's bulbs, stems, and fronds are all edible and can be added to any number of dishes. Dried fennel sticks are especially beloved in southern France, where they are often placed on the coals of open fires, imparting a delicate anise flavor to grilled and roasted fish, poultry, and meats. The French also use fennel sticks to season marinated olives.

You can buy fennel sticks at specialty markets or online (see Sources, page 210), but they can be hard to track down. Making your own, however, is very simple if you have access to fennel branches and have the time to let them cure for several weeks.

To dry your own fennel sticks, wash the branches from, preferably, wild fennel plants (these grow like weeds in many parts of the country, including northern California) in cold running water and dry thoroughly on paper towels. Place the fennel in a paper bag with the ends sticking out, or spread the sticks out on a screen tray (an old window screen works well for this), and store in a warm (70° to 80°F), dry place until completely dried, 2 to 4 weeks, depending on temperature and moisture levels. Once it's dried, transfer the fennel to an airtight container and store in a cool, dry place away from light and heat.

FENNEL POLLEN

This exotic ingredient has a self-explanatory name. Italian chefs are given credit for discovering that the intensely anise-flavored yellow dust collected from wild fennel blossoms could be dried and used as a seasoning, and the trend has spread. This ingredient is sold in gourmet stores, or you can order it online (see Sources, page 210). The pollen harvested in Tuscany is considered better than that from California. Finely ground fennel seeds or finely chopped fennel fronds make a far more affordable, if less intense, substitute.

TRIPE WITH SPICY YELLOW PEPPERS AND WATERCRESS

| MAKES 10 SERVINGS |

Even if you've never cooked tripe before, don't be intimidated by this recipe. Today—unlike several decades ago—honeycomb tripe (the most popular, for eating, of the four stomachs of a cow) is sold already very clean, so you don't have to do more than rinse it thoroughly before cooking. Then, braising tripe is like braising anything else, though the tripe does take several hours to tenderize.

Tripe is not only an acquired taste, but you also need to acquire a love for the texture, which is soft and chewy. I find it wonderful, and I think it goes well with very strong flavors. In Spain, for example, cooks use fresh chorizo and lots of garlic. In Latin America, where this recipe hails from, they use chilies and spices. By the way, the peanut butter in the sauce here just adds richness and helps to thicken it. You don't really taste the peanut butter, but it does bring the dish together (you can substitute other nut butters if you prefer). This dish is extremely filling, and the recipe makes a large amount, so invite all your best tripe-loving friends for a feast.

4 pounds honeycomb tripe, cleaned, cut into 1-inch squares, and thoroughly rinsed (see note)

1 tablespoon white wine vinegar

6 large tomatoes, cored, halved, and seeded (see note, page 37)

3 cups chicken stock (page 204) or low-sodium canned chicken broth

12 garlic cloves, peeled

10 sprigs fresh cilantro

3 avocado leaves (see note, page 52) or ½ teaspoon anise seed

2 poblano peppers, seeded and chopped

2 fresh or pickled ají mirasol or ají amarillo peppers (see note, page 61), seeded and chopped (or substitute 2 jalapeño chilies)

1 tablespoon ground turmeric

1 tablespoon ground annatto (see note, page 57) or paprika

½ cup smooth peanut butter

1. Center a rack in the oven and preheat the oven to 275°F.

2. Place the tripe in a large pot and add the vinegar and enough cold water to cover. Bring to a boil and cook for 10 minutes. Drain the tripe in a colander and let cool.

3. In a blender, combine the tomatoes, 1 cup of the chicken stock, the garlic, cilantro, avocado leaves, poblanos, ají mirasol, turmeric, and annatto and mix until smooth, blending in batches if necessary. In a small bowl, whisk together the peanut butter and milk.

4. In a large cast-iron pot or Dutch oven over high heat, warm the olive oil. Add the blanched tripe, the onions, and a large pinch each of salt and pepper. Cook, stirring frequently, until the tripe is golden brown, 15 to 20 minutes.

5. Add the tomato paste and cook for another minute. Stir in the remaining 2 cups chicken stock, the pureed tomato mixture, the peanut butter mixture, and the bell peppers and bring to a simmer.

6. Add the potatoes and carrots, cover the pot, transfer it to the oven, and braise until the tripe is tender, about 3 hours. Taste and adjust the seasoning if necessary. Sprinkle with the watercress leaves and serve.

½ cup whole milk

¼ cup extra-virgin olive oil

4 small onions, peeled and chopped

Coarse sea salt or kosher salt and freshly
ground black pepper

1 tablespoon tomato paste

3 red bell peppers, cored, seeded, and
cut into ½-inch dice

3 yellow bell peppers, cored, seeded, and
cut into ½-inch dice

1 pound Yukon Gold potatoes, peeled
and cut into ½-inch dice

2 medium carrots, peeled, trimmed, and
cut into ½-inch dice

Small bunch of watercress, leaves only,
for garnish

HONEYCOMB TRIPE

Tripe is a textural delicacy. The word in general refers to the stomach lining of a ruminant (cud chewer), and honeycomb tripe is the lining from the second stomach of a cow (cows have four stomachs). This is the meatiest variety of tripe and is always sold cleaned, so that the preparation time is substantially shortened. Still, tripe does require a long cooking time to become tender, but that allows it to take on the flavor of the seasonings it is cooked with—a good thing, because tripe itself is rather mild. Look for tripe at Hispanic or Chinese butcher shops, or have your butcher order some if necessary.

FEIJOADA

BRAZILIAN BLACK BEAN STEW

| MAKES 6 TO 8 SERVINGS |

Feijoada, the national dish of Brazil, is one of my favorite things about the country—and since I love Brazil, that is saying a lot. It's a rustic, hearty stew of black beans flavored with all kinds of meat, including bacon, pork sausage, ribs, blood sausage, beef sirloin, and tongue. Not exactly a dish for the timid, but I love its earthy, soulful character. There are many traditional accompaniments to feijoada, such as hearts of palm salad, orange slices, rice, and stewed greens: kale or collards, for instance. I like to stir chopped kale into the beans at the end of cooking because it adds a nice color, but you could cook the kale separately and serve it alongside.

If the long list of meats seems daunting to shop for, you could leave out some of the meats, or double the items that are easier to find (sirloin, fresh chorizo) and lessen the more unusual cuts (tongue). Feijoada is a very adaptable dish, since traditionally people simply used whatever they had on hand.

2 pounds dried black beans, picked over and rinsed

2 ounces double-smoked bacon, cut into 2-by-¼-inch strips

½ pound fresh chorizo, cut into ½-inch-thick slices (see note, page 19)

3 poblano peppers, seeded and finely chopped

3 garlic cloves, peeled and chopped

1 large white onion, peeled and sliced

1 tablespoon cumin seeds

1 teaspoon crushed red pepper flakes

1 pound baby back pork ribs, cut into individual servings

½ pound blood sausage (such as morcilla), cut into ½-inch-thick slices (see note)

½ pound boneless beef sirloin, cut into 16 pieces

½ pound smoked beef tongue, peeled and sliced (see note)

2 bay leaves

1. The day before you want to serve the dish, put the beans in a large bowl, cover with water by at least 2 inches, and refrigerate. The next day, drain before using.

2. Center a rack in the oven and preheat the oven to 275°F.

3. In a large cast-iron pot or Dutch oven over medium-high heat, cook the bacon and fresh chorizo until they render their fat and color lightly, about 10 minutes. Add the poblano peppers, garlic, onion, cumin seeds, and red pepper flakes and cook, stirring, for another 10 minutes. Add 2 quarts water, the black beans, pork ribs, blood sausage, sirloin, beef tongue, bay leaves, orange zest, and salt and pepper to taste.

4. Bring to a simmer, cover, and transfer to the oven. Braise for 2½ hours. Stir in the kale, parsley, and cilantro, and continue to braise, covered, for 30 minutes more.

MORCILLA

A Spanish blood sausage (also called blood pudding) made with pork blood and other pork parts, along with suet, grains (usually bread crumbs, rice, and/or oatmeal), and occasionally nuts, morcilla ranges from red-brown to very dark brown. It is seasoned with paprika and sometimes onions, and it has a sweet, spicy taste that varies in the degree of smokiness depending on how long it has been smoked. Look for morcilla in a good Hispanic butcher shop, or order it online (see Sources, page 210).

SMOKED BEEF TONGUE

The large tongues of full-grown cows are sold both fresh and smoked, but more often smoked. A traditional ingredient in feijoada, smoked tongue meat is lean, sweet, and versatile. Since it's already cooked, it is a convenient and flavorful addition to soups, stews, and beans; or it can be sliced as a cold cut. The best smoked beef tongue is produced in the Jura region of France, but tasty specimens are also sold at good butcher shops and in Eastern European markets. Often, smoked tongue is soaked before use, to lessen its saltiness.

Finely grated zest of 1 orange

Coarse sea salt or kosher salt and freshly ground black pepper

½ pound kale, stems removed, leaves roughly chopped

3 tablespoons chopped fresh flat-leaf parsley leaves

3 tablespoons chopped fresh cilantro leaves

STUFFED PIG'S FEET EN PAPILLOTE

| MAKES 4 TO 6 SERVINGS |

Pig's feet are delicious. Everyone knows that the meat around the bone is always the best; and trotters, like oxtail and lamb neck, have plenty of bones. In fact, picking out the bones is the most time-consuming part of preparing trotters (in terms of hands-on work). But it's not hard. The trick is to make sure not to let the feet cool entirely before you finish picking. They should be very warm: not too hot to touch, but not cold. Then the bones will just slip right out.

When I was growing up on a farm, we ate pig's feet every time a pig was killed. Sometimes we made sausage out of the pig's feet, along with the skin. I loved it, but then I was easy to feed. I liked everything as a child—except maybe chicken-blood omelets. My grandmother made those for dinner every Friday night. She'd mix chicken blood and eggs with vinegar, onions, herbs, and salt and pepper and fry it in a pan. Saturday was market day, so she'd kill the chickens on Friday and save the blood for supper. I haven't had one of those omelets for a long time, and that's just fine.

But pig's feet I still love. After poaching, you can fry them with bread crumbs until they are very crispy, or braise them and eat them when they are meltingly soft and tender, as in this recipe. They are very rich, so a little crisp salad (here I suggest celery root) with a sharp mustard vinaigrette is an excellent accompaniment.

FOR THE PIG'S FEET:

4 pig's feet, cut in half lengthwise and tied tightly back together with kitchen string

2 medium onions, peeled and halved

2 medium carrots, peeled, trimmed, and halved

1 stalk celery, cut into 4-inch segments

3 garlic cloves, peeled

Bouquet garni (1 sprig fresh thyme, 1 bay leaf, 1 sprig fresh savory, and 1 sprig fresh rosemary, tied with kitchen string)

3 cups dry white wine

5 tablespoons ruby port wine (see note, page 97)

2 tablespoons coarse sea salt or kosher salt

1½ teaspoons black peppercorns

1. Put a rack in the lower third of the oven and preheat the oven to 325°F.

2. Put the pig's feet, onions, carrots, celery, garlic, and bouquet garni into a large cast-iron pot or Dutch oven. Pour in 1 quart water, the white wine, port wine, salt, and peppercorns. Bring to a boil.

3. Cover the pot, transfer it to the oven, and braise for 3 hours, or until the feet are very tender and can be pierced easily with the point of a knife.

4. The feet should be boned while warm, so as soon as they're cooked through, delicately transfer them to a pan and cut the kitchen string. Wearing plastic gloves or using a fork, carefully pick out the bones and remove the nails—they'll come away easily, because the feet are so soft—but pay attention to the meat: it should remain attached to the skin. After cleaning each set of feet (expect to throw out more than you keep), transfer the cleaned feet to a pan to cool, arranging them side by side in a single layer. Strain the poaching liquid from the cooking pot through a fine-meshed sieve and reserve. Lower the oven temperature to 300°F.

5. For the stuffing: In a medium skillet over medium-high heat, warm 2 tablespoons of the olive oil. Add the thinly sliced mushrooms and cook for 5 to 7 minutes. Add the shallots, celery, carrot, and savory and cook until the vegetables are tender, 5 to 7 minutes more. Remove from the heat and let cool.

6. Using a spice grinder or mortar and pestle, grind the coriander seeds and clove.

7. In a large bowl, combine the cooled vegetables, the ground pork, and the lightly beaten eggs. Season with the ground coriander and clove, the allspice, mace (or nutmeg), and salt and pepper.

8. To stuff the pig's feet, put 8 (12-inch square) pieces of buttered parchment paper on a flat work surface. Put one half of a pig's foot on each paper, skin side down, and fill the foot with about ¼ cup of stuffing. Wrap the parchment paper around the pig's foot, roll tightly, twist the two ends, and secure with kitchen string. Cut the excess paper from each end.

9. In a medium cast-iron pot or Dutch oven over medium heat, warm the remaining 2 tablespoons olive oil. Add the wrapped pig's feet and cook, turning them every 2 minutes, until the parchment paper is light golden brown, 5 to 7 minutes. Add the whole mushrooms, pour in the reserved poaching liquid, and bring to a simmer. Cover the pot, transfer it to the oven, and braise for 1 hour.

10. To serve, unwrap the center of the parchment paper, keeping the two ends tied. Sprinkle the pig's feet with parsley and celery leaves and serve immediately with the salad.

FOR THE STUFFING AND BRAISING:

¼ cup extra-virgin olive oil

1 pound white button mushrooms, trimmed: ¼ pound thinly sliced; ¾ pound left whole

2 shallots, peeled and chopped

1 stalk celery, chopped

1 small carrot, peeled, trimmed, and chopped

1 sprig fresh savory (or marjoram), leaves only, chopped (see note, page 39)

1 teaspoon coriander seeds

1 whole clove

1 pound ground pork shoulder or lean pork sausage

2 large eggs, lightly beaten

Pinch of ground allspice

Pinch of ground mace or nutmeg

Coarse sea salt or kosher salt and freshly ground black pepper

Fresh flat-leaf parsley leaves, for garnish

Celery leaves, taken from the heart of the celery, for garnish

Celery Root Salad, for serving (see recipe, page 107)

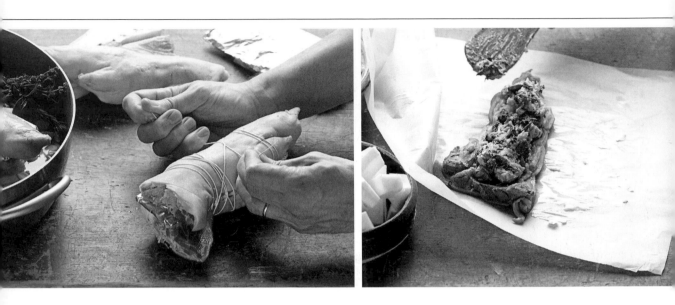

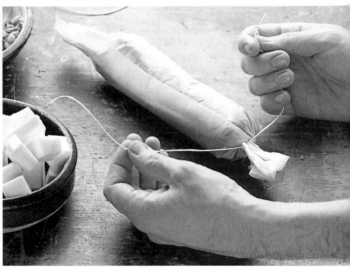

CELERY ROOT SALAD

| MAKES 4 TO 6 SERVINGS |

You can enrich this by stirring in 1 tablespoon of the sauce from the pig's feet pot.

1 (1-pound) celery root, peeled, trimmed, and julienned

3 tablespoons extra-virgin olive oil

Freshly squeezed juice of 1 lemon

1 tablespoon Dijon mustard

Coarse sea salt or kosher salt and freshly ground black pepper

1 tablespoon red wine vinegar

$1/2$ cup celery leaves, taken from the heart of the celery

12 cornichons, very thinly sliced (preferably on a mandoline)

4 stalks celery, cut into $1/4$-inch-thick slices

1. In a medium bowl, mix together the celery root, 1 tablespoon of the olive oil, the lemon juice, and 1½ teaspoons of the mustard. Season to taste with salt and pepper. Set aside.
2. Whisk together the remaining 2 tablespoons of olive oil, 1½ teaspoons mustard, and the vinegar. Add the celery leaves, cornichons, and celery and toss until well combined. Season to taste with salt and pepper.
3. Lightly toss the two mixtures together and serve.

POULTRY
AND
RABBIT

CUBANO CHICKEN LEGS WITH PEPPERS, TOMATOES, AND CITRUS

| MAKES 4 SERVINGS |

The orange, the lime, and a hefty amount of garlic and fresh oregano give this dish a particularly piquant, intense flavor. If you just saw the pot on the stove and didn't know what was in it, you might think this was the normal braised chicken and tomatoes. But taste it, and you'll see—it's very special.

4 chicken legs, thighs attached (about 2 pounds)

Coarse sea salt or kosher salt and freshly ground black pepper

8 garlic cloves, peeled and sliced paper-thin (use a mandoline, if you have one)

Finely grated zest and freshly squeezed juice of 2 large oranges

Finely grated zest and freshly squeezed juice of 2 limes

2 tablespoons chopped fresh oregano, preferably Cuban (see note, page 17)

1 tablespoon extra-virgin olive oil

2 green bell peppers, cored, seeded, and chopped

2 red bell peppers, cored, seeded, and chopped

1 large onion, peeled and chopped

1 (15½-ounce) can chickpeas, drained

4 plum tomatoes, halved lengthwise

4 piquillo peppers, sliced (see note)

1 tablespoon chopped fresh flat-leaf parsley leaves

Cucumber, Jicama, and Avocado Salad (see recipe, opposite)

1. The night before you plan to serve this dish, season the chicken with salt and pepper and place in a nonreactive pan (Pyrex is perfect for this). In a small bowl, stir together the garlic, the orange and lime juice and zest, and the oregano and pour the mixture over the chicken legs to coat them evenly. Cover the pan tightly with plastic wrap and refrigerate overnight.

2. Center a rack in the oven and preheat the oven to 300°F.

3. Heat the oil in a medium cast-iron pot or Dutch oven over medium-high heat. Remove the chicken legs from the marinade and reserve the marinade. Pat the legs dry, and sear until well browned on all sides, about 15 minutes. When the chicken is golden brown, transfer to a platter. Add the bell peppers and onion to the pot and cook, stirring, until the vegetables are tender, 8 to 10 minutes.

4. Return the chicken to the pot, along with the reserved marinade and the chickpeas, plum tomatoes, and piquillo peppers. Cover the pot and transfer to the oven to braise until the chicken is cooked through, about 1 hour. Sprinkle with the chopped parsley and serve with the Cucumber, Jicama, and Avocado Salad.

CUCUMBER, JICAMA, AND AVOCADO SALAD

3 tablespoons extra-virgin olive oil

Freshly squeezed juice of 1 lime

Coarse sea salt or kosher salt and freshly ground black pepper

1 small unpeeled English cucumber

1 ripe avocado, peeled and pitted

1 small head iceberg lettuce, cored and chopped

1/2 pound jicama, peeled and cut into 1/8-inch-thick matchsticks

1/4 cup celery leaves, taken from the heart of the celery

1. In a small bowl, whisk together the olive oil and lime juice. Season to taste with salt and pepper and set aside until needed.

2. Using a mandoline or a very sharp knife, cut the cucumber into paper-thin slices and place in a medium bowl. Using a vegetable peeler, peel the avocado into thin strips and add to the bowl, tossing with a bit of vinaigrette to keep the avocado from darkening. Add the lettuce, jicama matchsticks, and celery leaves and toss to combine.

3. To serve, whisk the vinaigrette and pour over the salad, tossing until the vinaigrette coats the salad evenly.

PIQUILLO PEPPERS

A pointed, triangular red chili pepper with a distinctive tangy flavor and slight heat, the piquillo is grown in only a small region of northern Spain. Piquillos roasted over a wood fire are a popular tapa, often served stuffed with fish, meat, or cheese, or simply marinated in olive oil and seasoned with salt. Look for jars of roasted piquillos in gourmet food stores, or order them online (see Sources, page 210).

TAMARIND CHICKEN
WITH SWEET POTATOES AND OKRA

| MAKES 4 SERVINGS |

Cooking any meat on the bone gives a lot of flavor, and chicken is no exception. Chicken with the bone in is a bit harder to eat than boned chicken, but if you and your guests aren't afraid to pick it up and chew near the bone, you can get the most taste. Here, you will also get the flavors of tangy tamarind, chilies, garlic, and spices, which make up the sauce. If okra is not in season, you can make this dish without it, though the sauce may not be as thick.

1 (4-pound) chicken, quartered

Coarse sea salt or kosher salt and freshly ground black pepper

1½ cups loosely packed fresh cilantro leaves

¼ cup vegetable oil

3 hot green chili peppers (such as serranos), seeded and finely chopped

1 tablespoon peeled, chopped garlic

1 tablespoon peeled, finely grated fresh gingerroot

1 tablespoon black mustard seeds (see note)

1 tablespoon tamarind paste (see note, page 55)

2 teaspoons coriander seeds

1½ teaspoons fenugreek seeds

1½ teaspoons ground turmeric

1½ teaspoons white poppy seeds (see note)

2 medium onions, peeled and cut into 1-inch wedges

8 plum tomatoes or 2 large beefsteak tomatoes, cored and roughly chopped

2 large sweet potatoes, peeled and cut into ¼-inch dice

1 pound fresh okra, trimmed

¼ pound white mushrooms, trimmed

1. The day before you plan to serve this dish, season the chicken with salt and pepper. Finely chop 1 cup of the cilantro leaves. Reserve the remaining leaves for garnish. Mix together 2 tablespoons of the vegetable oil with the chopped cilantro, chilies, garlic, gingerroot, black mustard seeds, tamarind paste, coriander seeds, fenugreek seeds, turmeric, and white poppy seeds. Rub this mixture over the chicken, cover tightly with plastic wrap, and refrigerate overnight.

2. Put a rack in the lower third of the oven and preheat the oven to 300°F.

3. Heat the remaining 2 tablespoons vegetable oil over medium-high heat in a cast-iron pot or Dutch oven large enough to hold the chicken in a single layer. Scrape the spice mixture off the chicken and reserve. Add the chicken, skin side down, and sear until golden brown, 7 to 8 minutes. Turn the chicken and cook for 2 to 3 minutes more. Transfer the chicken to a plate. Add the onions to the pot and sauté for 5 minutes. Add the tomatoes, sweet potatoes, okra, mushrooms, and reserved spice mixture and cook, stirring, for 3 to 4 minutes. Add 1½ cups warm water and bring to a simmer.

4. Return the chicken to the pot, cover, and transfer to the oven. Braise for 1 hour; then remove it from the oven.

5. Increase the oven heat to broil. Transfer the chicken from the pot to a broiler-proof pan, placing it skin side up. Mix together the lemon juice, honey, and cardamom. Brush the honey mixture over the chicken, then broil the chicken until the skin is crisp and golden brown. Be careful to watch it—this should take only about 5 minutes. Sprinkle with the reserved cilantro leaves and serve immediately.

Freshly squeezed juice of 1 lemon

1 tablespoon honey

1 teaspoon ground cardamom

BLACK MUSTARD SEEDS

Less common than the slightly larger brown mustard seeds of India, black mustard seeds are the approximate size of poppy seeds. They have a sharper, more bitter flavor than brown mustard seeds, though heating mutes this and causes the tiny black seeds to take on a nutty taste. Look for black mustard seeds at spice shops, or order them online (see Sources, page 210). Brown mustard seeds are an apt substitute if the black are unavailable.

WHITE POPPY SEEDS

Unlike the blue-black poppy seeds sprinkled on cakes, pastries, and bagels in Europe and the United States, these small ivory seeds, which come from a different variety of poppy plant, are used to give texture to Asian soups, stews, and sauces, especially in India. The flavor of the white seeds resembles that of the nutty black seeds. High in protein and oil, the seeds tend to go rancid quickly, so they should be purchased in small amounts or stored in the freezer. White poppy seeds are available at specialty spice markets or online (see Sources, page 210).

CHICKEN BASQUAISE
WITH ARTICHOKES

| MAKES 4 SERVINGS |

Piment d'Espelette is a spicy red pepper powder from the Basque region of France, where it is used in everything from sausages and hams to eggs, vegetables, and meat dishes. Here I've added it to a simple chicken braise with artichokes and fresh chorizo. It's a dish that's been part of my repertoire for years, ever since I worked in the Basque region as a young chef. It was wonderful to see how in love the Basques are with their peppers. You'd see peppers hanging everywhere, drying when they were in season or already dried during the rest of the year. The Basques even dedicated whole festivals to peppers.

If artichokes aren't in season when you want to make this dish, you can leave them out. It will still be delicious.

1 (3½-pound) chicken, cut into 8 pieces

Coarse sea salt or kosher salt and freshly ground black pepper

1 cup dry sherry

6 garlic cloves, peeled and thinly sliced

2 teaspoons piment d'Espelette (see note)

1 teaspoon crushed red pepper flakes

Freshly squeezed juice of 1 lemon

¼ pound fresh chorizo, cut into ¼-inch-thick slices (see note, page 19)

Extra-virgin olive oil, as needed

2 small red onions, each peeled and cut into 6 wedges

2 red bell peppers, cored, seeded, and cut into ½-inch-thick strips

1 cup chicken stock (page 208), low-sodium canned broth, or water

4 plum tomatoes, halved lengthwise

3 to 4 large globe artichokes or 8 baby artichokes, trimmed and sliced lengthwise into 6 wedges (see note)

Red Bell Pepper and Frisée Salad, for serving (see recipe, opposite)

1. The night before you plan to serve the dish, season the chicken with salt and pepper and arrange in a shallow, nonreactive baking pan. In a small bowl, mix together the sherry, garlic, piment d'Espelette, red pepper flakes, and lemon juice, and pour this mixture over the chicken. Cover the pan with plastic wrap and marinate overnight in the refrigerator, turning the chicken at least once during this period.

2. Place a rack in the lower third of the oven and preheat the oven to 325°F.

3. Remove the chicken from the marinade, reserving the marinade. Pat the chicken dry. In a medium cast-iron pot or Dutch oven over medium-high heat, sear the chorizo on all sides until it is golden brown and the fat has rendered, 4 to 5 minutes. Using a slotted spoon, transfer the chorizo to a plate lined with a paper towel.

4. If there is not enough fat in the pot, add 1 tablespoon extra-virgin olive oil; then add the chicken and sear on all sides until golden brown, 10 to 12 minutes. Transfer the chicken to a plate.

5. Add the onions and peppers to the pot and sauté until tender, 5 to 6 minutes. Pour the reserved marinade into the pot and, over high heat, reduce the liquid by half. Return the chicken and chorizo to the pot and stir in the stock, tomatoes, and artichokes. Bring to a simmer, cover the pot, and transfer it to the oven.

6. Braise until the chicken legs are tender, about 45 minutes. Serve with the Red Bell Pepper and Frisée Salad.

RED BELL PEPPER AND FRISÉE SALAD

| MAKES 4 TO 6 SERVINGS |

5 tablespoons extra-virgin olive oil

1$\frac{1}{2}$ tablespoons sherry vinegar

1 teaspoon piment d'Espelette (see note)

2 garlic cloves, peeled and finely chopped

Coarse sea salt or kosher salt

$\frac{1}{2}$ pound frisée, white and light yellow parts only

2 red bell peppers, cored, seeded, and diced

2 bunches scallions, trimmed and thinly sliced

1 small red onion, peeled and thinly sliced

$\frac{1}{2}$ cup fresh flat-leaf parsley leaves

1. In a small bowl, whisk together the olive oil, vinegar, piment d'Espelette, and garlic. Season to taste with salt.
2. In a large salad bowl, toss together the frisée, bell peppers, scallions, onion, and parsley. Add the vinaigrette and toss to combine. Adjust the seasoning if necessary.

PIMENT D'ESPELETTE

This long red chili pepper has a flavor that's more fruity than searing. It is usually associated with the southwestern Basque region of France, but, like all chilies, it originated in the New World and was brought back to Europe by Spanish explorers. For centuries, the peppers have thrived in the hot, dry Basque region, where they're quite beloved. Having recently gained AOC status, piment d'Espelette can now be grown only in this small area in France. Dried slowly in the sun, then often ground, the pepper, like its resulting powder, has a mild heat and a bright sunset color. It can be replaced by bittersweet smoked Spanish paprika, hot Hungarian paprika, or New Mexican red chili powder, though none has quite the same flavor. The real thing is available in gourmet markets or online (see Sources, page 210).

TRIMMING ARTICHOKES

Artichokes are actually flowers and are related to thistles, so eating them requires some work, either at the table or in the kitchen. But once you trim away their tough spiny leaves and their scratchy chokes, they become melting, tender, sweet, and a pleasure to eat. To trim an artichoke, first squeeze half a lemon into a bowl of water. Next, slice away the bottom of the artichoke stem and cut off the top third of the artichoke. Pull off the tough dark green outer leaves, and cut off any spiky tips from the remaining leaves. Trim the base of the artichoke, cutting off any remnants of the tough outer leaves. If the stems feel tough, peel them with a vegetable peeler. Halve the artichokes lengthwise, and use a melon baller, a tomato corer, or a spoon (a grapefruit spoon will work well) to scrape out the white chokes. Keep the trimmed artichokes in the lemon water to prevent them from turning brown.

For baby artichokes, which don't have mature chokes, you need to cut away only the tops and outer leaves, and then trim the stem and base as for mature artichokes.

SPICY PINEAPPLE CHICKEN WITH PAPAYA AND GINGER

| MAKES 4 SERVINGS |

I originally made this Latin American–inspired dish with rabbit, and it was terrific: a little spicy from the chili in the rocoto pineapple sauce, tangy from the Piquant Salsa Verde, and pungent from the fresh gingerroot. But then I realized that the earthy flavors would also work well with chicken thighs, which, of course, are easier to find. Either way, it's quick to make once you have all the ingredients. And if you don't have time to marinate the chicken overnight, you can skip that step. This dish goes well with black or red beans. Leftover Piquant Salsa Verde will keep for several weeks in the refrigerator and is great with grilled meats and fish. If you don't feel like making the Salsa Verde, it can be found at Latin American markets or online (see Sources, page 210).

4 pounds skinless bone-in chicken thighs or rabbit pieces

Coarse sea salt or kosher salt and freshly ground black pepper

½ cup rocoto pineapple sauce (see note), or substitute ½ cup pureed pineapple plus hot sauce to taste

¼ cup Piquant Salsa Verde (see recipe, opposite)

2 teaspoons chopped peeled fresh gingerroot

1 teaspoon ground turmeric

1 teaspoon paprika

Finely grated zest and freshly squeezed juice of 1 lime

½ cup toasted walnuts, finely chopped (see note, page 44)

3 tablespoons extra-virgin olive oil

1 yellow onion, peeled and chopped

1 cup chicken stock (see page 208) or low-sodium canned broth

2 ripe papayas, peeled, seeded, and cut into ½-inch dice

1. The day before you plan to serve this dish, season the chicken with 1 tablespoon salt and pepper to taste, and arrange in a nonreactive container such as a Pyrex dish. In a blender, mix the rocoto pineapple sauce, Piquant Salsa Verde, gingerroot, turmeric, paprika, and lime zest and juice until smooth. Transfer this marinade to a bowl and stir in the walnuts. Pour the marinade over the chicken, cover tightly with plastic wrap, and refrigerate overnight.

2. Center a rack in the oven and preheat the oven to 275°F.

3. Scrape the marinade off the chicken, reserving the marinade. Heat the olive oil in a medium cast-iron pot or Dutch oven over high heat. Add the chicken and sear until golden brown on all sides, 5 to 7 minutes, cooking in batches if necessary. Add the onion and cook until translucent, 3 to 5 minutes. Pour the reserved marinade over the chicken, and add the chicken stock and papayas. Cover, bring to a simmer, and transfer to the oven.

4. Braise until the chicken is cooked through and tender, about 1 hour 15 minutes. Serve immediately.

PIQUANT SALSA VERDE

| MAKES 2½ CUPS |

3 tomatillos, husks and cores removed and rinsed well

½ cup loosely packed fresh cilantro leaves

1 teaspoon fresh oregano leaves

½ garlic clove, peeled

Coarse sea salt or kosher salt

½ avocado, peeled, pitted, and cubed

2 tablespoons finely chopped white onion

½ jalapeño pepper, seeded and finely chopped

½ teaspoon ground cumin

Freshly squeezed juice of 1 lime

1 tablespoon extra-virgin olive oil

1. Put the tomatillos in a small saucepan of water and simmer, covered, until tender, 10 to 12 minutes. Drain and let cool.
2. In a blender or in the work bowl of a food processor, combine the tomatillos, cilantro, oregano, and garlic; season with salt. Process until smooth. Transfer the tomatillo mixture to a medium mixing bowl and stir in the remaining ingredients. Refrigerate until ready to use.

ROCOTO PINEAPPLE SAUCE

The rocoto is a brightly colored, thick-skinned red pepper that resembles a bell pepper but has pungent heat. When combined with pineapple, the result is a highly fruity hot sauce with the flavors of Peru. This unusual gourmet ingredient can be found in stores with a good hot sauce selection or ordered online (see Sources, page 210). Or make your own by puréeing fresh or canned pineapple with as much hot sauce as you can take.

MARINATED THAI-STYLE CHICKEN IN GREEN CURRY

| MAKES 4 SERVINGS |

This is a rich, mouth-searing, heady dish. It's based on a Thai green curry, which is one of my favorite Thai curries because of all the herbs—mint, cilantro, Thai basil, and Kaffir lime leaves, which give it the green color. The creamy sauce is based on coconut milk, and because of it, the dish has a nice sweetness. I especially like the way the coconut milk plays against the chilies, making them a little bit mellower. Although it's not traditional in Thailand to use crème fraîche, I added some here because I like the tangy dairy taste it contributes. This is a very complex and delicious dish that you would naturally serve with rice (see recipe, page 183).

4 pounds chicken thighs

2 cups unsweetened coconut milk

½ cup crème fraîche

3 tablespoons Thai or Vietnamese fish sauce (see note, page 55)

Freshly squeezed juice of 1 lemon

6 sprigs fresh Thai basil, torn

3 Kaffir lime leaves, torn (see note)

6 green bird's-eye chili peppers, split in half, seeds removed

4 cardamom pods

1 teaspoon white peppercorns

1 teaspoon coriander seeds

½ cup peeled, chopped red onion or shallots

10 sprigs fresh cilantro, leaves only

10 sprigs fresh mint, leaves only

Finely grated zest and freshly squeezed juice of 1 lime

2 tablespoons chopped fresh galangal or 1 teaspoon galangal powder (see note)

2 tablespoons chopped lemongrass (see note, page 55)

1. The night before you plan to serve this dish, put the chicken into a nonreactive container. In a small bowl, whisk together the coconut milk, crème fraîche, fish sauce, lemon juice, Thai basil, and 2 of the Kaffir lime leaves. Pour this marinade over the chicken, making sure the pieces are evenly coated. Cover tightly with plastic wrap and refrigerate overnight.

2. Center a rack in the oven and preheat the oven to 275°F.

3. In a spice grinder, finely grind the chili peppers, cardamom pods, white peppercorns, coriander seeds, and the remaining Kaffir lime leaf. Toss the red onion (or shallots) with the ground spices.

4. Transfer the seasoned red onion (or shallots) to a food processor and add the cilantro, mint, lime zest and juice, galangal, lemongrass, cumin seeds, mango, garlic, shrimp paste, and turmeric. Blend until a thick, smooth paste is formed. Season to taste with salt.

5. Scrape as much of the marinade off the chicken as possible, reserving the marinade, and pat the thighs dry. In a medium cast-iron pot or Dutch oven over high heat, warm the olive oil. Sear the chicken, skin side down, until the skin is golden brown, 5 to 6 minutes. Transfer to a plate. Reduce the heat to medium, add the onion mixture, and cook, stirring, for 3 to 4 minutes. Add the reserved marinade and bring to a simmer.

6. Return the chicken to the pot, cover, and transfer to the oven. Braise until the chicken is cooked through, about 1 hour 15 minutes.

1 tablespoon cumin seeds

1 tablespoon finely chopped fresh mango

1½ teaspoons peeled, finely chopped garlic

1 teaspoon shrimp paste (see note)

1 teaspoon ground turmeric

Coarse sea salt or kosher salt

2 tablespoons extra-virgin olive oil

KAFFIR LIME LEAVES

These sturdy, glossy green leaves are frequently used in Southeast Asian cuisine and are particularly common in Thai cooking. Typically they are used whole or slightly crushed. The bright citrus flavor is most intense when fresh rather than dried leaves are used. Kaffir lime leaves are available at Asian markets or online (see Sources, page 210).

GALANGAL

This rhizome, which resembles fresh ginger and is in the same family, is grown in tropical Asia. The spice, dried, had a vogue in Europe during the Middle Ages but now is associated mostly with Thai cooking. Fresh galangal can be found in markets that stock fresh Southeast Asian ingredients; dried galangal is sold in Asian markets and some well-stocked spice stores. If dried slices are available and the powder is not, the slices can be finely ground in an electric coffee mill or the work bowl of a small food processor. Dried galangal is available online (see Sources, page 210).

SHRIMP PASTE

This pungent condiment, made from fermented salted shrimp, has an ineffably funky flavor that adds depth to many Southeast Asian dishes. You can find it in Asian specialty markets or online (see Sources, page 210). Or substitute an equal amount of anchovy paste spiked with a dribble of Thai or Vietnamese fish sauce (for the funk).

HUNTER'S STEW WITH CHICKEN KIELBASA, SAUERKRAUT, AND APPLES

| MAKES 4 SERVINGS |

This classic Polish dish is the kind of bone-warming stew a hunter might make out of whatever game bird he was able to catch. The recipe calls for chicken, but it would be equally good with duck, pheasant, or partridge. The other flavors—a mix of sauerkraut, juniper, sausage, and apple—are influenced by Polish cuisine, though I also add tomatoes and Madeira to brighten up all that cabbage. Actually, I was struck by how similar the ingredients and preparation were to traditional French choucroute garnie. It's a wonderful combination.

1 cup apple juice

1½ cups Madeira

1 teaspoon Four-Spice Powder (see recipe, page 29)

1 teaspoon black peppercorns

¼ teaspoon freshly grated nutmeg

Small pinch of ground cloves

¼ cup extra-virgin olive oil

4 pounds chicken drumsticks (about 8 drumsticks)

Coarse sea salt or kosher salt and freshly ground black pepper

1 large onion, peeled and finely chopped

1 small head (about 1 to 1½ pounds) savoy cabbage, cored and thinly sliced

2 pounds sauerkraut, drained

1 pound kielbasa, cut into 1-inch cubes

3 medium tomatoes, halved, seeded, and roughly chopped

2 green apples, peeled, cored, and cut into ¼- to ½-inch dice

20 juniper berries (see note, page 5)

8 whole allspice

1. Combine the apple juice, ½ cup of the Madeira, the Four-Spice Powder, peppercorns, nutmeg, and cloves in a small saucepan and bring to a boil over high heat. Reduce the liquid until it becomes slightly syrupy, but not thick, about 15 minutes. Remove from the heat.

2. Center a rack in the oven and preheat the oven to 300°F.

3. Heat 2 tablespoons of the olive oil in a medium cast-iron pot or Dutch oven over medium-high heat. Season the drumsticks with salt and pepper. Working in two batches and adding the remaining 2 tablespoons olive oil as necessary, sear the drumsticks until golden brown on all sides, 12 to 15 minutes. Transfer the seared chicken to a platter.

4. Add the onion to the pot and sauté until translucent, 5 to 7 minutes. Add the cabbage and cook until wilted, about 3 minutes. Add the remaining 1 cup Madeira and cook for 5 minutes. Add the sauerkraut, kielbasa, 2 cups water, the tomatoes, apples, juniper berries, and allspice. Arrange the drumsticks on top of these ingredients and bring to a simmer.

5. Transfer the pot to the oven and braise, covered, for 1 hour 45 minutes. Uncover, brush the drumsticks with the apple-Madeira syrup, and continue to braise the drumsticks, uncovered, for 15 minutes, basting them every 5 minutes. Serve immediately.

CHICKEN WINGS WITH PANCETTA, BELL PEPPERS, AND MUSCAT RAISINS

| MAKES 4 SERVINGS |

Not your average spicy chicken wings, these have a lot of finesse from the sparkling wine, capers, and raisins. While you could still eat these on the couch with a beer watching a football game on television (and why not?), they are also refined enough for a more serious sit-down dinner.

1. Preheat the broiler.

2. Put the peppers on a foil-lined pan and broil about 2 inches from the heat, turning every few minutes, until the skins are charred and blistered. Transfer the peppers to a plastic bag and seal the bag, or drop them into a bowl and cover the bowl with plastic wrap. When the peppers are cool enough to handle, place them on a cutting board and use the back of a knife or your fingers to scrape off the skin, then slice open the peppers lengthwise. Core the peppers, remove the seeds, and cut away the veins. Cut into thick strips.

3. In a small cast-iron pot or Dutch oven over medium-high heat, cook the pancetta and red pepper flakes until the meat renders its fat, about 5 minutes. Transfer the pancetta to a plate, but leave the fat in the pot. Season the chicken wings with salt and pepper, add the chicken wings to the pot, and cook until golden brown on all sides, about 15 minutes. Transfer the chicken wings to a plate.

4. Add the olive oil to the pot, lower the temperature to medium, and add the onions, garlic, marjoram, and savory. Cook until the onions are translucent, 6 to 8 minutes. Add the roasted peppers, tomatoes, and wine and simmer until the liquid is reduced by one third. Add the capers and raisins, return the chicken wings and pancetta to the pot, and bring to a simmer.

5. Cover the pot and transfer it to the oven. Braise until the chicken is tender, about 45 minutes.

3 yellow bell peppers

3 red bell peppers

1/4 pound pancetta, diced

1/3 teaspoon crushed red pepper flakes

2 1/2 pounds chicken wings

Coarse sea salt or kosher salt and freshly ground black pepper

2 tablespoons extra-virgin olive oil

2 red onions, peeled and sliced

6 garlic cloves, peeled and chopped

2 tablespoons dried marjoram

1 teaspoon dried savory

8 plum tomatoes, roughly chopped

2 cups Italian sparkling white wine (such as Prosecco or Asti) or other dry white wine

1/3 cup capers, rinsed and drained

1/2 cup muscat or golden raisins

SOUTHERN-STYLE CORNISH HEN AND CRAB GUMBO

| MAKES 4 SERVINGS |

Michael Lawrence, the assistant director of operations for my restaurant group, is from Louisiana, and all the southern-inspired recipes in this book had to meet with his approval. Even though this isn't a strictly traditional gumbo (there's no filé powder, and I don't serve it with rice, although you could), it still passed muster. That's because we took great care with the roux, a long-cooked mixture of flour and fat that gives a depth of flavor to many a Creole and Cajun recipe. It's important to cook the roux slowly so that the flour toasts and turns a deep amber brown but doesn't burn. That rich flavor is the key to a good gumbo. Combining different kinds of pork, seafood, and poultry is common in gumbo. Here I use bacon, crab, oysters, and Cornish game hens, though you could substitute a large chicken for the hens if you'd like.

½ cup (1 stick) unsalted butter

¾ cup all-purpose flour

6 tablespoons extra-virgin olive oil

4 Cornish hens (about 1 pound each)

¼ pound slab bacon, cut into 1-inch strips

½ teaspoon freshly ground black pepper

2 small yellow onions, peeled and chopped

1 pound fresh okra, trimmed and split in half lengthwise

8 plum tomatoes, halved, seeded, and chopped

3 stalks celery, cut into ½-inch-thick slices

2 green bell peppers, cored, seeded, and cut into thin strips

1 medium leek, white and light green parts only, cut into thin strips, washed (see headnote, page 179)

1 teaspoon coarse sea salt or kosher salt

½ teaspoon cayenne pepper

20 oysters, shucked, liquor reserved, and shells discarded (see note)

½ pound lump crabmeat, picked over

1. Center a rack in the oven and preheat the oven to 275°F.

2. In an ovenproof saucepan or skillet over medium-high heat, melt the butter and cook until light golden brown, about 5 minutes. Whisk in the flour, making sure there are no lumps. Transfer the pan to the oven and bake until the roux is dark golden brown, about 1 hour. (The roux can be prepared and refrigerated up to 1 day in advance; allow to come to room temperature before using.)

3. Heat ¼ cup of the olive oil in a large cast-iron pot or Dutch oven over high heat. Sear 2 of the Cornish hens until golden brown on all sides, 10 to 12 minutes. Remove these Cornish hens from the pot, add the remaining 2 tablespoons olive oil, and sear the remaining hens. Remove the 2 Cornish hens, then pour off all the excess fat in the pot.

4. Wipe the inside of the pot clean with a paper towel. Lower the heat to medium-high, add the bacon and black pepper, and cook, stirring, for 3 minutes. Add the onions and sauté until translucent, about 5 minutes. Add the roux and cook, stirring, for 1 minute. Add the okra, tomatoes, celery, bell peppers, leek, salt, and cayenne pepper. Return the Cornish hens to the pot and add 3 cups water, the oysters, oyster liquor, and crabmeat. Bring to a simmer and cover.

5. Transfer to the oven and braise for 1 hour 30 minutes. Garnish with parsley leaves and serve.

SOUTHERN-STYLE BISCUITS

| MAKES ABOUT 18 (3-INCH) BISCUITS |

3½ cups all-purpose flour

1 tablespoon plus 1 teaspoon sugar

1 tablespoon plus ½ teaspoon baking powder

1½ teaspoons coarse sea salt or kosher salt

12 tablespoons (1½ sticks) unsalted butter, cut into cubes, at room temperature; plus melted butter for brushing

¾ cup buttermilk or milk

¾ cup crème fraîche or sour cream

1. Center a rack in the oven and preheat the oven to 375°F. Line a baking sheet with parchment paper or a silicone baking mat and set aside.

2. In a mixing bowl, sift together the flour, sugar, baking powder, and salt. Using your fingers, a pastry blender, or an electric mixer fitted with its paddle attachment, work the butter into the flour until the mixture resembles coarse crumbs. Add the buttermilk and crème fraîche and mix just until the dough comes together. Turn the dough out onto a lightly floured work surface and knead lightly, just until it forms a smooth mass. Cover the dough with a dish towel and let rest for 15 to 20 minutes.

3. Using a rolling pin, roll the dough ¼ inch thick. Cut the dough with a 3-inch round cutter (or an empty soup can) and place the biscuits on the prepared baking sheet. Gently knead the scraps until they just come together; let rest for 5 minutes, then gently reroll and cut. Bake until the biscuits are light golden brown, 15 minutes. Remove them from the oven and immediately brush the tops with the melted butter. Serve hot, warm, or at room temperature.

Fresh flat-leaf parsley leaves, for garnish

Southern-Style Biscuits, for serving (see recipe below)

SHUCKING OYSTERS

If you want to shuck fresh oysters, it's not hard, though it does take practice. Scrub them under cold running water, then lay them flat in the refrigerator for several hours before shucking so that their muscles relax. A thin, blunt-tipped oyster-shucking knife is useful, but any thin, strong blade will do. To shuck an oyster, hold it in a kitchen towel in one hand and insert the tip of the blade just into the shell near the hinge. Holding the oyster tightly, without tipping it (you don't want to spill the oyster liquor), twist the blade to pop open the shell. Slide the blade around the top half of the shell to detach it from the oyster, without inserting it into the shell enough to cut the oyster. Remove the top, and pour the oyster liquor through a cheesecloth-lined strainer to remove any grit. Pat away any particles remaining on the oyster, and cut the adductor muscle, which attaches it to the shell. Or ask your fish dealer to do this for you, making sure to keep the tasty oyster liquor.

BOMBAY-STYLE CAPON
WITH GINGERBREAD AND SNOW PEAS

| MAKES 4 TO 6 SERVINGS |

Capons are male chickens that have been castrated and allowed to get very fat, so the meat is extraordinarily tender and juicy. They are hard to find, but if you do have a source of capons, try this recipe with capon at least once. Otherwise, regular chicken makes a fine, readily available substitute. Thanks to a mix of garam masala, chilies, crumbled gingerbread (an excellent thickener), and vinegar, there is a sweet, sour, spicy taste that the bird readily takes on.

An unusual ingredient in this dish, and one that I use for other recipes in this book, is curry leaves. They are small, glossy green leaves that resemble tiny fresh bay leaves but have a curry-like flavor. I used to have a small curry plant that someone gave me, but curry plants don't grow well in apartments in New York City. Now I buy the leaves from a spice purveyor, and you can find them online either fresh or frozen. Like Kaffir lime leaves, they freeze very well.

I'm a big fan of Madhur Jaffrey's cookbooks. Her recipe for "Bombay-Style Chicken with Red Split Lentils" from her *Classic Indian Cooking* caught my eye one day and is the inspiration for this dish.

4 whole capon legs or chicken legs (about 2 pounds), skinned, drumsticks separated from thighs

Coarse sea salt or kosher salt and freshly ground black pepper

3 tablespoons unsalted butter

1 tablespoon ground cumin

1 teaspoon cumin seeds

1 teaspoon ground turmeric

½ teaspoon ground ginger

½ teaspoon freshly grated nutmeg

½ teaspoon cayenne pepper

½ teaspoon garam masala (see note and recipe, page 82)

¼ teaspoon ground cinnamon

1 teaspoon packed dark brown sugar

½ teaspoon white vinegar

1. Place a rack in the lower third of the oven and preheat the oven to 300°F.

2. In a medium saucepan, bring 4 cups water to a boil and keep at a slow, steady simmer.

3. Season the capon (or chicken) with salt and pepper. Melt the butter in a medium cast-iron pot or Dutch oven over medium heat. Add all the spices, the brown sugar, and vinegar and cook for 1 minute. Stir in the orange zest and juice. Add the capon (or chicken) and turn the pieces to coat with the spiced butter. Add the simmering water, lentils, pearl onions, jalapeño, curry leaves, and 2 teaspoons salt, and stir well.

4. Cover the pot and transfer it to the oven. Braise for 45 minutes. Remove the lid, sprinkle the gingerbread crumbs over the capon, and braise until the lentils and the capon are tender, about 15 minutes more. Turn the oven to broil and crisp the crust if needed.

5. Meanwhile, just before serving, bring a small pot of salted water to a boil. Add the snow peas and blanch until tender, about 2 minutes. Drain well. Scatter the snow peas and cilantro leaves over the capon and serve at once.

1 teaspoon finely grated orange zest

Freshly squeezed juice of 1 large orange

2 cups red split lentils, picked over and rinsed (see note)

16 pearl onions, peeled (see note, page 7)

1 jalapeño pepper, seeded (if desired) and finely chopped

1 teaspoon finely chopped curry leaves (see note, page 27)

½ cup fresh gingerbread or Pain d'Épices crumbs (see recipe, page 196) or gingersnap cookie crumbs

½ pound snow peas, trimmed

½ cup fresh cilantro leaves

RED LENTILS

Ranging in color from yellow to red to green to black, lentils have long been an important cooking staple in many countries, particularly as a source of protein for the largely vegetarian cultures of India and the Middle East. These slippery legumes vary in size but generally have a mild, earthy flavor that complements rich soups, stews, and meat dishes. Red lentils cook quickly and tend to break down easily, making them an ideal thickener. Unhulled, red lentils have a brownish-reddish hue; hulled, they are a vibrant salmon color that turns mustard yellow when cooked. Stored in a cool, dry place, lentils will last for up to 1 year. Red lentils can be purchased at Indian or Middle Eastern markets or online (see Sources, page 210).

TURKEY LEGS WITH MEXICAN MOLE

| MAKES 6 SERVINGS |

Mole is an ancient and very complex Mexican sauce often based on spices, bitter chocolate, and nuts. The list of ingredients may look very long, but these give a good mole its layered taste, which goes from fiery hot to sweet to toasty and earthy in every bite. That's why it's essential to use several different kinds of chilies, each of which gives the sauce a different character.

I like to serve a fresh, crisp salad of bell pepper, onion, and parsley on the side to help cut the heaviness of the mole, but this is optional if you don't feel like making it. Brining the turkey legs overnight helps keep them moist and tender while they are braising, and it also seasons them better than simply salting would. This recipe makes extra mole sauce, but it freezes well, and you can use it later on grilled chicken, or as a sauce for braising pork chops or other cuts of meat. You won't be sorry to have it on hand.

1 cup coarse sea salt or kosher salt, plus additional to taste

¼ cup honey

6 turkey drumsticks (about 5 pounds)

8 mulato chilies (see note)

6 guajillo chilies (see note, page 25)

3 pasilla chilies (see note, page 25)

2 ancho chilies (see note, page 25)

¼ cup sesame seeds

1 tablespoon coriander seeds

5 black peppercorns

2 whole cloves

2 large tomatoes, halved, seeded, and roughly chopped

1 large white onion, peeled and roughly chopped

¼ cup roasted peanuts

¼ cup raisins

3 ounces Mexican chocolate, finely chopped (see note)

2 tablespoons dried oregano

3 garlic cloves, peeled and chopped

1 (2-inch) piece canela or cinnamon stick (see note, page 52)

1. The night before you plan to serve this dish, bring 2 quarts water, the salt, and honey to a boil in a large pot and stir until dissolved. Let the brine cool to room temperature. Put the turkey legs into a large container, pour the brine over them, and refrigerate overnight (alternatively, add the turkey legs to the pot with the cooled brine and refrigerate).

2. Remove the stems, if any, from the chilies. For each chili, make a slit down one side and remove the seeds and veins. Spread out and flatten the chilies as much as possible. Warm a large skillet over medium heat. Press the chilies down lightly onto the hot surface and cook for a few seconds; turn and repeat on the other side for a few seconds more. The inside flesh of the chilies should be golden brown. Transfer the chilies to a bowl and cover with hot water. Let soak for 10 to 15 minutes, or until fleshy and soft.

3. Center a rack in the oven and preheat the oven to 275°F.

4. To make the mole: Warm a small skillet over medium-high heat. Add the sesame and coriander seeds, black peppercorns, and cloves and toast the spices until they are fragrant and start to smoke, 2 to 3 minutes. Transfer the spices to a food processor or blender and add the drained softened chilies, tomatoes, onion, peanuts, raisins, chocolate, oregano, garlic, canela, and bread and blend until smooth (you will need to do this in two batches if your food processor is not large enough for a single batch). Pour the mixture into a large bowl and add 4 cups, stirring until incorporated. Add salt to taste.

5. Remove the turkey legs from the brine and drain them on paper towels to remove excess moisture. In a large cast-iron pot or Dutch oven over high heat, warm the olive oil. Add the turkey legs and sear until golden brown on all sides, 12 to 15 minutes. Spoon off as much of the excess fat as possible. Pour the mole over the turkey legs, making sure it covers the meat evenly, and bring to a simmer over high heat.

6. Cover the pot, transfer it to the oven, and braise until the meat is tender, about 2 hours. Serve with the salad, if desired.

1 slice white bread or brioche

¼ cup extra-virgin olive oil

Bell Pepper, Onion, and Parsley Salad
 (see recipe below), optional

BELL PEPPER, ONION, AND PARSLEY SALAD

| MAKES 6 SERVINGS |

1 yellow bell pepper, cored, seeded, and thinly sliced

1 small red onion, peeled and thinly sliced

10 sprigs fresh flat-leaf parsley, leaves only

2 tablespoons extra-virgin olive oil

Coarse sea salt or kosher salt and freshly ground black pepper

Right before serving the turkey, toss together the bell pepper, onion, and parsley with the olive oil in a small bowl. Season to taste with salt and pepper.

MULATO CHILIES

A chocolate-brown chili related to the poblano, the mulato is fully ripened before being picked and dried. Mulato peppers are triangular and average about 5 inches in length. They should remain flexible when dried and are soaked to rehydrate them before use. Mulato chilies are a common ingredient in mole sauce, where they add a bittersweetness that backs up or replaces the flavor of chocolate. Look for dried mulatos in stores with a Mexican clientele, or order them online (see Sources, page 210).

MEXICAN CHOCOLATE

Handmade in Oaxaca, the best Mexican chocolate is a gritty cake of cacao beans that have been ground with almonds, sugar, cinnamon, and vanilla and dried in molds in the sun. It is sold in boxes containing segmented cakes, to be broken and dissolved in hot water or milk. Two well-distributed brands are Ibarra and Abuelita.

PARTRIDGE WITH ALMONDS AND KABOCHA SQUASH

| MAKES 4 SERVINGS |

Partridges are little birds with a lot of flavor, somewhere between the intensity of a quail and that of a squab. If you can find wild partridge, it has the best taste, since wild partridges fly around feeding on wild berries—like juniper, which really spices up the flesh. In this braise, I use winter squash, almonds, sherry, and cream as a mellow contrast to the bird. But the sweet flavors also work well with a milder meat, such as quail or even chicken.

1. The night before you plan to serve this dish, season the partridges (or chicken) with salt and pepper. Combine the lemon juice, thyme leaves, and cayenne and rub this marinade over the partridges. Place in a nonreactive container, cover tightly with plastic wrap, and refrigerate overnight.

2. Center a rack in the oven and preheat the oven to 275°F.

3. In a medium cast-iron pot or Dutch oven over high heat, warm the olive oil. Sear the partridges, in batches if necessary to avoid overcrowding the pot, until golden brown on all sides, 7 to 10 minutes. Remove from the pot and reserve.

4. Add the onions to the pot and cook for 6 to 8 minutes. Add the sherry and cook until almost all the liquid in the pot has evaporated. Add the reserved partridges, the chicken stock, heavy cream, almonds, squash, and tomato and bring to a simmer.

5. Cover the pot and transfer it to the oven. Braise until the partridge is tender, about 60 minutes.

4 (³⁄₄ to 1 pound) partridges or 1 (4-pound) chicken, cut into quarters

Coarse sea salt or kosher salt and freshly ground black pepper

Freshly squeezed juice of 1 lemon

2 teaspoons fresh thyme leaves

1 teaspoon cayenne pepper

¼ cup extra-virgin olive oil

2 cups peeled, thinly sliced onions

½ cup dry sherry

3 cups chicken stock (page 208) or low-sodium canned broth

1 cup heavy cream

1 cup blanched whole almonds

1 kabocha squash or other winter squash (about 3 pounds), peeled, seeds removed, and cut into 1½-inch cubes

1 large tomato, peeled, seeded, and roughly chopped (see note, page 37)

INDIAN-STYLE QUAIL IN BEET, APRICOT, AND TOMATO CHUTNEY

| MAKES 4 SERVINGS |

Because they are such small birds, quail cook relatively quickly. In fact, you can grill or broil a split quail in just a few minutes. But for this recipe I braise them very slowly, at a low temperature, so that they can absorb all the spicy flavors of the chutney. Make sure to buy jumbo quail, which are nice and plump, and then cook them immediately if they aren't still frozen (most quail you buy at a butcher will have been frozen). Quail have a very short shelf life.

If you happen to be making this in July—apricot season—go ahead and substitute fresh fruit for the dried fruit in the salad. But out of season, dried apricots are better.

2 medium yellow beets

12 dried apricots

½ cup packed fresh mint leaves

3 tablespoons unsalted butter

1½ cups coarsely chopped peeled onion

2 tablespoons finely grated peeled fresh gingerroot

4 teaspoons garam masala (see note and recipe, page 82)

2 teaspoons crushed coriander seeds

1 teaspoon ground turmeric

½ teaspoon saffron threads (see note, page 77)

4 star anise pods

1 hot green chili pepper (such as serrano), split and seeded

8 plum tomatoes, peeled (if desired), seeded, and chopped (see note, page 37)

Freshly squeezed juice of 2 oranges

2 red apples (such as Rome), peeled, cored, and quartered

Coarse sea salt or kosher salt and freshly ground black pepper

8 whole jumbo quail (6 to 8 ounces each), each with the breast deboned but the legs bone-in (ask your

1. Put a rack in the lower third of the oven and preheat the oven to 350°F. Wash the beets and wrap in aluminum foil. Place in a baking pan and roast until they are easily pierced with a paring knife, 1½ to 2 hours. Remove the beets from the oven. When they are cool enough to handle, peel them, and cut them into ½-inch cubes.

2. Meanwhile, bring 1 cup of water to a boil. Add the apricots and mint leaves, remove the pan from the heat, and let cool to room temperature. Puree the mixture in a blender or food processor.

3. Lower the oven temperature to 300°F. In a large cast-iron pot or flameproof roasting pan over medium heat, melt 2 tablespoons of the butter. Add the onion, gingerroot, garam masala, coriander seeds, turmeric, saffron, star anise, and chili pepper and sweat until the onion is lightly colored, about 5 minutes. Add the tomatoes, toss, and cook for 4 minutes more. Pour the orange juice and apricot puree into the pot, and stir to combine. Add the diced beets, bring to a simmer, and season to taste with salt. Transfer to the oven and bake for 60 minutes.

4. While the sauce is cooking, melt the remaining 1 tablespoon butter in a large nonstick skillet over medium-high heat. Add the apples and cook until golden brown, 3 to 5 minutes. Remove from the heat. When the apples are cool enough to handle, stuff each quail with an apple piece, and, for a nicer presentation, run a skewer through both legs, just below the knee, fitting 2 quail onto a skewer. Alternatively, you can skip the skewers; if a piece of apple pops out of a quail cavity, simply pop it back in.

5. In a large nonstick skillet over medium-high heat, warm the vegetable oil. Season the quail with salt and pepper and press the mustard seeds evenly all over the quail. Add 4 quail to the skillet and sear on all sides until golden brown, 7 to 8 minutes. Remove to a plate and repeat with the remaining 4 quail, adding more oil to the skillet if needed.

6. Put the quail, breast side down, in the tomato-beet chutney, pressing them into the mixture. Return the pot to the oven and braise, uncovered, for 60 minutes. Serve with the salad.

butcher to do this preparation for you)

¼ cup vegetable oil, plus additional

1 tablespoon black mustard seeds (see note, page 113)

Fennel, Apricot, and Tomato Salad, for serving (see recipe below)

FENNEL, APRICOT, AND TOMATO SALAD

| MAKES 4 TO 6 SERVINGS |

1 teaspoon saffron threads (see note, page 77)

¼ cup extra-virgin olive oil

Finely grated zest and freshly squeezed juice of 1 lime

1½ teaspoons white wine vinegar

6 fresh mint leaves, julienned

Coarse sea salt or kosher salt and freshly ground black pepper

2 small fennel bulbs, trimmed and thinly sliced lengthwise (preferably on a mandoline)

2 dried apricots or 2 pitted fresh apricots, thinly sliced lengthwise

1 cup cherry tomatoes, halved

1. In a small pot on the stove, or in a small bowl in the microwave, warm 2 tablespoons water until hot. Remove from the heat, add the saffron, and let infuse until the water turns bright yellow, about 10 minutes. Strain through a fine-mesh sieve, discard the saffron threads, and set the liquid aside.

2. Whisk together the olive oil, lime zest and juice, vinegar, mint leaves, and saffron water. Season to taste with salt and pepper.

3. In a salad bowl, toss the fennel, apricots, and tomatoes together with the vinaigrette and season to taste with salt and pepper.

ASIAN-STYLE DUCK LEGS
À L'ORANGE

| MAKES 6 SERVINGS |

This is not your run-of-the-mill duck à l'orange—not at all what I grew up eating and was trained to make in France: the sweet, glazed bird with orange liqueur. Instead, the inspiration for this dish comes from China, and the recipe depends on jolts of black vinegar, hoisin sauce, soy, ginger, and Szechuan pepper for its flavor.

If you want to keep the extra duck fat for rendering, you can put it in the freezer in a little container until you are ready to render it. Duck fat is great for frying potatoes and even shellfish like scallops and shrimp, so it's a good thing to have around.

6 duck legs (3 to 4 pounds)

2 tablespoons finely grated peeled fresh gingerroot

2 tablespoons black vinegar (see note, page 55)

2 tablespoons hoisin sauce (see note, page 33)

1 tablespoon coarse sea salt or kosher salt

2 teaspoons hot chili sauce

2 teaspoons five-spice powder (see note)

Finely grated zest and freshly squeezed juice of 1 large orange

2 teaspoons Szechuan pepper (see note, page 10)

1 tablespoon vegetable or extra-virgin olive oil

¼ cup rice wine vinegar (see note, page 49)

2 tablespoons dark soy sauce (see note, page 11)

2 tablespoons light soy sauce (see note, page 11)

1. The night before you plan to serve this dish, remove most of the fat from the duck legs. In a small bowl, combine the gingerroot, black vinegar, hoisin sauce, salt, hot chili sauce, five-spice powder, orange zest, and orange juice. Rub the duck legs with the Szechuan pepper and place them in a nonreactive container. Pour the marinade over the duck, cover tightly with plastic wrap, and refrigerate overnight.

2. Center a rack in the oven and preheat the oven to 275°F.

3. Scrape the marinade off the duck, reserving the marinade. In a large cast-iron pot or Dutch oven over high heat, warm the vegetable or olive oil. Add the duck legs and sear until golden brown on all sides, about 10 minutes.

4. Pour in the rice wine vinegar, dark and light soy sauce, and the reserved marinade and deglaze the pot, scraping up any browned bits stuck to the bottom. Let the mixture bubble for a few seconds, then cover and transfer to the oven. Braise until the duck is cooked through but still slightly pink, about 2½ hours. To remove the excess fat, chill for at least 4 hours, or overnight. Reheat either on the stovetop over medium heat or in a preheated 350°F oven for 30 minutes.

FEIJOADA—BRAZILIAN
BLACK BEAN STEW (PAGE 102)

STUFFED PIG'S FEET EN PAPILLOTE (PAGE 104)

SPICY OXTAILS WITH PEARS
AND SWEET POTATOES (PAGE 32)

INDIAN-STYLE QUAIL IN BEET,
APRICOT, AND TOMATO CHUTNEY
(PAGE 132)

GRILLED TOFU WITH CHINESE SAUSAGE
AND BLACK BEANS (PAGE 186)

BRAISED VEAL SWEETBREADS
WITH FENNEL AND TOMATO
(PAGE 98)

TRIPE WITH SPICY YELLOW PEPPERS
AND WATERCRESS (PAGE 100)

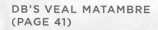
DB'S VEAL MATAMBRE
(PAGE 41)

LAMB SHANKS ROGAN JOSH (PAGE 81)

FIVE-SPICE POWDER

This Chinese spice blend, containing cinnamon, star anise, cloves, fennel, and Szechuan peppercorns, is usually paired with meats. Used sparingly, it contributes a mild spiciness and a slightly sweet anise flavor. It is sold in Chinese markets, or you can order it online (see Sources, page 210). Allspice is a satisfactory substitute in a pinch, or you can make your own five-spice powder as follows: Roast Szechuan peppercorns in a dry skillet, then grind them in a spice mill. Repeat this process with star anise. Then combine 1 tablespoon each ground star anise and ground cinnamon with 1 teaspoon each ground Szechuan peppercorns and fennel seeds and ½ teaspoon ground cloves.

SPICE-STUFFED SQUAB WITH COUSCOUS AND BUTTERNUT SQUASH

| MAKES 4 SERVINGS |

Some people call squab the red meat of poultry, and its flesh is indeed red. That's because squabs are usually smothered, not shot, and aren't bled before being brought to market. The blood gives the meat a very rich, gamy flavor that can stand up to assertive spicing. Here I use a mix of Middle Eastern flavors including mint, figs, cinnamon, and coriander, and I stuff the birds with couscous to absorb their juices. The combination of tastes is similar to what you'd find in a Moroccan pastilla, although instead of being cooked, shredded, and layered in pastry, the squabs are simply braised and served in their sauce.

If you are used to being served very rare squab in restaurants, you'll find this recipe a little different. The birds are cooked longer, until they are only a touch pink and not at all red.

---

4 (1-pound) squabs, legs, neck, and wings (wing tips cut off)

Coarse sea salt or kosher salt and freshly ground black pepper

2 oranges

½ cup couscous, soaked in ½ cup warm water for 30 minutes and drained

⅓ cup golden raisins, soaked in water to cover for 30 minutes, drained, and chopped

⅓ cup chopped blanched almonds

2 tablespoons chopped fresh flat-leaf parsley leaves

3 sprigs fresh mint, leaves only, chopped

3 tablespoons extra-virgin olive oil

1 tablespoon Tagine Spice Mix (see recipe, opposite)

1 tablespoon unsalted butter

1 small butternut squash, peeled, seeded, and cut into ½-inch cubes

2 medium yellow onions, peeled and chopped

1 tablespoon coriander seeds

2 star anise pods

1. Center a rack in the oven and preheat the oven to 300°F.

2. Rinse the inside of the squabs and pat dry. Season the squabs, inside and out, with salt and pepper. Finely grate the zest of 1 orange, and juice both oranges.

3. For the stuffing, combine the couscous, raisins, almonds, parsley, mint, 1 tablespoon of the olive oil, half of the Tagine Spice Mix, the orange zest, and salt and pepper to taste. Spoon one-fourth of the stuffing mixture into each squab, and secure the legs with kitchen twine.

4. Heat the butter and the remaining 2 tablespoons olive oil in a medium cast-iron pot or Dutch oven over high heat. Add the squabs and sear until golden brown on all sides, 10 to 15 minutes. Remove the squabs. Lower the temperature to medium-high. Add the squash, onions, coriander seeds, star anise, and cinnamon and sweat, stirring, for 8 to 10 minutes. Add the remaining spice mix and the honey and let glaze for 5 minutes. Add the vinegar and orange juice and reduce for 2 minutes; then add the dried figs and 1 cup water.

5. Return the squabs to the pot and transfer it to the oven to braise until they are cooked through but still slightly pink, 1 hour to 1 hour 15 minutes.

TAGINE SPICE MIX

1 teaspoon saffron threads (see note, page 77)

1 whole clove

5 whole allspice

1 teaspoon cumin seeds

$1/2$ teaspoon ground mace

2 cardamom pods

1 teaspoon black peppercorns

$1/4$ teaspoon cayenne pepper

Finely grind the saffron, clove, allspice, cumin seeds, mace, cardamom, black peppercorns, and cayenne in a spice grinder.

1 (3-inch) cinnamon stick

1 tablespoon honey

2 tablespoons fig vinegar or sherry vinegar

12 dried figs

DUCK WITH
GREEN PICHOLINE OLIVES

| MAKES 4 SERVINGS |

This duck recipe is almost a cross between a braise and a confit, since I leave all the fat under the skin during the cooking, then take it off the next day when it's hardened on the surface of the contents of the pot. The fat gives a lot of flavor to the sauce and keeps the duck legs extremely tender. This is an ideal dish to make ahead for a dinner party, since you do all the heavy lifting the day before.

Cooking duck with olives has been a classic method ever since olives became fashionable in France about 100 years ago. Their brininess and acidity work well with the richness of the duck meat. Serve this with crusty bread, because there will be plenty of good sauce for mopping up.

---

4 to 6 duck legs (about 3 pounds)

Coarse sea salt or kosher salt and freshly ground black pepper

2 tablespoons extra-virgin olive oil

¼ pound sliced bacon, cut into ¼-inch pieces

3 carrots, peeled, trimmed, and diced

2 small onions, peeled and chopped

2 small turnips, peeled and diced

½ cup green picholine olives, pitted

2 sprigs fresh thyme

1 bay leaf

2 cups chicken stock (page 208) or low-sodium canned broth

1. The night before you plan to serve this dish, place a rack in the lower third of the oven and preheat the oven to 350°F.

2. Season the duck with salt and pepper. Heat the olive oil in a medium cast-iron pot or Dutch oven over medium-high heat. Add the duck legs and sear until golden brown on all sides, 7 to 10 minutes.

3. Transfer the duck to a platter. Pour off the excess fat from the pot. Return the duck to the pot along with the bacon and cook, stirring, over medium-high heat for 5 to 6 minutes. Spoon any fat out of the pot. Add the carrots, onions, turnips, olives, thyme, and bay leaf, and pour in the stock. Transfer the pot to the oven and braise, covered, for 2 hours, until the duck is tender. Chill overnight.

4. Preheat the oven to 350°F. Remove the layer of fat from the top of the sauce and heat the duck in the oven for 30 minutes. Remove the thyme sprigs and bay leaf and serve.

BRUNSWICK STEW
WITH GREEN TOMATOES

| MAKES 4 SERVINGS |

This old-fashioned American stew is traditionally made with squirrel meat. Here I use rabbit, which is what most modern recipes call for, though you could also substitute chicken. I've replaced the usual ripe tomatoes with green tomatoes because I like their acidity and the way they give the dish a little tang. It's a warming dish with a nice thick sauce that would be very good over polenta (cornmeal mush), which is actually a classic, historical American way to serve it.

1. Center a rack in the oven and preheat the oven to 300°F.

2. Place the rabbit pieces in a shallow dish and season with salt and pepper to taste. Add the flour and toss to coat the rabbit.

3. Heat the olive oil in a large cast-iron pot or Dutch oven over high heat. Add the rabbit and bacon and sear until the rabbit is golden brown on all sides, 10 to 15 minutes.

4. Lower the heat to medium-high. Add the onion and cook, stirring, until translucent, about 8 minutes. Add the celery, carrot, bell pepper, basil, garlic, thyme, red pepper flakes, and salt and pepper to taste and cook until the vegetables are softened, about 10 minutes. Pour the wine into the pot and deglaze, stirring up all the brown bits stuck to the bottom of the pot, until the wine is almost completely evaporated, 2 to 3 minutes.

5. Stir in 1 cup water, the tomatoes, and bay leaves. Bring the liquid to a simmer, cover the pot, and transfer it to the oven. Braise until the rabbit is tender, 40 to 45 minutes. Skim off excess fat if necessary, and serve.

1 (4- to 5-pound) rabbit, cut into 12 pieces (see Lapin à la Dijonnaise, page 140)

Coarse sea salt or kosher salt and freshly ground black pepper

1 tablespoon all-purpose flour

2 tablespoons extra-virgin olive oil

3 ounces slab bacon, cut into thin strips

1 medium onion, peeled and cut into large dice

3 stalks celery, cut into ½-inch-thick slices

1 medium carrot, peeled, trimmed, and cut into small dice

1 green bell pepper, peeled, cored, seeded, and cut into ½-inch-thick slices

1 cup loosely packed fresh basil leaves

1 tablespoon peeled, chopped garlic

2 sprigs fresh thyme

¼ teaspoon crushed red pepper flakes

½ cup dry white wine

4 large green tomatoes, cut into ¾-inch cubes

3 small bay leaves

LAPIN À LA DIJONNAISE

DIJON-STYLE RABBIT

| MAKES 4 TO 6 SERVINGS |

When I was growing up on a farm, we had rabbit for dinner at least once a week. It was a meal we could depend on. If you buy a pair of rabbits, male and female, you can be sure to feed your whole family for an entire year—that's how quickly and often rabbits reproduce. They are cheap to raise, too, since they love to eat grass and whatever vegetable trimmings you have around. When I was young, rabbits were never pets. You just can't get attached to anything on a farm except the dog, because of course you won't eat the dog.

The problem with rabbits is that the meat is very, very lean and often dry. And it's a little bland, so you have to be careful about how you prepare it. You need to add some fat, such as bacon or butter, and then cook it slowly and evenly, and not for too long. The meat should be done (rabbit is no good rare), but not overdone. If it's overdone, it gets stringy. But cooked just right, it's tasty and moist and very good to eat.

This recipe is a classic way to prepare rabbit, and it's excellent. Serve it with crusty bread or over noodles.

---

2 (3-pound) rabbits or 8 rabbit legs

4 cups chicken stock (page 208) or low-sodium canned broth

2 cups dry white wine, preferably chardonnay or white burgundy

¼ cup extra-virgin olive oil or vegetable oil

2 tablespoons unsalted butter

Coarse sea salt or kosher salt and freshly ground black pepper

2 tablespoons all-purpose flour

2 dozen small pearl onions, peeled (see note, page 7)

½ pound button mushrooms, trimmed and quartered

1 tablespoon mustard seeds

2 teaspoons tarragon leaves: half left whole; half finely chopped

¼ cup Dijon mustard

1 tablespoon dried mustard

1. Place a rack in the lower third of the oven and preheat the oven to 325°F.

2. If you bought whole rabbits, place 1 rabbit flat on a cutting board. Cut off the 2 back legs. Cut the 2 front legs from the shoulders. Cut the back loin into 3 pieces, cutting across the backbone; then cut the rack into 3 pieces. Cut each of the back legs in half. Repeat with the second rabbit. (You can also ask your butcher to do this.)

3. In a large saucepan, bring the stock and wine to a boil. Reduce the heat to medium-low and keep the liquid at a slow, steady simmer.

4. Heat the olive oil and butter in a large cast-iron pot or Dutch oven over medium-high heat. Season the rabbit with salt and pepper and dust with the flour. Add the rabbit to the pot and sear until golden brown on all sides, about 10 minutes. Add the onions and mushrooms and sweat, stirring, for 5 to 7 minutes. Add the mustard seeds and the whole tarragon leaves, toss well, and cook for 10 minutes. Pour in the hot stock-and-wine mixture and stir to scrape up the browned bits on the bottom of the pot. Cover the pot and place it in the oven to braise for 30 minutes. Raise the oven temperature to 375°F, uncover the pot, and braise for 10 minutes more. To check for doneness, use a small knife to pierce the thickest part of the thigh. The meat should feel tender.

5. Meanwhile, in a small bowl, whisk together the Dijon mustard, dried mustard, crème fraîche, and the chopped tarragon leaves. Remove the pot from the oven, stir in the mustard mixture, and let rest for 15 minutes.

6. If you would like a richer sauce, transfer the rabbit to a platter and keep it warm while you boil the braising liquid for 5 to 10 minutes. Season to taste with salt and pepper. Return the rabbit to the pot, garnish with the croutons and chives, and serve.

2 tablespoons crème fraîche

½ cup small croutons

2 tablespoons finely chopped fresh chives, for garnish

FISH
AND
SEAFOOD

SMOKED SABLE CHOWDER

| MAKES 4 SERVINGS |

This is a very homey New England–style corn and potato chowder that gets a deep smoky taste from the sable (smoked black cod) and double-smoked bacon. I think it has a lot more oomph than the usual clam version, and the scallions and thyme give it freshness. You could serve it with little oyster crackers if you like, but it doesn't need them.

3 cups milk and 2 cups cream, or 5 cups half-and-half

3 ounces double-smoked bacon, diced

1 teaspoon crushed black pepper

1 medium red onion, peeled and thinly sliced

4 medium Yukon Gold potatoes (about 1½ pounds), halved and cut into ¼-inch-thick slices

1 cup fresh or frozen corn kernels

1 red bell pepper, cored, seeded, and cut into ¼-inch cubes

1 bunch scallions, trimmed, white and green parts separated and finely chopped

2 bay leaves

1 sprig fresh thyme

1½ pounds smoked sable or smoked haddock (see note)

Coarse sea salt or kosher salt

1. Center a rack in the oven and preheat the oven to 300°F.

2. In a medium saucepan over high heat, bring the milk and cream (or half-and-half) to a simmer. Immediately reduce the heat to low and keep warm.

3. In a small cast-iron pot or Dutch oven over medium-high heat, cook the bacon until the fat is rendered. Add the black pepper and cook for 1 to 2 minutes. Add the onion and cook, stirring, for 10 minutes. Add the potatoes, corn, bell pepper, white part of the scallions, bay leaves, and thyme and stir to combine. Add the hot milk mixture and bring to a simmer. Arrange the sable on top of the vegetables, sprinkle with the scallion greens, cover, and transfer to the oven.

4. Braise until the fish is cooked through, about 30 minutes. Taste the chowder and season with salt if necessary. To serve, cut the sable into large pieces and divide the chowder among warm soup bowls.

SMOKED SABLE AND HADDOCK

Sable, also known as black cod, is a rich white fish often sold smoked at specialty markets. Smoked haddock, also known as finnan haddie, is sold split, its backbone still attached. Though this velvet-fleshed delicacy originated in Scotland, it is also made in Canada, Denmark, and New England. Its smoky flavor is sometimes tempered by simmering in milk. Look for smoked haddock or sable at delicatessens and specialty food stores, or order it online (see Sources, page 210).

SKATE CIOPPINO

BRAISED SKATE IN A WINE AND TOMATO BROTH

| MAKES 2 SERVINGS |

One of the first fish I caught in the Atlantic was skate, which is now quite fashionable in America but was overlooked here for many years. In Lyon, we cook skate wings in brown butter with capers and vinegar—a traditional, very good preparation. For this recipe, I use the wings in a savory tomato-based stew that originated with Mediterranean fishermen in San Francisco. At the restaurant, we blanch the skate in boiling water with a splash of vinegar for 1 or 2 minutes and then peel off the skin, which is a little tough. Most fish dealers will have done this for you, but you can easily do it yourself if you need to. You don't have to worry about deboning the skate after it is cooked. The bones are cartilaginous and soften while cooking, so it's easy to eat around them.

1 tablespoon unsalted butter

1 medium red onion, peeled and thinly sliced

3 garlic cloves, peeled and finely chopped

1 teaspoon crushed black pepper

1 green bell pepper, cored, seeded, and cut into ½-inch squares

1 yellow bell pepper, cored, seeded, and cut into ½-inch squares

1 teaspoon saffron thread (see note, page 77), crushed

1 pound cockles, scrubbed and rinsed well (see note)

½ cup dry white wine

8 plum tomatoes (about 1 pound), peeled, seeded, and chopped (see note, page 37)

1 orange, peeled and segmented

Finely grated zest and freshly squeezed juice of 1 lemon

3 sprigs fresh basil

3 bay leaves

2 sprigs fresh oregano

1 (2- to 3-pound) skinless skate wing, on the bone

1. Center a rack in the oven and preheat the oven to 300°F.

2. In a medium cast-iron pot or Dutch oven over medium-high heat, melt the butter. Add the onion, garlic, and black pepper and cook, stirring, for 3 minutes. Add the bell peppers and saffron and cook for 3 minutes more. Add the cockles, pour in the white wine, and reduce the liquid by half. Cook until the cockles open, about 5 minutes. Transfer the open cockles to a bowl.

3. To the pot, add the tomatoes, ¼ cup water, the orange segments, lemon zest, basil, bay leaves, and oregano. Season the skate with salt and arrange the fish on top of the vegetables. Bring to a simmer, cover, and transfer to the oven.

4. Braise until the fish is just cooked through, 20 to 25 minutes. Return the open cockles to the pot, add the lemon juice, and continue to braise until heated through, 4 to 5 minutes. Sprinkle the fish with the parsley and serve immediately.

COCKLES

Several varieties of small bivalves resembling clams are called cockles. All have ridged shells and sweet, delicate flesh. Cockles are gathered everywhere from the Mediterranean to the Pacific Ocean and are particularly common in the British Isles. They are sought in Spain for paella; can be eaten raw or cooked; and are available, though somewhat rare, at good fish stores in America. If you can't find them, substitute small clams.

Coarse sea salt or kosher salt

3 sprigs fresh flat-leaf parsley, leaves only, finely sliced, for garnish

BRAISED COD WITH TAHINI HERBS AND GARLIC

| MAKES 6 TO 8 SERVINGS |

Fish cooked in tahini is a traditional Middle Eastern dish. It's very simple. You basically make a garlicky tahini sauce in the blender and use it as the liquid for braising. But the flavors of the final dish are much more complex than you'd think from the straightforwardness of the preparation. It's both elegant enough for guests and quick, easy, and accessible enough to serve on a weeknight for just the family.

⅔ cup tahini (see note)

2 tablespoons extra-virgin olive oil

Finely grated zest and freshly squeezed juice of 2 lemons

2 garlic cloves, peeled and finely chopped

3 pounds cod fillets

Coarse sea salt or kosher salt and freshly ground black or white pepper

2 teaspoons ground coriander

½ tablespoon chopped fresh dill, for garnish

½ tablespoon chopped fresh cilantro, for garnish

1. Center a rack in the oven and preheat the oven to 275°F.

2. In a blender, combine 1 cup water, the tahini, olive oil, lemon zest and juice, and garlic and puree until smooth. Pour the mixture into a cast-iron pot or Dutch oven large enough to hold the fish in one layer. Season the cod with salt, pepper, and the ground coriander. Arrange the fish in the pot, cover, and transfer to the oven. Braise until tender, 35 to 40 minutes. (Check the fish occasionally to see that the tahini does not come to a boil, or the sauce will break up.) Sprinkle the dill and cilantro leaves over the fish and serve.

TAHINI

A ground paste made simply from sesame seeds that have been soaked, crushed, and milled, tahini is a staple in Middle Eastern cuisine, where it lends its nutty flavor to a variety of sweet and savory dishes, such as halvah and hummus. Used primarily as a condiment and a base for soups and sauces, tahini is available in light and dark varieties; the lighter variety is considered a higher-quality paste. Tahini can be purchased fresh, canned, and jarred and is available at most specialty food markets or online (see Sources, page 210).

SPICY COD WITH BLACK BEAN SAUCE AND CHESTNUTS

| MAKES 2 SERVINGS |

If you have eaten salt cod, you know how firm, silken, and dense the meat of this fish can be. You can enhance these qualities in fresh cod by seasoning the fillet with salt and, in this case, five-spice powder; wrapping the fish in a towel; and letting it rest on a plate in the refrigerator for a few hours (or even overnight). This will partly cure the cod, so it is less flaky but more toothsome and meaty. If you don't have time for this partial curing, the recipe is delicious prepared with fresh, uncured fish. Either way, you end up with a full-flavored, spicy dish that's pungent from the black bean paste and vinegar, and sweet from the chestnuts and sherry.

1. Center a rack in the oven and preheat the oven to 275°F.

2. Season the fish with salt and the five-spice powder. Warm the olive oil in a small cast-iron pot or Dutch oven over high heat. Place the fish, skin side down, in the pot and sear until golden, 3 to 4 minutes. Transfer the fish to a plate.

3. Add the turnips, artichokes, and celery to the pot and cook, stirring, until softened, 8 to 10 minutes. Add the garlic and gingerroot and cook, stirring, for 2 minutes. Add the chestnuts, sherry, jalapeño pepper, bean paste, vinegar, and bay leaf. Return the fish to the pot, pour in ¾ cup water, and bring the liquid to a simmer. Cover the pot and transfer it to the oven. Braise until the fish is just cooked through, 18 to 20 minutes. Serve immediately.

1 (1-pound) firm cod fillet, skin on

Coarse sea salt or kosher salt

1 teaspoon five-spice powder (see note, page 135)

1 tablespoon extra-virgin olive oil

4 baby turnips or 1 large turnip, peeled, trimmed, and cut into ¼-inch-thick slices

3 baby artichokes or 2 large globe artichoke hearts, trimmed and cut into ¼-inch-thick slices (see note, page 116)

2 stalks celery, julienned

3 garlic cloves, peeled and finely grated

1 (2-inch) piece fresh gingerroot, peeled and finely grated

¾ cup peeled fresh chestnuts or peeled dry-packed bottled or vacuum-sealed chestnuts

½ cup dry sherry

1 jalapeño pepper, seeded and chopped

1 tablespoon fermented black bean paste (see note, page 10)

1 teaspoon black vinegar (see note, page 55)

1 bay leaf

SPICED GROUPER WITH FENNEL, CASHEWS, AND MANGO

| MAKES 6 SERVINGS |

Grouper is a good braising fish. It's not very fatty, but somehow—as if it had a lot of fat—it still keeps its moisture well and doesn't dry out. I don't know what groupers like to eat, but their plumpness makes me think they favor shrimp and scallops! That's what their dense flesh reminds me of. If you can't get grouper, you could substitute monkfish, but monkfish will be more bland. Grouper has a well-balanced saltiness that stands up to assertive, diverse flavors, like the curry spices and raisins I use here. It also, by the way, makes a nice fish soup.

FOR THE MARINADE:

2 tablespoons vegetable oil

1 teaspoon coriander seeds

1 teaspoon fennel seeds

½ teaspoon cumin seeds

½ teaspoon caraway seeds

½ teaspoon fenugreek seeds

½ teaspoon ground turmeric

½ teaspoon cayenne pepper

½ teaspoon garam masala (see note and recipe, page 82)

6 black peppercorns, preferably Tellicherry (see note)

6 plum tomatoes, cored and roughly chopped

1 cup plain whole-milk yogurt

¼ cup chopped fennel bulb

¼ cup peeled, chopped onion

¼ cup raw unsalted cashew nuts

1½ teaspoons peeled, finely grated fresh gingerroot (1-inch piece, approximately)

2 garlic cloves, peeled and roughly chopped

1. To make the marinade: Warm the vegetable oil in a small nonstick skillet over medium heat. Add the coriander seeds, fennel seeds, cumin seeds, caraway seeds, fenugreek seeds, turmeric, cayenne, garam masala, and peppercorns. Cook, stirring, until fragrant, about 3 minutes. Transfer this spice oil to a blender and add ¼ cup water and the remaining marinade ingredients. Blend, starting on low speed and working up to puree, until smooth, about 5 minutes.

2. Salt the grouper well and lay the fillets flat in a large dish. Pour the marinade over the grouper, cover with plastic wrap, and marinate for 3 hours in the refrigerator.

3. Put a rack in the lower third of the oven and preheat the oven to 300°F.

4. Warm the olive oil in a medium cast-iron pot or Dutch oven over medium-high heat. Add the pearl onions, mushrooms, and fennel and cook, stirring occasionally, until the vegetables are lightly colored, 6 to 8 minutes. Stir in the tomatoes. Lay the fish fillets, skin side up, over the vegetables, and pour the marinade over the fish. Sprinkle the cashews and raisins over the top of the dish, cover, and transfer to the oven.

5. Braise until the vegetables are tender and the fish is just cooked, 30 to 35 minutes.

6. Meanwhile, toss the mango with the lime zest, lime juice, and cayenne pepper.

7. Stir in the heavy cream. Sprinkle the mango mixture, mint, basil, and cilantro over the fish and serve immediately.

TELLICHERRY PEPPERCORNS

These black peppercorns, grown in Tellicherry on the Malabar coast of India, are large and have a particularly fruity taste. They are harvested later than most other peppercorns and so develop a fuller flavor. They are available in gourmet markets or online (see Sources, page 210).

SMYRNA AND OTHER RAISINS

Raisins are made by drying different varieties of grapes and are produced in most grape-growing areas, though California has become the world's leader in production. While the common, dark, medium-size Thompson seedless raisin is found in most supermarkets, other varieties offer more nuance. Light gold Smyrna raisins provide a delicate balance between sweetness and acidity and have a tender texture. Sultana raisins resemble Thompson seedless but are larger and lighter, with a tarter, brighter flavor. Brown muscats are particularly large and flavorful. Different varieties of raisins are sold in stores with a good bulk-foods section, such as natural food stores and markets that cater to an Indian or Middle Eastern clientele.

FOR THE GROUPER:
Coarse sea salt or kosher salt

6 (6-ounce) grouper fillets, skin on, or monkfish, skinned

2 tablespoons extra-virgin olive oil

10 ounces pearl onions (about 24), peeled (see note, page 7)

½ pound white button mushrooms, trimmed and quartered

1 fennel bulb, quartered lengthwise, cored, and cut crosswise into ¼-inch-thick slices

2 plum tomatoes, seeded and cut into 1-inch dice

¼ cup raw unsalted cashew nuts

¼ cup Smyrna raisins or regular raisins (see note)

1 small mango, peeled, pitted, and diced

Finely grated zest of ½ lime (about 1 teaspoon)

Freshly squeezed juice of 1 lime

¼ teaspoon cayenne pepper, or to taste

¼ cup heavy cream

1 tablespoon finely chopped fresh mint leaves, for garnish

1 tablespoon finely chopped fresh purple basil (or substitute green basil), for garnish

1 tablespoon finely chopped fresh cilantro leaves, for garnish

PESCADO VERACRUZANA

RED SNAPPER IN A SPICY TOMATO, OLIVE, AND CAPER SAUCE

| MAKES 4 TO 6 SERVINGS |

In this recipe, red snapper is imbued with the typical flavorings of Veracruz, Mexico. After marinating in a mix of jalapeño, citrus, tomatoes, olives, and capers, the snapper is cooked under a banana leaf, which makes for a very dramatic presentation and also keeps the fish very moist. Any thick fish of similar size, such as grouper, can be prepared this way; or you can use a chunk of a larger fish, such as halibut, as long as it's on the bone. The low oven temperature also contributes to the moistness of the fish—if you like, take the fish out after 40 or 45 minutes and let it rest for 15 minutes more, so that it will finish cooking as gently as possible.

---

1 (3- to 3½-pound) red snapper, cleaned

2 oranges

2 limes

3 tablespoons annatto seed, finely ground (see note, page 57)

Coarse sea salt or kosher salt

1 teaspoon crushed black pepper

1 ripe banana, peeled

1¼ banana leaves, optional (see note)

¼ cup extra-virgin olive oil

2 teaspoons ground cumin

1 teaspoon ground coriander

3 small Spanish onions, peeled and thinly sliced

4 garlic cloves, peeled and chopped

2 jalapeño peppers, seeded and finely minced

2 bay leaves

½ cup green olives, pitted

¼ cup capers, rinsed and drained

12 ripe plum tomatoes, quartered and seeded

1 tablespoon dried oregano

Freshly ground black pepper

1 tablespoon chopped fresh cilantro, for garnish

1. Score the top of the fish with 3 vertical slashes. Put the fish into a large nonreactive dish, such as Pyrex. Zest 1 of the oranges and set the zest aside. Zest 1 of the limes and place the lime zest in a small bowl. Juice both oranges and both limes into the bowl as well. Whisk in the annatto seed, 1 tablespoon salt, and the crushed pepper and pour this marinade over the fish. Cover with plastic wrap and refrigerate for 3 hours.

2. Center a rack in the oven and preheat the oven to 275°F.

3. Remove the fish from the refrigerator and scrape off the marinade (reserve the marinade). Wrap the banana in the ¼ banana leaf, if you are using this ingredient. Split the fish in half along its belly and stuff it with the banana.

4. In a large cast-iron pot or Dutch oven over high heat, warm 2 tablespoons of the olive oil. Add the cumin and coriander and stir for 10 seconds. Add the onions, garlic, jalapeños, and bay leaves and cook, stirring, until the onions are lightly colored, 6 to 8 minutes. Add the olives, capers, and 2 cups water. Arrange the fish on top and pour the reserved marinade over the fish. Add the plum tomatoes and oregano.

5. In a small bowl, combine the remaining 2 tablespoons olive oil and the reserved orange zest and season to taste with salt and pepper. Sprinkle the oil mixture over the fish, and top with the remaining banana leaf, if you are using it, making sure that it completely covers all the other ingredients. (Alternatively, partially cover the pot with its lid, leaving a crack open for evaporation.)

6. Transfer the pot to the oven and braise until the fish is cooked through, 45 to 60 minutes. Discard the banana—it's only used as flavoring. Sprinkle with the cilantro and serve immediately.

BANANA LEAF

A convenient product in the tropics, mature banana leaves are enormous, green, and very strong. Pieces of the leaves can be used to wrap foods into parcels before cooking, and the flavor of the leaf will imbue the cooked foods. Banana leaves are waterproof, so they are also used to line serving plates and platters. Look for fresh or frozen banana leaves in Asian or Latin American markets, and thaw them in the refrigerator overnight if necessary. They are also available online (see Sources, page 210).

STRIPED BASS WITH ZAATAR GINGER AND DRIED FRUITS

| MAKES 4 SERVINGS |

I use striped bass in this highly flavored Middle Eastern dish because it has enough flavor to stand up to the spices, mustard, and dried fruit. The dish can also be made with striped bass steak, on the bone, if that is more convenient. Use 2 pounds of the thickest bass steaks you can find, and reduce the cooking time, checking on the fish after about 30 minutes.

1 (2-pound) striped bass tail on the bone

Coarse sea salt or kosher salt

2 bunches scallions, trimmed and finely chopped

1 cup dried fruits (such as figs, prunes, apricots, and cherries), pitted if necessary

¼ cup balsamic vinegar

¼ cup pine nuts or chopped blanched almonds

2 tablespoons Dijon mustard

1½ tablespoons finely grated peeled fresh gingerroot

1 tablespoon honey

2 teaspoons zaatar (see note)

1 teaspoon freshly ground black pepper

1. Center a rack in the oven and preheat the oven to 275°F.

2. Season the fish with salt. In a small cast-iron pot or Dutch oven over high heat, bring the scallions, dried fruits, vinegar, nuts, mustard, gingerroot, honey, zaatar, black pepper, and ¾ cup water to a boil. Arrange the fish on top, cover, and transfer to the oven.

3. Braise until the fish is cooked through, 45 to 55 minutes.

ZAATAR

Zaatar is Arabic for wild thyme, but the word is usually used in reference to a tangy mix of thyme, sumac, and sesame seeds that is sprinkled on yogurt, breads, and other foods. Zaatar mix is sold in Middle Eastern food stores or online (see Sources, page 210).

STUFFED TROUT WITH MEDJOOL DATES, RICE, AND ALMONDS

| MAKES 6 SERVINGS |

A whole fish like a trout will keep its shape beautifully in a braise and won't flake apart. But here, as extra insurance, and to help keep the sweet stuffing of rice, fat dates, and almonds from falling out into the sauce, I've wrapped each trout in fresh fig leaves (though grape leaves, which you can buy in supermarkets, work well too). This way, you serve a nice contained packet that your guests will enjoy opening; and since the rice is already inside the fish, you don't have to make a side dish. It's a great presentation for a dinner party.

2 teaspoons ground sumac (see note, page 79)

1 teaspoon coriander seeds, crushed with a mortar and pestle

1 teaspoon ground cumin

6 (8-ounce) trout, deboned, head on, split horizontally in half, and patted dry

Coarse sea salt or kosher salt and freshly ground black pepper

2 cups cooked long-grain white rice

1 cup Medjool dates, pitted and cut into small dice

½ cup sliced blanched almonds

2 tablespoons chopped fresh cilantro leaves, plus additional leaves for garnish

1 tablespoon peeled, chopped shallot

3 tablespoons extra-virgin olive oil, plus additional for garnish

3 oranges: 2 juiced; 1 sliced into thin rounds

2 pinches of cayenne pepper

9 large fresh fig leaves or 12 to 18 brined grape leaves, rinsed and patted dry

6 scallions, trimmed and cut into 1-inch segments

½ pound baby turnips, trimmed, peeled, and thinly sliced

1 tablespoon date molasses (see note) or regular molasses

1 lemon, cut into 6 wedges, for garnish

1. In a small bowl, combine the sumac, coriander seeds, and ground cumin. Season the trout, inside and out, with half the spice mixture and salt and pepper.

2. In a medium bowl, combine the rice, ¾ cup of the dates, half of the almonds, the cilantro, shallot, 1 tablespoon of the olive oil, and half of the orange juice; season to taste with a pinch of the cayenne and salt and black pepper. Open the split trout fillets and divide the stuffing among the 6 trout, from head to tail, mounding the stuffing tightly in the center of the fillet. Fold the fillet back over the filling to close.

3. Center a rack in the oven and preheat the oven to 300°F.

4. On a clean surface, lay out the fig leaves (if you are using grape leaves, overlap 2 or 3 leaves per trout). Place each stuffed trout over a leaf (or leaves) and wrap the leaf tightly around the fish. (The fish can be made a few hours ahead up to this point and refrigerated.)

5. Heat a large skillet with a cover or a wide braiser, large enough fit the trout in one layer, over medium heat. Add 1 tablespoon of the olive oil, the scallions, turnips, the remaining spice blend, and the remaining pinch of cayenne and cook, stirring, for 3 to 4 minutes. Add the remaining dates and orange juice and the date molasses. Arrange the trout tightly side by side, sprinkle them with the remaining almonds, and drizzle with the remaining 1 tablespoon olive oil.

6. Top with the orange slices, cover, and transfer to the oven. Braise for 30 minutes.

7. To serve, place each wrapped trout on a warm dinner plate. After your guests have unwrapped their trout, offer them the lemon wedges to squirt, the cilantro leaves to sprinkle, and the olive oil to drizzle over the fish.

DATE MOLASSES

A dark, viscous sweetener, date molasses is sold either as syrup (called pataly) or in a thickened "hard" form composed of a crust of crystallized sugar and a runny, sticky interior. Made by extracting and boiling date juice, date molasses tastes, not surprisingly, like concentrated dates. It is used in Lebanese, Iraqi, and Bangladeshi cooking, primarily in desserts. Look for jars of date molasses in Middle Eastern, Indian, and natural food stores, or order it online (see Sources, page 210).

MACKEREL
WITH HERB CURRY

| MAKES 4 SERVINGS |

People think of mackerel as a strong, fishy fish, but that's not exactly true. It has a more assertive character than, say, a delicate white fish like sole. But I think it also has a rich meatiness, rather like tuna. In any case, braised with yogurt, herbs, tomatoes, and spices, it's one of my favorites. I reserve some of the yogurt marinade for the very end because I find that when you drizzle it or stir it into the mackerel just before eating, it lends a bit of freshness to the dish. You could serve this dish with regular or Israeli couscous.

---

4 Spanish mackerel fillets (about 2 pounds), skin on, small pinbones removed and each fillet cut on the bias into 4 pieces

2 oranges

1 cup plain whole-milk yogurt

1 small bunch fresh cilantro, leaves only, plus additional for garnish

10 sprigs fresh mint, leaves only, plus additional for garnish

10 sprigs fresh flat-leaf parsley, leaves only, plus additional for garnish

1½ teaspoons fresh dill leaves

6 fresh or dried curry leaves (see note, page 27)

1 Kaffir lime leaf (see note, page 121)

1 hot green chili pepper (such as jalapeño or serrano), seeds removed

Coarse sea salt or kosher salt

2 tablespoons vegetable oil

1 teaspoon cumin seeds

1 teaspoon coriander seeds

1 teaspoon ground turmeric

1 tablespoon peeled, chopped garlic

1 tablespoon finely grated peeled fresh gingerroot

1 bunch scallions, trimmed and cut into ¼-inch-thick slices

1. The day before you plan to serve this dish, arrange the mackerel in a large nonreactive bowl or Pyrex dish. Finely grate the zest of ¼ orange, and juice both of the oranges. Using a blender, puree the yogurt, cilantro, mint, parsley, dill, curry leaves, Kaffir lime leaf, chili, two-thirds of the orange juice, and all of the orange zest until smooth. Season to taste with salt. Reserve ½ cup of the marinade in the refrigerator until ready to serve. Pour the remaining marinade over the mackerel. Cover tightly with plastic wrap and marinate overnight in the refrigerator.

2. Put a rack in the lower third of the oven and preheat the oven to 300°F.

3. In a small cast-iron pot or Dutch oven over medium heat, warm the vegetable oil. Add the cumin seeds, coriander seeds, and turmeric and toast until fragrant, 2 to 3 minutes. Add the garlic and gingerroot and cook, stirring, for 1 minute. Add the scallions and red bell pepper and continue to cook for 8 to 10 minutes. Add the tomatoes, tomato juice, and the remaining orange juice; season to taste with salt, cayenne, and sugar (the sugar is to help balance the acidity of the tomatoes). Bring the mixture to a boil. Put the mackerel on top of the vegetables, cover, and transfer to the oven.

4. Braise until tender, about 30 minutes. Sprinkle the lime juice and the cilantro, mint, and parsley leaves over the fish. Serve with the reserved yogurt marinade on the side.

1 red bell pepper, cored, seeded, and cut into ¼-inch dice

4 plum tomatoes or 1 large beefsteak tomato, cut into ¼-inch dice

¼ cup canned or fresh tomato juice

Cayenne pepper

Sugar

Freshly squeezed juice of 2 limes

MONKFISH WITH SAVOY CABBAGE AND JUNIPER BERRIES

| MAKES 6 SERVINGS |

Even though the bulk of this recipe comes from the rather humble ingredients—the cabbage, potatoes, and onions—the monkfish in its creamy beurre blanc sauce transforms this into a more formal dish. I added juniper berries because of their affinity for cabbage, and it turned out to be quite a nice but unusual pairing with the fish. Juniper, which is the principal flavoring of gin, is very fragrant, with a pine scent. But since it's not at all pungent or spicy, it really lets the brininess of the fish come through. It reminds me of the combination of olives in a gin martini.

Coarse sea salt or kosher salt

1 cup peeled, sliced shallots

1 cup dry white wine

$^1/_4$ cup white wine vinegar

1 tablespoon gin

12 juniper berries: 4 finely crushed; 8 left whole

1 teaspoon crushed black pepper

1 small head savoy cabbage (about 2 pounds), quartered, cored, and cut into 1-inch wedges

$1^1/_2$ pounds Yukon Gold potatoes, peeled and cut into $^1/_8$-inch-thick slices

$^3/_4$ pound unsalted butter (3 sticks), cut into tablespoon-size pieces and chilled

1 ($3^1/_2$-pound) monkfish tail, on the bone (have your fish dealer remove the skin and membrane)

Freshly ground black pepper

$^1/_4$ pound smoked country bacon, cut into $^1/_2$-inch-thick strips

1 large onion, peeled and thinly sliced

2 bay leaves

1 small bunch round red radishes, thinly sliced, for garnish (optional)

1. Put a rack in the lower third of the oven and preheat the oven to 300°F. Bring a large pot of salted water to a boil.

2. To make the beurre blanc: In a medium saucepan, bring the shallots, wine, vinegar, gin, crushed juniper berries, and black pepper to a boil and simmer until reduced to $^1/_4$ cup, about 20 minutes.

3. Meanwhile, add the cabbage and potatoes to the pot of boiling water and blanch until tender, 5 to 7 minutes. Transfer to a colander to drain.

4. When the beurre blanc reduction has finished, reduce the heat to low and add the butter, 1 piece at a time, whisking until just melted before adding more. The sauce should have the consistency of a hollandaise. Strain the beurre blanc through a fine-mesh sieve, pressing on the solids to extract as much liquid and flavor as possible. Season to taste with salt and cover to keep warm (the sauce will break if it gets too hot or too cold).

5. Wash the monkfish, pat it dry, and season it with salt and pepper. In a medium cast-iron pot or Dutch oven, cook the bacon over medium heat until it is translucent (adjust the heat so it does not brown), 5 to 7 minutes. Add the onion, bay leaves, and whole juniper berries and cook, stirring, until the onion is translucent, about

10 minutes. Add the cabbage and potatoes, pour the beurre blanc over the vegetables, and arrange the monkfish on top (cut the monkfish tail crosswise in half if it is too long for the pot). Cover the pot and transfer it to the oven.

6. Braise until the fish is cooked through, 25 to 35 minutes. Garnish with the radish slices, if using, and serve.

MONKFISH WITH EGGPLANT AND PINE NUTS

| MAKES 6 SERVINGS |

Monkfish is a very meaty fish that pairs well with eggplant, a very meaty vegetable. To give the eggplant a better, firmer texture, and to reduce any bitter flavor, I cure it with salt for several hours before cooking. The flavors of this dish hail from Spain—particularly the smoked paprika, which gives some spice as well as heat to the fish. If you cannot find smoked paprika, use hot Hungarian paprika, or add a small pinch of ground cayenne pepper to sweet paprika. The bones of monkfish are actually cartilage and will nearly melt when you cook them, so you don't need to worry about deboning the fish before you serve it. And cooking the fish on the bone adds plenty of flavor. Any part of a good, fresh monkfish—or even a whole headless baby monkfish—will work here. Alternatively, you can use several pieces of monkfish cut into 2-inch chunks (as if for osso buco). In that case, simply reduce the cooking time slightly.

---

2 pounds eggplant, trimmed, peeled, and cut into ¼- to ½-inch cubes

Coarse sea salt or kosher salt

1 (3½- to 4-pound) monkfish tail, on the bone (have your fish dealer remove the skin and membrane)

1 tablespoon smoked Spanish paprika (see note) or sweet paprika

Freshly ground black pepper

½ cup extra-virgin olive oil

2 medium onions, peeled and finely chopped

4 garlic cloves, peeled and chopped

1 tablespoons dried oregano

⅓ cup sherry vinegar

6 tablespoons pine nuts, toasted (see note, page 44)

2 tablespoons chopped fresh flat-leaf parsley leaves, for garnish

1. In a bowl, toss together the eggplant and 1 tablespoon salt. Transfer to a colander and let drain for 2 to 3 hours.

2. Center a rack in the oven and preheat the oven to 275°F.

3. Season the monkfish with salt, the paprika, and pepper. Heat 3 tablespoons of the olive oil in a medium cast-iron pot or Dutch oven over high heat. Add the monkfish and sear for 3 to 4 minutes on each side. Transfer the monkfish to a plate. Lower the temperature to medium, add the onions, and cook, stirring, for 2 to 3 minutes. Raise the temperature to high; add the eggplant, garlic, oregano, ¼ teaspoon black pepper, and the remaining 5 tablespoons olive oil, and cook, stirring, for 5 to 6 minutes. Add the sherry vinegar, bring to a simmer, and scrape up any browned bits sticking to the bottom of the pot. Add the pine nuts and 2 cups water and return the monkfish to the pot. Bring to a simmer, and transfer to the oven.

4. Braise until the fish is cooked through, about 1 hour. Sprinkle the parsley leaves over the fish and serve immediately.

SMOKED SPANISH PAPRIKA
This Spanish product is indispensable in paella and is the seasoning responsible for the smokiness of Spanish chorizo. The best smoked paprika (also called pimentón) comes from la Vera, Spain, where peppers are gradually dried in smokehouses, then ground to a red powder. The spice is available in sweet, bittersweet, and spicy varieties and can be found in some specialty food stores or online (see Sources, page 210).

SEA SCALLOPS WITH SALSIFY, SHIITAKE MUSHROOMS, AND WHITE MISO

| MAKES 4 SERVINGS |

Good, fresh sea scallops are a pristine food requiring very little preparation. In this recipe, I sear the scallops on one side for a caramelized flavor before braising them, then broil them at the end to regain a wonderful crisp texture. These little added steps give this Asian-influenced braise all the dimensions that scallops have to offer.

There are many wonderful varieties of scallop—in Japan, I was introduced to a black-shelled scallop the size of a man's shoe, which looked like a mussel and had firm, sweet flesh that we ate raw, as sashimi. At my restaurants, I buy live scallops in the shell so I can be sure they are fresh and not preserved, but they are not always easy to find. To choose fresh scallops out of their shells, look for ones that are *not* all the exact same shade— opaque and pale white—as this indicates preservatives, which bleach them. Scallops should run the gamut of shades from pearly to tan. Next, make sure that they are fairly dry and are not surrounded by milky liquid. This liquid is injected into them to plump them up, and it will seep out again when you sear them. And finally, you must ask to smell them, since this is the best way to know they are fresh—you want a clean, mild smell of the sea, and nothing more.

---

2 tablespoons white miso (see note, page 13)

2 tablespoons sake or dry white wine

2 teaspoons yuzu juice (see note)

2 tablespoons extra-virgin olive oil

2 tablespoons unsalted butter

3 salsify roots, peeled and cut on the bias into ¼-inch-thick slices

6 ounces large shiitake mushrooms, stemmed and cut into ¼-inch-thick slices

12 jumbo sea scallops (about 1 pound)

Coarse sea salt or kosher salt and freshly ground white pepper

½ pound Swiss chard, stems removed, coarsely chopped

½ cup small stale bread cubes, for croutons

2 teaspoons white sesame seeds

1. Center a rack in the oven and preheat the oven to 275°F.

2. In a small bowl, whisk together ½ cup water and the miso, sake, and yuzu juice.

3. In a medium cast-iron pan, a flameproof gratin dish, or a Dutch oven, warm 1 tablespoon of the olive oil and 1 tablespoon of the butter over medium-low heat. Add the salsify and sauté, stirring occasionally, until deep golden brown, 12 to 15 minutes. Add the shiitake mushrooms and cook, stirring, until softened, 3 to 5 minutes. Transfer the vegetables to a plate, raise the heat to high, and heat the remaining 1 tablespoon olive oil.

4. Season the scallops with salt and pepper and sear, on one side only, until golden brown, about 1½ minutes (do not cook too long). Transfer them to a plate and pour the miso-sake mixture into the pan, scraping up any browned bits sticking to the bottom. Add the chard and cook until wilted, 1 to 2 minutes. Return the scallops, golden side up, to the pan, along with the salsify and the mushrooms. Cover the pan with a lid or aluminum foil and transfer it to the oven.

5. Braise until the scallops offer no resistance when pierced with a fork, 12 to 15 minutes.

6. Meanwhile, melt the remaining 1 tablespoon butter in a small skillet over medium-high heat. Add the bread cubes, sesame seeds, and cilantro and toss to coat with the butter. Cook until the croutons just barely begin to color, about 2 minutes.

7. Remove the scallops from the oven and preheat the broiler. Scatter the crouton mixture over the scallops and broil for 1 minute, until the croutons are golden. Serve immediately.

2 teaspoons black sesame seeds (see note, page 13)

1 tablespoon chopped fresh cilantro leaves

YUZU JUICE

A citrus fruit about the size of a lemon, yuzu grows in Asia and is used often in Japanese cooking. The fruit has a thick, stippled, orange-yellow skin, many seeds, and highly acidic juice. Yuzu juice is often combined with soy sauce to make a dipping sauce and is a key ingredient in Japanese ponzu sauce. Yuzu zest is used as a seasoning. The juice is sold in bottles in Asian markets, or you can order it online (see Sources, page 210). Alternatively, substitute lime juice spiked with some grated lime zest.

SHRIMP WITH ZUCCHINI, ONIONS, COCONUT, AND TAMARIND

| MAKES 4 TO 6 SERVINGS |

I love to cook with tamarind, which is used in Thai, Vietnamese, and Mexican preparations, as well as in this Indian-inspired recipe. In its natural state tamarind has the kind of tart, complex flavors that balance sweetness in a dish. It gives a dimension similar to what you get from reducing wine.

Here, marinated shrimp are cooked with tamarind and nutty coconut, along with some typical Indian spicing, for a well-rounded, highly complex flavor. The shrimp must be very large to stand up to the marination and braising without losing their firm texture, so buy the biggest ones you can find and adjust the cooking time as necessary. To finish the dish, instead of adding heavy cream or crème fraîche, as I would in a French sauce, I add yogurt, which smooths out all the flavors in the marinade and helps to tenderize the shrimp, while keeping the dish light. Serve this with rice.

FOR THE MARINADE:

1 cup fresh cilantro leaves

½ cup fresh mint leaves

½ cup plain whole-milk yogurt

Freshly squeezed juice of 1 orange

Freshly squeezed juice of 2 lemons

20 fresh curry leaves (see note, page 27)

2 garlic cloves, peeled and finely chopped

2 green chili peppers (such as jalapeño or serrano), seeded and finely chopped

½ teaspoon ground turmeric

¼ teaspoon ajwain seeds (see note, page 83)

Coarse sea salt or kosher salt to taste

3 pounds extra-large shrimp, peeled and deveined (see note)

1. To make the marinade: In a large bowl, combine all the marinade ingredients. Pour the marinade over the shrimp, cover tightly with plastic wrap, and refrigerate for 1 hour.

2. To make the braise: Microwave the fresh tamarind (if you're using tamarind concentrate, skip ahead to step 3) and ½ cup water on high for 2 minutes. Mash well with a fork and then push the tamarind and its liquid through a fine-mesh sieve. Discard the fibrous residue and set aside the strained pulp.

3. Put a rack in the lower third of the oven and preheat the oven to 275°F.

4. In a medium cast-iron pot or Dutch oven over medium-high heat, warm the vegetable oil. Add the tamarind pulp or concentrate, gingerroot, spices, co-conut, onions, tomatoes, and yogurt. Cook, stirring, until the onions are tender, 10 to 12 minutes. Add the shrimp, with its marinade, and the zucchini, cover, and transfer to the oven.

5. Braise until the shrimp are just cooked through, 40 to 45 minutes.

DEVEINING SHRIMP

Deveined shrimp can usually be purchased at fish markets. However, if the long black digestive tube running along the shrimp's back has not been removed, it is necessary to do so during preparation. First, peel off the shrimp's hard outer shell. Then, use a paring knife to cut a slit along the curved, convex back of the shrimp, from head to tail. Using the tip of your knife, remove the vein under cold running water.

FOR THE BRAISE:

Walnut-size piece of seedless fresh tamarind (about 2 ounces) or 2 tablespoons tamarind concentrate (see note, page 55)

1/4 cup vegetable oil

1 (1/2-inch) piece fresh gingerroot, peeled and finely grated

1 teaspoon coriander seeds

3/4 teaspoon ground turmeric

1/2 teaspoon cumin seeds

1/2 teaspoon garam masala (see note and recipe, page 82)

1/2 teaspoon cayenne pepper

1/4 teaspoon freshly ground black pepper

1/4 teaspoon fenugreek seeds

1/4 teaspoon black mustard seeds (see note, page 113)

2 tablespoons desiccated coconut

2 medium onions, peeled and chopped

6 plum tomatoes, roughly chopped

1/2 cup plain whole-milk yogurt

2 medium zucchini, trimmed and cut into 1/4-inch dice

OCTOPUS WITH GINGER, GARLIC, AND SOY SAUCE

| MAKES 6 TO 8 SERVINGS |

Because its chewy flesh needs long, slow cooking to tenderize properly, braising is the best way to cook an octopus. Many cultures have their own methods and flavorings. In Italy, cooks simmer octopus with wine and wine corks (they say that the corks help tenderize the flesh). Cooks in northern Spain favor paprika, and cooks in Greece use a lot of lemon and olive oil. Octopus is also popular in many parts of Asia, and Asian flavors were the inspiration for this dish. Thai or Vietnamese fish sauce, sesame seeds, Korean chili pepper, and ginger combine to give the cephalopod a very savory, layered taste. The only trick to this recipe is to keep the temperature very low; just under a boil is best. If you heat it too much, the meat will toughen.

1 (5-pound) cleaned fresh or frozen octopus (or use 2 to equal that weight combined), thawed if frozen

2 tablespoons extra-virgin olive oil

1 large onion, peeled and chopped

6 garlic cloves, peeled and crushed

1 (4-inch) piece fresh gingerroot, peeled and (with the base of a small heavy pan) crushed

1 tablespoon pink peppercorns (see note, page 15)

2 teaspoons freshly ground black pepper

1 to 2 teaspoons crushed red Korean chili pepper, to taste (see note)

3 tablespoons light soy sauce (see note, page 11)

1½ tablespoons Thai or Vietnamese fish sauce (see note, page 55)

3 small lemons, peeled, seeded, and cut into ¼-inch-thick slices

1 bunch scallions, trimmed and sliced

1½ tablespoons packed dark brown sugar

1 tablespoon toasted sesame seeds, plus additional for garnish (see note, page 33)

1 teaspoon cornstarch

1. Bring a large pot of water to a boil. Add the octopus, reduce the heat to very low, and simmer very gently for 30 minutes. Do not let the water come back to a boil. Drain the octopus, and using a needle, prick it all over. Remove the skin from the tentacles for a prettier presentation, if desired.

2. Center a rack in the oven and preheat the oven to 275°F.

3. Warm the olive oil in a large cast-iron pot or Dutch oven over medium heat. Add the onion, garlic, gingerroot, pink peppercorns, black pepper, and red chili pepper. Cook, stirring, until the onion is softened, about 5 minutes (adjust the heat so that the onion cooks without taking on any color). Pour in the soy sauce and fish sauce and simmer, scraping up any browned bits from the bottom of the pot. Pour in 1 cup water and add the lemons, scallions, brown sugar, sesame seeds, and octopus. Bring the liquid to a simmer, cover, and transfer the pot to the oven.

4. Braise until the octopus is completely tender, about 2 hours.

5. Remove the octopus from the pot. Strain the sauce through a fine-mesh sieve into a medium saucepan. Mix together the cornstarch and 1 teaspoon water. Bring the sauce to a boil and add the cornstarch mixture. Stir well. Continue to cook until the sauce is thick enough to coat the back of a spoon, 2 to 3 minutes. Pour the sauce over the octopus, garnish with the additional sesame seeds, and serve.

KOREAN RED PEPPER

A traditional ingredient in kimchi, red flecks of Korean crushed red peppers contribute a lot of flavor and a moderate level of spice. The pepper is usually sold in bags at stores that cater to a Korean clientele, or you can find it online (see Sources, page 210).

VEGETABLES
AND
BEANS

CABBAGE KIMCHI-STYLE

| MAKES 6 TO 8 SERVINGS |

One has to acquire a taste for kimchi, the fiery Korean pickled cabbage condiment, and if you start with a bad kimchi, you may never go back. But when it's well made, with really good ingredients, it's an exciting taste that livens up all kinds of meats, soups, and stews. This recipe is not at all traditional. It's more of a European-style, kimchi-inspired cabbage braise, made from fresh instead of pickled cabbage, with a little Asian pear for sweetness. But we didn't hold back on the chilies and garlic, so it's somewhat authentic in that way. It's a terrific side dish with grilled meats or fish; or just serve it with rice (see recipe, page 183) or noodles.

1 (4-pound) head napa cabbage

1¼ cups coarse sea salt or kosher salt

2 tablespoons extra-virgin olive oil

1 large onion, peeled, halved, and thinly sliced

5 garlic cloves, peeled and finely grated

1 (4-inch) piece fresh gingerroot, peeled and finely grated

1 jalapeño pepper, finely diced

2 bunches scallions, trimmed and thinly sliced

1 small (about 10 ounces) daikon radish, peeled, trimmed, and diced

1 large red bell pepper, cored, seeded, and diced

1 large Asian pear, peeled, cored, and diced

1 cup freshly squeezed lemon juice

3 ounces rock candy (see note) or ⅓ cup plus 1 tablespoon packed brown sugar

1 to 2 tablespoons Korean red pepper flakes, to taste (see note, page 169)

1 tablespoon oyster sauce (see note, page 173)

1 teaspoon saffron threads (see note, page 77)

1. Wash the cabbage and drain. Trim off the very bottom of the cabbage, leaving enough of the root end intact to hold the head together. Carefully separate the leaves without breaking them from the root, and sprinkle 1 cup of the salt in between and over them. Tightly press and reshape the cabbage and place it in a nonreactive container, such as a Pyrex dish. Dissolve the remaining ¼ cup salt in 6 cups water and pour over the cabbage. Let the cabbage sit for 3 hours, giving it a quarter turn every 15 minutes. Rinse for several minutes under cold running water. Gently squeeze out any excess water.

2. Center a rack in the oven and preheat the oven to 275°F.

3. In a large cast-iron pot or Dutch oven over medium heat, warm the olive oil. Add the onion, garlic, gingerroot, and jalapeño pepper and cook, stirring, for 5 minutes. Lay the cabbage on its side in the pot. Add 1 cup water and the remaining ingredients and bring to a simmer. Cover and transfer to the oven.

4. Braise for 2½ hours. Turn the cabbage over, baste with the pan juices, and continue to braise for 2½ hours more.

OYSTER SAUCE

An essential ingredient in Chinese and Southeast Asian cooking, oyster sauce is a thick, salty-sweet condiment of oyster extract, soy sauce, and sugar. Originally made of fermented oysters, today's oyster sauce usually derives its seafood flavor from simmering dried oysters in brine. Dark brown in color, it is used as a marinade for meats and poultry and is also a common addition to stir-fried dishes. Oyster sauce can be purchased bottled and canned, and it should be refrigerated after opening. It is available at Asian markets or online (see Sources, page 210).

ROCK CANDY

Sold in large crystal formations, rock candy is a hard lump sweetener used in Asian cooking, particularly to sweeten and glaze savory dishes. It is actually a blend of refined and raw sugars and honey, and it is slightly less sweet than pure sugar. You can find both yellow and clear rock sugar, sometimes called Chinese rock sugar, at Asian markets; or you can substitute the slightly less pure rock sugar sold on sticks or strings at old-time candy stores. (You will need to pulverize the sugar by hitting it with something hard, like the base of a frying pan, to remove the sugar from the string or stick onto which it has been crystallized.) You can also find rock sugar online (see Sources, page 210).

RED CABBAGE WITH APPLES AND HONEY

| MAKES 8 SERVINGS |

It takes a long time to braise a red cabbage, but after 2 hours the formerly crunchy veg-etable turns silky and sweet. I play up that sweetness in this recipe by adding apples and honey, and then stir in some vinegar for a tangy taste. This red cabbage is an ideal accom-paniment for roasted or braised pork, duck, or game. Or, to keep things vegetarian, serve it on its own with a selection of other vegetables, and maybe some dark bread to highlight the recipe's northern European origins.

4 cardamom pods

1 teaspoon coriander seeds

½ cup honey

4 cups apple juice

⅓ cup white wine vinegar

4 ounces smoked country bacon, cut into 1-by-½-inch strips

2 medium onions, peeled and thinly sliced

1 head red cabbage, quartered, cored, and thinly sliced

2 Granny Smith apples, cored and diced

1. Put a rack in the lower third of the oven and preheat the oven to 300°F.

2. In a spice grinder or clean coffee grinder, finely grind the cardamom and coriander seeds. Bring the honey to a boil in a small saucepan. Add the ground spices, apple juice, and white wine vinegar, bring to a boil, and reduce the liquid by half.

3. In a medium cast-iron pot or Dutch oven, cook the ba-con over medium-high heat until translucent, 5 to 7 min-utes. Add the onions and cook for 5 minutes more. Add the red cabbage and apples and cook, stirring, until soft-ened, about 15 minutes. Pour the reduced honey-apple mixture over the cabbage and toss to coat. Cover the pot and transfer it to the oven.

4. Braise for 2 hours, or until the cabbage is very tender.

ENDIVE BRAISED IN CRÈME FRAÎCHE

| MAKES 4 TO 6 SERVINGS |

Since endive is a bitter vegetable, I like to pair it with cream and cheese to tame the assertive flavor. The ham adds a salty meatiness and also makes the dish more substantial, though you can leave it out if you'd rather. Served with just bread and a salad, this dish is a light meal on its own. That's how my mother and grandmother would serve it, though it also works well as part of a larger meal. If you pair it with a salad, try dressing some raw endive with vinaigrette for a good crisp contrast.

1. Center a rack in the oven and preheat the oven to 300°F.

2. In a large skillet over medium heat, melt the butter and sugar. Add the endive leaves and lemon juice and cook until almost all the liquid in the pan has evaporated, making sure that the leaves do not color, 3 to 4 minutes.

3. Pour in the white wine and continue to cook until the endive leaves are evenly coated with the reduced pan liquid, about 2 minutes more. Season to taste with salt and pepper and let cool to room temperature.

4. Divide the endive leaves into 3 equal portions. Divide the ham and cheese into 3 equal portions as well. Put 1 portion of the endive leaves in an even layer on the bottom of a small cast-iron pot, Dutch oven, or casserole, followed by 1 portion of the ham. Brush one-third of the crème fraîche over the ham layer, season with salt, pepper, and mace, and put 1 portion of cheese on top. Repeat the layering two more times.

5. Cover with a buttered parchment round and transfer to the oven. Braise for 1 hour.

6. Preheat the broiler. Remove the parchment and broil for 15 minutes, or until the cheese is golden brown and bubbling.

½ cup (1 stick) unsalted butter

1 teaspoon sugar

14 heads Belgian endive, leaves separated

Freshly squeezed juice of 1 lemon

¼ cup dry white wine

Coarse sea salt or kosher salt and freshly ground black pepper

1 pound French ham (such as Bayonne) or prosciutto, sliced

½ pound Gruyère cheese, thinly sliced

½ cup crème fraîche

¼ teaspoon ground mace

MIXED GREENS WITH RHUBARB, LEEKS, AND DILL

| MAKES 4 TO 6 SERVINGS |

My Chef de Cuisine at DANIEL is married to an Afghan woman, and she gave us the traditional Afghan vegetable recipe—from her mother—that inspired this dish. It's an unusual mix of greens made tart with rhubarb and flavored with a lot of dried dill. When we tested it here at the restaurant, my chef and cooks couldn't stop eating it! You can serve it as it is, or with a spoonful of plain whole-milk yogurt on top.

2 tablespoons extra-virgin olive oil

1½ pounds leeks, white and light green parts, washed (see headnote page 179) and diced (about 4 cups)

2 pounds mixed greens (collard greens, kale, Swiss chard, mustard greens, beet leaves), trimmed

1 pound rhubarb, trimmed and cut into ½-inch-thick slices (about 4 cups)

5 tablespoons dried dill

1½ teaspoons coarse sea salt or kosher salt, plus additional to taste

1 teaspoon Aleppo pepper (see note)

Freshly ground black pepper

ALEPPO PEPPER

Syrian Aleppo pepper flakes are mild and fruity, without the slightly bitter seeds found in standard crushed red pepper flakes. If you can't find Aleppo pepper, use half the quantity of regular red pepper flakes. Aleppo pepper is sold in Middle Eastern markets and in some well-stocked spice markets, or you can order it online (see Sources, page 210).

1. Center a rack in the oven and preheat the oven to 275°F.

2. In a medium cast-iron pot or Dutch oven over medium heat, warm the olive oil. Add the leeks and cook, stirring, for 4 to 5 minutes. Add the greens, cover, and cook just until they are slightly wilted, 2 to 3 minutes. Add the rhubarb, dill, salt, Aleppo pepper, and freshly ground black pepper to taste and continue to cook until the rhubarb is slightly softened, 12 to 15 minutes. Pour in 2 cups water and bring to a simmer. Cover and transfer to the oven.

3. Braise until the greens have broken down and the liquid has reduced, about 1½ hours. Adjust the seasoning if necessary and serve.

BROCCOLI RABE
WITH ANCHOVIES

| MAKES 4 SERVINGS |

We don't eat a lot of broccoli rabe in France, but ever since I first tasted it, I've been in love with its bitter flavor. Here I stay true to the vegetable's Italian roots and cook it with anchovies and olives, plus a little fontina cheese to smooth out the other forceful tastes.

1. Center a rack in the oven and preheat the oven to 300°F.

2. Heat the olive oil in a small cast-iron pot or Dutch oven over medium heat. Add the onions and cook, stirring, until translucent, 6 to 8 minutes. Add the remaining ingredients and stir to combine. Cover and transfer to the oven.

3. Braise until the broccoli rabe is very tender and most of the liquid has evaporated, 1 to 1½ hours.

2 tablespoons extra-virgin olive oil

2 medium white onions, peeled and thinly sliced

2 pounds broccoli rabe, trimmed

8 anchovy fillets

¼ cup green olives, pitted and thinly sliced

1 cup red wine

¼ cup crumbled fontina cheese

SPICED SWEET POTATOES
WITH ALMONDS

| MAKES 6 SERVINGS |

I use a lot of sweet potatoes during the autumn and winter, and I especially like to serve them with game and other rich cold-weather dishes. Because of their sweetness, they can take a lot of spicing, whereas regular potatoes cannot. If you tried to use cinnamon, ginger, and brown sugar with a white potato, it would taste awful. But the sweet potato can accept all those flavors. In this dish, I also add almonds and orange zest, to give a fruity nuttiness. It is an interesting alternative to the usual sweet potato gratin.

3 oranges

5 tablespoons ground almonds

2 tablespoons packed dark brown sugar

1 teaspoon ground mace

½ teaspoon ground cinnamon

½ teaspoon ground ginger

1 tablespoon extra-virgin olive oil

3 medium onions, peeled, halved, and thinly sliced

Coarse sea salt or kosher salt and freshly ground black pepper

6 to 7 sweet potatoes (5 to 6 pounds), peeled and cut crosswise into ½-inch-thick slices

6 tablespoons unsalted butter, cut into small pieces

1. Put a rack in the lower third of the oven and preheat the oven to 300°F.

2. Finely grate the zest of 1 orange. Juice all 3 oranges (there should be about 1½ cups juice). In a small bowl, combine the orange zest, almonds, dark brown sugar, mace, cinnamon, and ginger.

3. In a medium cast-iron pot or Dutch oven, warm the olive oil. Add the onions and cook, stirring, until translucent, about 10 minutes. Transfer half the onions to a plate. Spread the remaining onions over the bottom of the pot and season to taste with salt and pepper. Put half the sweet potatoes in a layer on top of the onions. Pour half the orange juice over the potatoes and season to taste with salt and pepper. Sprinkle half the almond-spice mixture evenly over the sweet potatoes. Repeat the layering with the remaining onions, sweet potatoes, orange juice, and almond-spice mixture. Dot the top with the butter. Cover the pot and transfer it to the oven.

4. Braise until the potatoes are tender, about 1 hour. Uncover and bake until golden brown, about 10 minutes more.

LEEKS, PRUNES, AND PLUMS

| MAKES 4 TO 6 SERVINGS |

Leeks are good to braise because they will hold their shape, yet they take on a very silky texture when cooked at a low temperature. I think they have a very gentle, green flavor that works well with the spices and tart plums in this recipe. Take care to clean your leeks well before cooking them. Usually they are dirtiest at the top, dark green part of the stem, so pay particular attention when you are rinsing them there. It's a good idea to split a leek lengthwise before rinsing. Then you'll really be able to flush out any clinging soil.

1. Center a rack in the oven and preheat the oven to 300°F.

2. Heat the olive oil in a small cast-iron pot or Dutch oven over medium-high heat. Add the leeks and cook, stirring, until light golden brown on all sides, about 5 minutes. Add the onion, fennel, cinnamon sticks, fennel seeds, mace, and salt and pepper to taste. Cook, stirring, for 5 minutes. Add the plums, prune juice, prunes, and lemon juice. Bring to a simmer, cover, and transfer to the oven.

3. Braise for 1 hour, or until the leeks are tender and easily pierced with a knife, turning the leeks over halfway during the braise. Discard the cinnamon sticks. Serve the braise warm or cold as an appetizer or a side dish.

¼ cup extra-virgin olive oil

2 pounds leeks, white and light green parts, trimmed, washed, and cut into 3-inch pieces

1 onion, peeled, halved, and sliced

1 fennel bulb, trimmed and cut lengthwise into ¼-inch-thick slices

2 (3-inch) cinnamon sticks

1 teaspoon fennel seeds

¼ teaspoon ground mace

Coarse sea salt or kosher salt and freshly ground black pepper

1 pound firm red plums, pitted and cut into eighths

1 cup prune juice

½ cup prunes, pitted and diced

Freshly squeezed juice of 1 lemon

ARTICHOKES STUFFED
WITH FETA CHEESE

| MAKES 6 TO 8 SERVINGS |

Stuffed with a good amount of feta and greens, these citrus-and-wine-braised artichokes would make a wonderful savory vegetarian main course, or an appetizer for a light meal.

5 tablespoons extra-virgin olive oil

1 large onion, peeled and chopped

4 garlic cloves, peeled and chopped

Pinch of cayenne pepper

1 pound mustard greens, Swiss chard, or lacinato kale, trimmed

1/2 pound spinach, stems removed

Finely grated zest of 1 orange

Finely grated zest of 1 lemon

1/2 pound feta cheese, cubed

10 large globe artichokes, trimmed and cleaned (see note, page 116)

2 fennel bulbs, trimmed: 1 diced; 1 cut into 10 wedges

3 fennel sticks, optional (see note, page 99)

3 sprigs fresh thyme

2 sprigs fresh savory, optional

1 teaspoon coriander seeds

1 teaspoon fennel seeds

1/2 teaspoon freshly ground black pepper

1 cup dry white wine

2 cups freshly squeezed orange juice

1. Center a rack in the oven and preheat the oven to 300°F.

2. Heat 3 tablespoons of the olive oil in a large skillet over medium-high heat. Add the onion, garlic, and cayenne pepper and cook, stirring, until the onion is translucent, about 8 minutes. Add the greens, spinach, orange zest, and lemon zest and cook, stirring, until the vegetables are tender, 12 to 15 minutes. Transfer the vegetables to a bowl. Add the feta cheese to the vegetables and mix to combine. Stuff the center of each artichoke with the vegetable-cheese mixture, using about 1/3 cup stuffing for each artichoke.

3. Heat the remaining 2 tablespoons olive oil in a large cast-iron pot or Dutch oven over medium-high heat. Add the fennel, fennel sticks if using, thyme, savory, coriander seeds, fennel seeds, and black pepper and cook, stirring, for 6 to 8 minutes. Pour in the white wine and stir to remove any browned bits clinging to the bottom of the pot. Reduce the wine to 1/3 cup. Add the orange juice and place the stuffed artichokes in the pot. Bring to a simmer, cover, and transfer to the oven.

4. Braise until the artichokes are tender, about 1 1/2 hours.

SOUTHERN-STYLE BLACK-EYED PEAS WITH BACON

| MAKES 4 SERVINGS |

In the South, everyone has his or her own way of cooking black-eyed peas, but most recipes have bacon, onions, and hot sauce in common. My recipe makes a spicy but not tongue-searing dish, although you can increase the heat by adding more hot sauce, or by serving extra hot sauce on the side for your guests to add to their taste. Some people can take the heat better than others. If you would like to make a vegetarian version of this dish, substitute 2 tablespoons of extra-virgin olive oil for the bacon.

---

1. The day before you plan to serve this dish, put the peas in a bowl, cover with water by at least 2 inches, and refrigerate. The next day, drain well before using.

2. Center a rack in the oven and preheat the oven to 275°F.

3. Place the bacon in a small cast-iron pot or Dutch oven over medium-high heat and cook until it renders its fat, about 5 minutes.

4. Add the onions, garlic, oregano, and black pepper and cook, stirring, for 8 minutes. Add the drained peas, bay leaves, salt, and 6 cups water. Bring to a simmer, cover, and transfer to the oven.

5. Braise until the peas are tender, about 1 hour 15 minutes. Stir in the Tabasco, sprinkle with the parsley, and serve.

1 pound dried black-eyed peas

5 ounces slab bacon, cut into cubes

2 red onions, peeled and sliced

4 garlic cloves, peeled and chopped

1 tablespoon dried oregano

1/4 teaspoon freshly ground black pepper

2 bay leaves

2 teaspoons coarse sea salt or kosher salt

2 teaspoons Tabasco or other hot sauce

Fresh flat-leaf parsley leaves, for garnish

RED BEANS WITH BACON
AND FRESH CHORIZO

| MAKES 6 TO 8 SERVINGS |

Whereas Southern-Style Black-Eyed Peas with Bacon (page 181) is more of a side dish, this hearty braise of red beans and fresh chorizo (or andouille sausage if you can find a good one; see note) is a full meal. Beans always taste better if you make them ahead and then reheat them, but don't cook the rice until just before serving. If the beans get too thick as they cool, add a little water when reheating.

1 pound dried red beans

7 ounces fresh chorizo, diced (see note, page 19)

4 ounces bacon, diced

¼ teaspoon crushed black pepper

¼ teaspoon cayenne pepper

2 onions, peeled and thinly sliced

4 garlic cloves, peeled and chopped

½ teaspoon dried mustard

2 stalks celery, thinly sliced

1 red bell pepper, cored, seeded, and cut into ½-inch squares

1 green bell pepper, cored, seeded, and cut into ½-inch squares

6 tomatoes, chopped

2 tablespoons molasses

2 teaspoons dried oregano

2 bay leaves

1 sprig fresh thyme

2 teaspoons coarse sea salt or kosher salt, plus more to taste

2 tablespoons ketchup

Cooked rice, for serving (see recipe, opposite)

1. The day before you plan to serve this dish, place the beans in a bowl, cover them with cold water by at least 2 inches, and refrigerate overnight. The next day, drain well before using.

2. Center a rack in the oven and preheat the oven to 275°F.

3. In a small cast-iron pot or Dutch oven over medium-high heat, cook the fresh chorizo and bacon until the bacon colors lightly and a good part of the fat has rendered, about 6 minutes. Spoon out half the fat and discard.

4. Add the black pepper and cayenne pepper to the pot and cook for 1 minute. Add the onions and garlic and cook, stirring, until translucent, about 5 minutes. Stir in the dried mustard. Add the celery and bell peppers and cook, stirring, until softened, about 4 minutes. Add 6 cups water and the drained beans, tomatoes, molasses, oregano, bay leaves, and thyme and bring to a simmer. Cover and transfer to the oven.

5. Braise for 2 hours, adding the salt after 1½ hours. Stir in the ketchup and serve immediately, with the rice.

BRAISED CHESTNUTS AND APPLES
IN SPICED APPLE CIDER (PAGE 194)

PEPPERY PEACHES WITH SAUTERNES (PAGE 192)

CABBAGE KIMCHI-STYLE (PAGE 172)

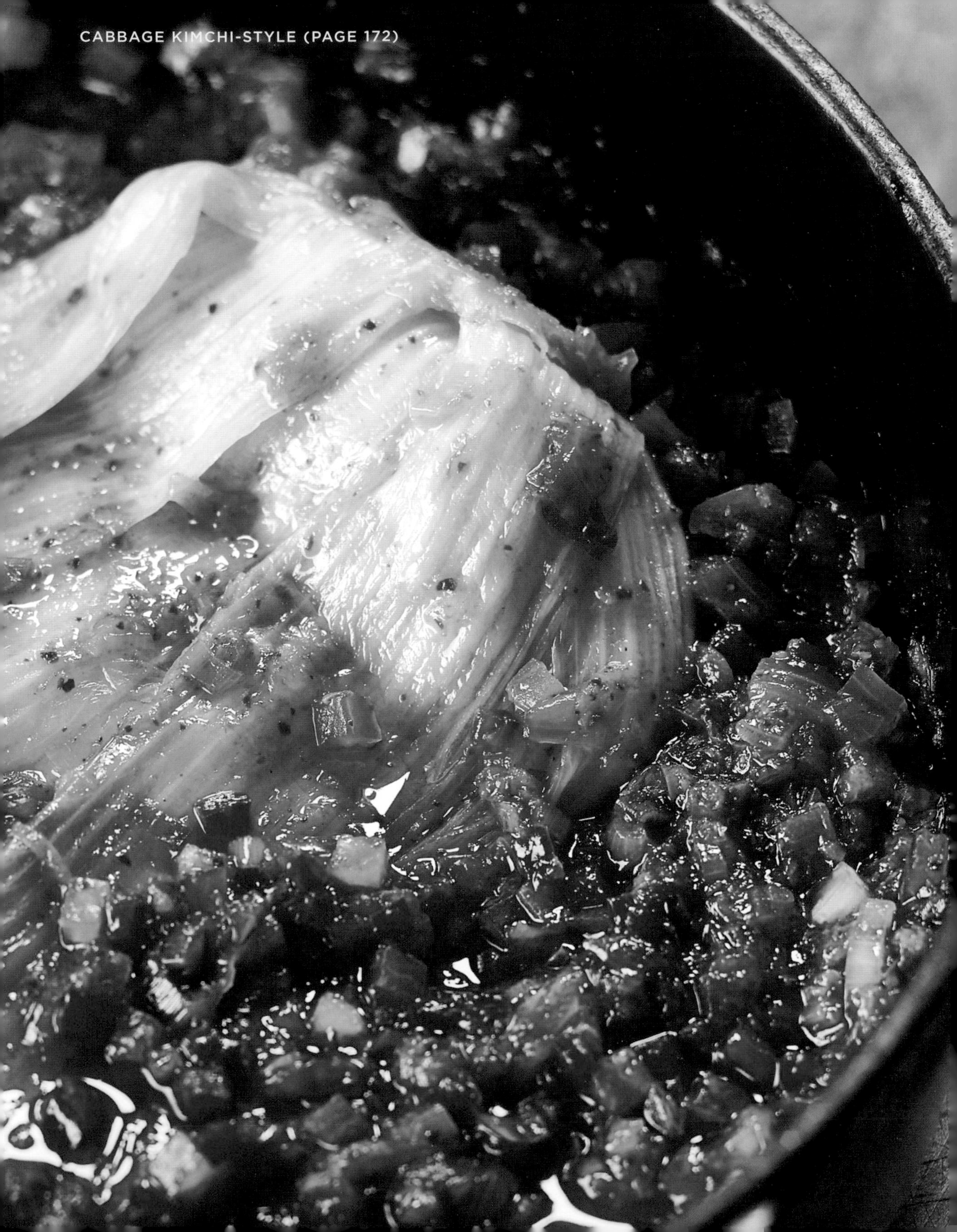

LEEKS, PRUNES, AND PLUMS (PAGE 179)

ARTICHOKES STUFFED
WITH FETA CHEESE
(PAGE 180)

ENDIVE BRAISED IN
CRÈME FRAÎCHE
(PAGE 175)

MIXED GREENS WITH RHUBARB, LEEKS, AND DILL (PAGE 176)

COOKED RICE

| MAKES 6 TO 8 SERVINGS |

Coarse sea salt or kosher salt

2 cups long-grain white rice

In a large heavy-bottomed saucepan over high heat, bring 3¾ cups salted water to a boil. Stir in the rice and reduce the heat to medium-low. Cover the pan and simmer until the rice is tender and most of the liquid has evaporated, 15 to 20 minutes.

ANDOUILLE SAUSAGE

Andouille is a spicy, garlicky smoked sausage made of several different cuts of pork. It originated in France, where it is traditionally stuffed with tripe and served cold or hot with beans and cabbage. French settlers brought andouille to Louisiana, where it was spiced up and has since become a mainstay in Cajun cooking. It is integral in recipes for gumbo, jambalaya, and red beans and rice. Germans and Italians also produce their own variation of andouille. If it is not available where you shop, substitute spicy Italian sausage; or you can order Cajun andouille online (see Sources, page 210).

EGGPLANT WITH WHITE MISO, KAFFIR LIME, LEMONGRASS, AND GINGER

| MAKES 6 SERVINGS |

Kaffir lime leaves are lemony and delicious, especially when paired with anything mild and creamy, like eggplant cooked until very soft and silky, as it is here. I started using Kaffir lime leaves a long time ago—over twenty years, when I was the chef at Le Cirque and Sottha Khunn, from Cambodia, was my sous-chef. He introduced me to all kinds of what were then unusual herbs and spices. The important thing about using Kaffir lime is being careful not to overdo it. Just a little bit adds a nice perfume. Too much can be overpowering.

3 pounds eggplant, cut into 1-inch cubes

2 tablespoons extra-virgin olive oil

1 large red onion, peeled and cut into cubes

4 garlic cloves, peeled and finely chopped

2 tablespoons peeled, finely grated fresh gingerroot

2 teaspoons grated lemongrass (see note, page 55)

1 teaspoon five-spice powder (see note and recipe, page 135)

½ cup rice wine vinegar (see note, page 49)

¼ cup white miso (see note, page 13)

4 bunches scallions, trimmed and thinly sliced

2 Kaffir lime leaves (see note, page 121)

¼ cup fresh cilantro leaves, for garnish

1. Center a rack in the oven and preheat the oven to 300°F.

2. In a nonstick skillet over medium-high heat, cook the eggplant, in batches, with 1 inch water until the eggplant is golden brown and all the liquid in the pan has evaporated, 10 to 15 minutes per batch.

3. Heat the olive oil in a small cast-iron pot or Dutch oven over medium heat. Add the onion, garlic, gingerroot, lemongrass, and five-spice powder and cook, stirring, for 3 to 4 minutes. Add the rice wine vinegar, white miso, and scallions and whisk until the miso has dissolved into the liquid. Add the eggplant, Kaffir lime leaves, and 2 cups water and bring to a simmer. Cover and transfer to the oven.

4. Braise for 45 minutes. Sprinkle the cilantro leaves over the dish and serve immediately.

MOUSSAKA-SPICED EGGPLANT, ARTICHOKE, AND TOMATO CASSEROLE

| MAKES 8 SERVINGS |

This atypical but delicious moussaka recipe includes artichokes along with the usual eggplant and tomato, giving the dish a pleasing textural variation. It also uses yogurt in place of béchamel for a lighter, tangier sauce. For this dish, I use a buttered parchment round instead of the pot's cover. Since vegetables exude a lot of water, this allows for evaporation. If you can't find baby eggplant, use 3 pounds of small regular eggplant instead.

1. Center a rack in the oven and preheat the oven to 300°F.

2. Finely grind the oregano, coriander seeds, cumin seeds, caraway seeds, cinnamon, black peppercorns, bay leaves, and allspice together in a spice grinder. Mix together the ground spices, yogurt, gingerroot, lemon zest, and lemon juice. Cover with plastic wrap and refrigerate until needed.

3. Toss the eggplant rounds with the flour. Heat the olive oil in a large skillet over high heat. Add half the eggplant rounds and sauté until golden brown, 5 to 6 minutes. Transfer to a plate. Sauté the remaining eggplant rounds, adding more olive oil to the pan if needed, and transfer the cooked rounds to the plate.

4. Add more olive oil to the pan if needed. Add the artichokes to the pan and cook until golden brown, working in batches if necessary. Transfer the artichokes to a separate plate. Repeat with the onion and garlic, cooking until the onion is golden.

5. Put one-third of the eggplant on the bottom of a medium cast-iron pot or Dutch oven, and season lightly with salt and pepper. Add a layer of half the onion, followed by half the artichokes, tomatoes, and yogurt mixture, seasoning each layer lightly with salt and pepper. Repeat, finishing with a layer of eggplant on top. Cover with a buttered parchment round and transfer to the oven.

6. Braise until the eggplant is tender, about 2 hours.

1 teaspoon dried oregano

1 teaspoon coriander seeds

1 teaspoon cumin seeds

1 teaspoon caraway seeds

1 teaspoon ground cinnamon

¼ teaspoon black peppercorns

2 bay leaves

3 whole allspice

2 cups plain whole-milk yogurt, preferably Greek

1 tablespoon finely chopped peeled fresh gingerroot

Finely grated zest and freshly squeezed juice of 1 lemon

8 baby eggplants (about 3 pounds), trimmed and cut into ⅓-inch-thick rounds

2 tablespoons all-purpose flour

6 tablespoons extra-virgin olive oil, plus more as needed

8 globe artichokes, trimmed and cut into ¼-inch-thick slices (see note, page 116)

1 onion, peeled and chopped

4 garlic cloves, peeled and chopped

Coarse sea salt or kosher salt and freshly ground black pepper

8 plum tomatoes, peeled if desired, and cut into ¼-inch-thick slices (see note, page 37)

GRILLED TOFU WITH CHINESE SAUSAGE AND BLACK BEANS

| MAKES 4 SERVINGS |

I never cooked much with tofu until my daughter became a vegetarian. Now I have really gotten to know tofu. It has a very particular, mild taste, and there is nothing comparable to it in Europe—especially to its texture, which can go from silky and soft to firm and dry or anything in between. Here I grill slices of firm tofu until they become meaty and crispy around the edges, then I braise them with Chinese sausage, ground beef, garlicky bean paste, and Szechuan pepper. The tofu keeps its shape in the braise and acts as a sponge, soaking up and softening all those assertive flavors. It's a very unusual, multidimensional dish.

If you've never used Szechuan peppercorns, you'll be surprised at how different they taste from the usual peppercorns. If you use just a touch, they'll give the dish a fragrant, pine-like fruitiness. Use too many, and their camphor-like qualities come out; then it's like biting into a mothball. You can substitute black peppercorns if necessary. The flavor will still be good, but slightly less exotic.

1 teaspoon Szechuan peppercorns (see note, page 10)

1 pound firm or medium tofu

1 tablespoon extra-virgin olive oil

½ pound ground beef

3 garlic cloves, peeled and finely chopped

1 (1-inch) piece fresh gingerroot, peeled and finely grated

¼ cup fermented black bean paste (see note, page 10)

2 tablespoons packed light soy sauce (see note, page 11)

1 teaspoon packed dark brown sugar

1 bunch scallions, trimmed

3 Chinese sausage links, cut into ½-inch-thick slices (see note)

1. Center a rack in the oven and preheat the oven to 275°F.

2. Warm a small skillet over medium heat. Add the Szechuan peppercorns and toast for 20 seconds, or just until you can smell them. Let cool. Finely grind the peppercorns in a spice grinder.

3. Place a grill pan over high heat. Add the tofu and grill for 12 minutes on one side, or just until you can see grill marks on it. Remove from the heat.

4. In a small cast-iron pot or Dutch oven over medium-high heat, warm the olive oil. Add the ground beef, garlic, and gingerroot. Cook, stirring and breaking up the meat with a fork, until the meat is browned, 4 to 5 minutes. Stir in the bean paste, soy sauce, brown sugar, and 1 cup water. Add the tofu, scatter the scallions and sausage around the tofu, and bring to a simmer.

5. Cover and transfer the pot to the oven. Braise for 1½ to 2 hours, or until the sauce is thickened to taste. Serve this dish hot or warm.

CHINESE SAUSAGE

This sweet and spicy sausage, called *lop cheung* by the Chinese, is usually made with chopped pork, pork liver, and hefty quantities of fat. Sometimes available smoked, Chinese sausage is dry and hard in texture and lends excellent flavor to stir-fries and noodle dishes. Lop cheung are long (about 6 inches) and thin and usually come in links of two. The sausage is also sometimes made with duck liver, although this variety tends to be scarce outside China. Chinese sausage can be purchased in many Asian markets and some butcher shops or online (see Sources, page 210). Mild hard fresh chorizo, mild pepperoni, or German Landjaeger (a dried, smoked, German sausage made with beef and pork) may be substituted.

FRUIT AND OTHER DESSERTS

APRICOTS BEAUMES-DE-VENISE, WITH OR WITHOUT CLAFOUTIS

| MAKES 4 SERVINGS |

Fresh apricots have a limited season, but good dried ones are available all year long. Here I braise dried apricots very simply to highlight their natural fruity, tart taste, and I top them with a light, creamy clafoutis batter. Beaumes-de-Venise, a sweet, aromatic wine from the South of France, is an excellent cooking medium, and the lemongrass heightens the perfume. Serve this warm, with ice cream if you'd like.

FOR THE APRICOTS:

2 cups Beaumes-de-Venise or other sweet white wine

1 stalk lemongrass, crushed (see note, page 55)

20 dried apricots

1 tablespoon plus 1 teaspoon granulated sugar

1. The night before you plan to serve the dessert, bring the Beaumes-de-Venise and lemongrass to a boil in a medium saucepan. Add the apricots, cover with a lid or plastic wrap, and refrigerate overnight. Drain the apricots, reserving the syrup; discard the lemongrass.

2. Center a rack in the oven and preheat the oven to 325°F.

3. In a medium ovenproof skillet over high heat, melt the sugar with 1 teaspoon water, swirling it in the pan until the sugar dissolves. Reduce the heat and caramelize until the sugar turns golden, about 4 minutes. Add the apricots and toss to coat evenly with the caramel. Add the lemongrass syrup and bring to a boil.

4. Transfer the skillet to the oven and braise until the syrup thickens slightly, about 40 minutes. Serve as is, with cookies or ice cream, or top with the clafoutis batter (see opposite) and bake.

1. The day before you plan to make the dessert, whisk together the eggs and sugar in a bowl. Add the remaining batter ingredients and mix just until combined. Refrigerate overnight. Rewhisk before using.

2. Center a rack in the oven and preheat the oven to 375°F.

3. Spray the insides of four 4-inch gratin dishes (or, alternatively, you can use an 8-inch cake pan) with nonstick cooking spray. Fill each gratin dish (or the cake pan) a third full with clafoutis batter. Bake just until a skin forms on top of the batter, about 4 minutes.

4. Arrange 5 apricots in a circular pattern on top of the batter in each gratin dish, spoon 1 tablespoon of the braising syrup over each, and cover the apricots with the remaining clafoutis batter. If using, sprinkle the sliced almonds over. Bake for 10 to 15 minutes, until golden brown (5 minutes longer for the 8-inch cake pan).

5. Let the clafoutis cool for 10 minutes before serving. Pass the remaining braising syrup and whipped cream on the side.

FOR THE CLAFOUTIS BATTER:

2 eggs

¼ cup sugar

⅓ cup all-purpose flour

½ cup heavy cream

½ cup milk

½ cup almond flour

Finely grated zest of 2 lemons

2 tablespoons sliced almonds (optional)

Whipped cream or crème fraîche, for serving

PEPPERY PEACHES
WITH SAUTERNES

| MAKES 8 SERVINGS |

Long pepper has a peppery, piney flavor that works extremely well with the sweet fragrance of vanilla bean. Here I combine the two to season ripe peaches braised gently in syrupy white dessert wine. If you can't find or don't want to spend the money on a true Sauternes, a late-harvest Riesling is another good choice that will underscore the spiciness of the pepper.

1 long peppercorn (see note)

8 ripe peaches

2 cups Sauternes or other sweet white wine

1 vanilla bean, split, seeds scraped out and reserved

1. Center a rack in the oven and preheat the oven to 275°F.

2. In a spice grinder or clean coffee grinder, finely grind the peppercorn.

3. Bring a large pot of water to a boil. Fill a large bowl halfway with ice cubes and cold water. Cut a small X in the bottom of each peach. Carefully lower the peaches into the boiling water and blanch for 30 seconds. Using a slotted spoon, transfer them to the prepared ice bath. Drain the peaches, and when they are cool enough to handle, slip the skin off each peach.

4. Put the blanched peaches, Sauternes, vanilla bean pod and seeds, and ground pepper into a small cast-iron pot or Dutch oven. Bring to a gentle simmer, and transfer to the oven to braise for 2 hours.

5. Using a slotted spoon, very gently transfer the peaches to a plate. Return the pot to the stove top over medium heat. Cook until the liquid in the pot has reached a syrupy consistency, 10 to 15 minutes. Remove the vanilla bean pod. Serve the peaches warm or at room temperature, with the syrup.

LONG PEPPER

More pungent than typical peppercorns, the dark brown, rod-shaped
long pepper has a hot, sweet flavor
like a cross between black pepper and
cinnamon with a piney undertone. (In
fact, a good substitute for long pepper
would be ground white pepper mixed
with a pinch of mace.) The fruit of a
flowering vine, long peppers actually
consist of many tiny seed-like berries
clustered together to form the charac-
teristic cylindrical shape. Prized in
ancient Rome for their sweet-savory
taste, long peppers are not often used
today in Europe or the United States.
They are more common in North
Africa, where they are pounded into
spice blends such as *ras el hanout,*
and in Asia, where they give fiery
sweetness to Indian vegetable pickles
and Thai, Malaysian, and Indonesian
cooking. The peppers should be
crushed before use. They can be purchased at Indian or Asian markets or
online (see Sources, page 210).

BRAISED CHESTNUTS AND APPLES IN SPICED APPLE CIDER

| MAKES 4 TO 6 SERVINGS |

This is an excellent dessert to make in autumn, when apples and chestnuts are both in season—and when it starts getting chilly outside, so that you don't mind having your oven on for an hour or more. That's how long it takes the chestnuts to soften and absorb the spiced apple cider, which gives them a very fruity flavor. You can use preserved, already peeled chestnuts for this recipe, but if you don't mind peeling them, fresh chestnuts are best. Peeling fresh chestnuts is easy, though it will take some time. The best way I've found is to make an incision on both sides of the shell, and then toast the chestnuts in a dry skillet or roast them in the oven. (I've heard you can use the microwave, but I've never tried it myself.) Make sure to peel the chestnuts while they are still warm; once cooled, the shell is very hard to take off.

If you can find quinces, you can substitute them for the apples. They add more pectin to the sauce, thickening it like jam.

I like to serve this dessert with slices of toasted gingerbread. If you don't have time to make it yourself, you can buy it; or you can serve it with crisp gingersnap cookies.

5 tablespoons unsalted butter

3 pounds Granny Smith apples, peeled, quartered, and cored

¼ cup packed light brown sugar

½ pound peeled fresh chestnuts or dry-packed bottled, vacuum-sealed, or frozen peeled chestnuts

3 strips freshly peeled orange zest, plus 1 teaspoon finely grated

2 (3-inch) cinnamon sticks

1 vanilla bean, split, seeds scraped out and reserved

2 cups apple cider

¼ cup pomegranate juice (see note, page 79)

Freshly squeezed juice of 1 orange

¼ cup granulated sugar

1. Put a rack in the lower third of the oven and preheat the oven to 300°F.

2. In a medium cast-iron pot or Dutch oven, melt 3 tablespoons of the butter over high heat. Add the apples and brown sugar and cook, stirring occasionally, until the apples are caramelized, 10 to 15 minutes. Add the chestnuts, orange zest strips, cinnamon sticks, and vanilla bean seeds and pod. Pour the apple cider, pomegranate juice, and orange juice into the pot and bring to a boil. Stir to loosen any browned bits of apple on the bottom of the pot.

3. Cover the pot and transfer it to the oven. Braise until the apples and chestnuts are tender, 60 to 70 minutes.

4. Meanwhile, in a large nonstick skillet over medium-high heat, melt the remaining 2 tablespoons butter. Sprinkle the granulated sugar on both sides of the Pain d'Épices or gingerbread. Add the Pain d'Épices to the pan and cook until each slice is crispy on the outside yet still soft on the inside, 3 to 4 minutes for each side.

5. Mix together the crème fraîche and grated orange zest. Serve the apples and chestnuts warm, with the toasted gingerbread and orange crème fraîche on the side.

6 (½-inch-thick) slices Pain d'Épices (see recipe page 196) or store-bought gingerbread, for serving

6 tablespoons crème fraîche

PAIN D'ÉPICES

| MAKES 4 TO 6 SERVINGS |

$^3/_4$ cup lavender honey or your choice of honey

$^1/_2$ cup sugar

2 tablespoons molasses

2 cups all-purpose flour

1$^1/_2$ teaspoons baking powder

1 teaspoon baking soda

1$^1/_2$ teaspoons ground anise seeds

1$^1/_2$ teaspoons ground allspice

1$^1/_2$ teaspoons ground cinnamon

1$^1/_2$ teaspoons freshly grated nutmeg

1$^1/_2$ teaspoons ground ginger

$^1/_2$ teaspoon ground cloves

Finely grated zest of 1 lemon

$^1/_2$ cup whole milk

3 large eggs

2 teaspoons vanilla extract

1. Center a rack in the oven and preheat the oven to 350°F. Butter a 9-by-5-inch loaf pan.

2. In a medium saucepan over medium-high heat, bring the honey, sugar, molasses, and ¼ cup water to a boil. Reduce the heat to medium and simmer, stirring once or twice, for 5 minutes. Remove from the heat and gradually whisk in 1 cup of the flour.

3. In a large bowl, combine the remaining 1 cup flour, the baking powder, baking soda, anise seeds, allspice, cinnamon, nutmeg, ginger, cloves, and lemon zest. In another large mixing bowl, whisk the milk and eggs until frothy. Stir in the honey mixture and the vanilla, then fold in the sifted ingredients until just combined.

4. Pour the batter into the loaf pan. Bake until the bread is firm to the touch and has begun to pull away from the sides of the pan, about 45 minutes. Transfer to a wire rack to cool.

BANANAS WITH NUTMEG, HONEY, AND COCONUT CRUMBLE

| MAKES 4 SERVINGS |

Everyone loves bananas except me. A banana is the only thing I don't like to eat. But for anyone else who tastes this, it's a terrific recipe. The bananas caramelize and soak up the flavor of the spices and honey, and they get very soft inside, which is a nice contrast to the crunchy crumble topping. Serve this with crème fraîche or ice cream, if you like.

1. For the crumble: In the bowl of a mixer fitted with the paddle attachment, combine the sugar and butter. Add the remaining ingredients and mix until combined. Spread the mixture on a baking sheet and refrigerate for at least 2 hours.

2. Center a rack in the oven and preheat the oven to 350°F.

3. Remove the baking sheet from the refrigerator and break up the crumble between your fingers into an even layer. Bake the crumble for 8 to 10 minutes, until golden brown. Let cool. If not using right away, store in an airtight container for up to 3 days.

4. To prepare the bananas: Center a rack in the oven and preheat the oven to 300°F.

5. Warm the honey in an ovenproof skillet or Dutch oven over low heat. Add the bananas and cook, turning occasionally, for 15 minutes, or until the bananas begin to caramelize. Add the orange juice, lemon juice, and nutmeg to the pan and bring to a simmer, stirring gently.

6. Transfer to the oven and braise, basting occasionally, until the sauce thickens and becomes syrupy, about 25 minutes. Sprinkle the coconut crumble over the top and bake for 4 to 5 minutes more. Serve warm.

FOR THE CRUMBLE:
3 tablespoons Muscovado sugar or packed light brown sugar

3 tablespoons unsalted butter, at room temperature

1/3 cup plus 1 tablespoon all-purpose flour

1/3 cup unsweetened desiccated coconut

1 1/2 tablespoons almond flour

FOR THE BANANAS:
1/3 cup honey

4 ripe bananas

Freshly squeezed juice of 2 oranges

Freshly squeezed juice of 1/2 lemon

1/4 teaspoon ground nutmeg

LICORICE PEARS
WITH FENNEL SABLÉS

Pears are wonderful to use in desserts because they keep their own personality no matter what other flavors you add. Here, I use licorice, and during the long, slow braising, the pears absorb the flavor nicely and still maintain their shape. The Fennel Sablés, if you decide to make them, are an elegant accompaniment, though pound cake or Pain d'Épices (page 196) would be delicious, too.

FOR THE FENNEL SABLÉS:

9 tablespoons unsalted butter, at room temperature

⅓ cup confectioners' sugar

1 large egg white, at room temperature

1 cup all-purpose flour

Pinch of salt

1½ teaspoons fennel seeds

1. For the sablés: Center a rack in the oven and preheat the oven to 350°F. Line a baking sheet with parchment paper.

2. In the bowl of a mixer fitted with the paddle attachment, cream the butter and sugar until fluffy. Add the egg white and mix well. Add the flour and salt and mix just until combined. Spoon the batter into a pastry bag fitted with a large star tip. Pipe the batter into six 3-inch circles on the prepared baking sheet. Sprinkle each cookie with fennel seeds.

3. Slide the baking sheet into the oven and bake for 15 minutes, until golden brown. Let cool.

1. For the pears: Combine the pears, ½ cup of the sugar, the lemon juice, licorice stick, licorice candies, and 1¾ cups water in a medium saucepan and bring to a boil. Remove from the heat and let the pears infuse in the liquid for at least 4 hours, or preferably overnight (refrigerate the pears overnight).

2. Center a rack in the oven and preheat the oven to 325°F.

3. Remove the pears from the poaching liquid. Cut each pear in half and remove the core. Strain the poaching liquid through a fine-mesh sieve into a bowl; discard the licorice stick and candies.

4. In a medium ovenproof saucepan over high heat, melt the remaining 2 tablespoons sugar with 1 teaspoon water, swirling the pan until the sugar dissolves. Reduce the heat and caramelize until the sugar turns golden, about 4 minutes. Add the pears and butter to the pan and cook until the pears are caramelized on all sides, about 10 minutes. Deglaze with the strained poaching liquid and bring to a simmer.

5. Cover, transfer the saucepan to the oven, and braise, basting the pears occasionally, until the pears are tender and the syrup has thickened slightly, about 40 minutes.

6. To serve, place each fennel sablé in the center of a dessert plate and top with a braised pear half. Spoon some syrup over each pear and let sit for 10 to 15 minutes before serving, to allow the cookies to soften slightly.

FOR THE PEARS:

3 ripe Comice pears, peeled

½ cup plus 2 tablespoons sugar

Freshly squeezed juice of ½ lemon

1 licorice stick (see note)

7 small French licorice candies (such as Cachou la Jaunie, see Sources, page 210)

1 teaspoon unsalted butter

LICORICE STICKS

Actually the root of a perennial shrub related, interestingly, to the pea plant, licorice sticks have been cultivated in their native China for over 2,000 years and in Europe for nearly 1,000. An acquired taste, licorice has a distinct earthy, sweet, and slightly medicinal flavor with an anise-fennel tang. It is not uncommon for licorice root to season savory dishes in China and the Middle East; it is also used in confections and liqueurs. The roots can be dried and used whole or ground into a pale green powder. They are also turned into an extract made by boiling crushed or sliced roots and then reducing the resulting liquid. Licorice sticks can be purchased at Asian markets and specialty spice markets, and they are also available online (see Sources, page 210).

PINEAPPLE MARTINIQUE

PINEAPPLE BRAISED WITH PINK PEPPERCORNS

| MAKES 6 SERVINGS |

Pineapple is sometimes better cooked than fresh. You definitely have more options with a cooked pineapple. Fresh, there's not too much you can do to it, and if it isn't perfectly ripe, it may not be very enjoyable. Cooked with sugar until it is almost a confit, it's juicy and sweet but still retains its acidity. And it will absorb any spices or flavorings you cook it with. Here, rum, allspice, and cinnamon, plus Coconut Sorbet on the side, give a Caribbean taste, while pink peppercorns add a touch of heat.

½ teaspoon whole allspice

¼ teaspoon pink peppercorns (see note, page 15)

12 kumquats, pierced with a small knife

3 tablespoons unsalted butter

1 (4-pound) pineapple, peeled, quartered, cored, and each quarter halved crosswise

¼ cup packed light brown sugar

2 vanilla beans, split, seeds scraped out and reserved

1 (3-inch) cinnamon stick

½ cup light rum

1½ cups fresh or canned pineapple juice

Coconut Sorbet, for serving (see recipe, opposite)

1. Center a rack in the oven and preheat the oven to 300°F.

2. In a spice grinder, finely grind the allspice and pink peppercorns.

3. In a medium saucepan over medium-high heat, bring 1 quart water to a boil. Add the kumquats and simmer for 5 minutes. Drain well.

4. Melt the butter in a small cast-iron pot or Dutch oven over high heat. Add the kumquats, pineapple pieces, brown sugar, ground spices, vanilla bean pods and seeds, and cinnamon stick. Cook, stirring, until the pineapple is golden brown on all sides, 10 to 12 minutes. Pour in the rum and, holding the pan away from the heat, light the liquid with a match. Wait for the flame to burn out, then return the pan to the stove. Add the pineapple juice and bring to a simmer.

5. Cover and transfer to the oven to braise for 1 hour. Serve warm, with the Coconut Sorbet.

COCONUT SORBET

| MAKES ABOUT 1 QUART |

1 (15-ounce) can coconut cream (like Coco Lopez)

2 cups whole milk

Combine the coconut cream and milk in the bowl of an ice cream machine and freeze according to the manufacturer's instructions.

SWEET EGGPLANT
WITH PISTACHIOS

| MAKES 4 TO 6 SERVINGS |

Serving it for dessert may not be the first thing you think of when you think of eggplant, but this dish works very well. The grape and pomegranate juices add fruitiness, while the nuts, toasted brioche, butter, and spices enrich the mixture, which you wouldn't necessarily guess contains eggplant unless you look for it. Your guests certainly won't have tasted anything like it.

2 pounds Japanese or regular eggplant, trimmed and cut into ⅓-inch cubes

2 cups red grape juice

½ cup pomegranate juice (see note, page 79)

¼ cup granulated sugar

2 tablespoons packed light brown sugar

½ vanilla bean, split, seeds scraped out and reserved

1 cup diced crustless brioche

½ cup roughly chopped pistachios or hazelnuts

6 tablespoons unsalted butter, melted

⅓ cup ginger marmalade

¼ cup pomegranate molasses (see note, page 79)

2 teaspoons honey

½ teaspoon ground cinnamon

Pinch of ground cloves

Fromage Blanc Sorbet, for serving (see recipe, opposite)

1. The night before you plan to serve this dessert, place the eggplant cubes in a large bowl. In a medium saucepan, bring the grape juice, pomegranate juice, granulated sugar, light brown sugar, and vanilla bean seeds and pod to a boil. Pour the hot syrup over the eggplant, cover, and refrigerate overnight.

2. Center a rack in the oven and preheat the oven to 275°F.

3. In a large bowl, combine the brioche, pistachios (or hazelnuts), ¼ cup of the melted butter, the ginger marmalade, pomegranate molasses, honey, cinnamon, and cloves.

4. Drain the eggplant, reserving the marinade. Pour the remaining 2 tablespoons butter into a small cast-iron pot or Dutch oven over medium-high heat. Add the drained eggplant and sauté until caramelized, 5 to 10 minutes. Pour the reserved marinade into the pot, sprinkle the brioche mixture over the eggplant, and cover with a buttered parchment round.

5. Transfer to the oven and braise for 1 hour. Remove the parchment paper and continue to bake until the crust is light golden brown, 10 to 15 minutes. Serve with the Fromage Blanc Sorbet.

FROMAGE BLANC SORBET

| MAKES 1½ PINTS |

¼ cup sugar

½ cup fromage blanc

¼ cup sour cream

¼ cup plain whole-milk yogurt

Finely grated zest of 1 lime

1. Combine 1¼ cups water and the sugar in a small saucepan and warm over medium heat until the sugar has dissolved. Let cool.

2. Using a handheld immersion blender, mix together the cooled syrup, fromage blanc, sour cream, yogurt, and lime zest in a bowl until well combined. Freeze in an ice cream maker according to the manufacturer's instructions. Transfer to a covered container and freeze for at least 1 hour before serving.

MANGOES AND CARROTS
WITH HONEY
AND GINGER-LIME WHIPPED CREAM

| MAKES 4 SERVINGS |

You wouldn't necessarily think of pairing carrot and mango in a dessert, but the acidity of the mango and the sweetness of the carrot balance each other very well. I also add both fresh gingerroot and crystallized ginger for a touch of spice. By adding the crystallized ginger to the whipped cream at the very end, you make sure that the ginger is not going to melt and soften up too much but will stay present and a little chewy.

2 tablespoons unsalted butter

³⁄₄ pound carrots, peeled, trimmed, and cut into ¹⁄₄-inch-thick rounds

2 tablespoons honey

2 star anise pods

3 mangoes (about 12 ounces each), peeled, pitted, and cut into ¹⁄₂-inch cubes

¹⁄₂ cup fresh or bottled carrot juice (see note, page 27)

¹⁄₄ cup toasted blanched whole almonds (see note, page 44)

1 tablespoon finely grated peeled fresh gingerroot (about a 2-inch piece)

Freshly squeezed juice of 1 lime

1 cup heavy cream

Finely grated zest of ¹⁄₂ lime

1 tablespoon finely chopped crystallized ginger

1. Place a rack in the lower third of the oven and preheat the oven to 300°F.

2. In a small cast-iron pot or Dutch oven over medium heat, melt the butter. Stir in the carrots, 1 tablespoon of the honey, and the star anise pods and cook, covered, for 20 minutes. Add the mangoes, carrot juice, almonds, 2 teaspoons of the grated gingerroot, and the lime juice. Stir to combine, and bring the liquid to a boil.

3. Cover the pot and transfer to the oven to braise until the carrots are meltingly tender and the mangoes soften, 35 to 45 minutes.

4. In the bowl of an electric mixer fitted with the whisk attachment (or using a hand whisk), whip the cream with the remaining 1 teaspoon gingerroot and the lime zest to medium peaks. Whisk in the remaining 1 tablespoon honey and the crystallized ginger.

5. Serve the mangoes and carrots warm, with the ginger-lime whipped cream on the side.

SWEET SPAGHETTI SQUASH WITH TOASTED WALNUTS AND GOLDEN RAISINS

| MAKES 6 TO 8 SERVINGS |

Winter squash is often used in dessert—think of pumpkin pie or pumpkin bread. And with its soft, velvety texture and mild sweet flavor, it's not surprising. In this dish, the squash breaks down until it's almost porridge-like, and is then mixed with crumbled halvah, spices, and walnuts for a Middle Eastern flavor.

1. Center a rack in the oven and preheat the oven to 275°F.

2. In a small cast-iron pot or Dutch oven over medium-high heat, melt the butter. Add the squash and sweat for 10 to 15 minutes.

3. Stir in the remaining ingredients except the walnuts. Cover and transfer to the oven, and braise until the squash is very tender, about 2 hours. Sprinkle the walnuts over and serve warm.

2 tablespoons unsalted butter

1 (4-pound) spaghetti squash, peeled, halved, seeds discarded, and thinly sliced

¾ cup sugar

½ cup golden raisins

1 teaspoon ground cinnamon

1 teaspoon ground ginger

½ teaspoon ground fennel seeds

1 vanilla bean, split, seeds scraped out and reserved

½ cup crumbled halvah (see note)

Freshly squeezed juice of 1 lemon

1 quart freshly squeezed orange juice

½ cup toasted walnuts (see note, page 44)

HALVAH

Halvah is an Arabic word for sweetmeat, but it is used in English for a candy made from the by-product of sesame oil production. After their oil has been pressed out, sesame seeds are pulverized, sweetened, and formed into rich cakes with a deep, nutty taste and a dry, flaky, crunchy texture. Halvah is available in bulk at Middle Eastern and Jewish specialty stores, and it can also be found packaged in many supermarkets.

APPENDIX

STOCKS

CHICKEN STOCK

| MAKES ABOUT 1 GALLON |

4 pounds chicken necks, backs, and wings or chicken parts, skinned, fat trimmed, and rinsed

2 medium onions, peeled, and quartered

2 small carrots, peeled and cut into 2-inch pieces

1 stalk celery, trimmed and cut into 2-inch pieces

1 medium leek, trimmed, split lengthwise, and washed (see headnote, page 179)

1 head garlic, split in half crosswise

1 bay leaf

5 sprigs fresh flat-leaf parsley

1 teaspoon white peppercorns

1. Put the chicken and 7 quarts cold water in a tall stockpot and bring to a boil. Add 3 quarts more cold water (it should be very cold) and bring to a boil; skim off any fat that rises to the top. Lower the heat so that the water simmers, and simmer—skimming regularly—for 10 minutes.

2. Add the remaining ingredients to the pot and simmer for 3 hours, continuing to skim so that the stock will be clear. Strain the stock through a colander. Allow the solids to drain for a few minutes before discarding them, then strain the stock through a chinois or fine-mesh sieve. Let cool to room temperature, then cover tightly and refrigerate. (The stock can be kept tightly covered in the refrigerator for up to 4 days or frozen for up to 1 month.)

BEEF STOCK

| MAKES ABOUT 5 QUARTS |

1. Heat a griddle or small cast-iron skillet over high heat. Place the onion halves in the pan, cut side down, and cook until blackened (they should be as dark as you can get them). Transfer the onion to a plate and stick 1 whole clove in each half.

2. Season the beef with salt and pepper. Heat the oil in a large nonstick skillet over high heat. Working in batches, sear the beef until well browned on all sides, about 20 minutes per batch. As the pieces of meat are browned, transfer them to a large stockpot.

3. When all the meat is browned and in the stockpot, pour in 6 quarts water, add the remaining ingredients, and bring the liquid to a boil. Lower the heat to a simmer and cook for 2 hours, frequently skimming off the foam and fat that bubble to the surface.

4. Strain the stock through a colander and then pass it through a chinois or fine-mesh sieve. Let cool to room temperature, then cover and refrigerate. (The stock can be kept tightly covered in the refrigerator for up to 4 days or in the freezer for up to 1 month.) When the stock is chilled, the fat will rise to the top. Before reheating the stock, spoon off and discard the fat.

1 large onion, peeled, and halved crosswise

2 whole cloves

1 (6-pound) bone-in beef shank, cut crosswise into 2-inch-thick slices and trimmed of excess fat (ask your butcher to do this for you)

Coarse sea salt or kosher salt and freshly ground black pepper

2 tablespoons vegetable oil

6 large white mushrooms, trimmed, cleaned, and halved

4 stalks celery, trimmed and cut into 2-inch pieces

3 carrots, peeled, trimmed, and cut into 1-inch pieces

6 garlic cloves, peeled and crushed

5 sprigs fresh flat-leaf parsley

2 sprigs fresh thyme

2 bay leaves

1 teaspoon coriander seeds, toasted (see note, page 31)

SOURCES

KALUSTYAN'S
www.kalustyans.com
1-800-352-2451

Juniper berries; preserved lemon; ancho chili powder; pasilla chili pepper and powder; whole guajillo chilies; habanero chili peppers, dried whole and powdered; whole poblano peppers; fresh and dried curry leaves; canela; plum sauce; annatto powder, paste, and seeds; epazote; ají amarillo paste; ají mirasol; quinoa, saffron threads; black cumin seeds; sumac powder and berries; pomegranate molasses; quince paste; fennel pollen; Kaffir lime leaves; dried galangal; mulato chilies; five-spice powder; Tellicherry peppercorns; smoked paprika; Aleppo pepper; harissa; ginger marmalade; licorice sticks

ZINGERMAN'S
www.zingermans.com
1-888-636-8162

Spanish fresh chorizo, Mexican chocolate, smoked Spanish paprika, long pepper, fennel pollen, Tellicherry peppercorns

ZABAR'S
www.zabars.com
1-800-697-6301

Smoked sable

KITCHEN MARKET
www.kitchenmarket.com
1-888-468-4433

Dried Mexican oregano; annatto; avocado leaves, ancho chilies, pasilla chilies, guajillo chilies, chilies de árbol, pequín chilies, habanero chilies, dried poblano peppers, salsa verde picante, ají amarillo, ají mirasol; canela; epazote; salsa verde picante

GOURMET SLEUTH
www.gourmetsleuth.com
408-354-8281

Szechuan peppercorns, pink peppercorns, Mexican sugar, canela, fish sauce, tamarind paste, annatto, epazote, saffron, black cardamom pods, ajwain seeds, black mustard seeds, quince paste, Mexican chocolate, banana leaf, yuzu juice

LA TIENDA
www.tienda.com
888-472-1022

Spanish fresh chorizo, saffron threads, quince paste, morcilla, smoked Spanish paprika, serrano ham

BARNEY GREENGRASS
www.barneygreengrass.com
1-212-724-4707

Smoked sable

LOBEL'S
www.lobels.com
1-877-783-4512

German Landjaeger

ETHNIC GROCER
www.ethnicgrocer.com
630-860-1733

Chinese barbecue sauce, plum sauce, fish sauce, soy sauce, five-spice powder, rice wine vinegar, ajwain, saffron, tamarind paste, dried ancho chilies, dried mulato chilies, red chili paste, fish sauce, dried lemongrass, tahini, red lentils

PENZEY'S
www.penzeys.com
800-741-7787

Juniper berries, Szechuan peppercorns, pink peppercorns, dried whole and ground ancho chilies, whole dried guajillo chilies, chilies de árbol, four-spice, dried epazote, sumac, ajwain seed, white poppy seeds, five-spice powder, Tellicherry peppercorns, zaatar, Aleppo pepper

ASIAN FOOD GROCER
www.asianfoodgrocer.com
888-482-2742

Black bean paste, dark soy sauce, red miso, white miso, fish sauce, hoisin sauce, black sesame seeds, wasabi paste

NIMAN RANCH
www.nimanranch.com
866-808-0340

Pork caul fat, fatback

TEMPLE OF THAI
www.templeofthai.com
  Red chili paste, black soy sauce, fish sauce, dried galangal root, Kaffir lime leaves, shrimp paste, fresh lemongrass

ZAMOURI SPICES
www.zamourispices.com
1-866-329-5988
  Ajwain, annatto, juniper berries, preserved lemon, four-spice, sumac, black cumin seeds

CHEF SHOP
www.chefshop.com
1-877-337-2491
  Pink peppercorns, pomegranate molasses, quince paste, fennel pollen, piment d'Espelette

KOA MART
www.koamart.com
  Korean red pepper

RUSS AND DAUGHTERS
www.russanddaughters.com
212-475-4880
  Halvah, smoked sable, smoked haddock

PERU COOKING
www.perucooking.com
  Rocoto pineapple sauce

COOKIN' CAJUN
www.cookincajun.com
1-800-786-0941
  Andouille sausage

THE BAKER'S CATALOGUE
www.shop.bakerscatalogue.com
1-800-827-6836
  Masa harina

PACIFIC RIM GOURMET
www.pacificrim-gourmet.com
  Black vinegar, black bean paste, dark soy sauce, black sesame seeds, red miso, white miso, chili de árbol, guajillo chilies, red chili paste, annatto, Mexican chocolate, Mexican oregano, ancho chili powder, Chinese barbecue sauce, plum sauce, shrimp paste, dried galangal

CANDY CRATE
www.candycrate.com
1-866-422-6399
  Rock candy

ABINA GOURMET FOOD
www.abinagourmetfood.com
  Chinese sausage, Spanish chorizo, merguez sausage

KAMDAR PLAZA
www.kamdarplaza.com
773-338-8100
  Indian paprika

APHRODISIA HERB STORE
212-989-6440
  Licorice sticks

LICORICE INTERNATIONAL
www.licoriceinternational.com
1-800-542-6742
  French licorice candy

MELISSA GUERRA
www.melissaguerra.com
1-877-875-2665
  Mexican sausage

INDEX

(Page references in *italic* refer to the black-and-white illustrations.)